NIETZSCHE, FREUD, BENN,
AND THE AZURE SPELL OF LIGURIA

GERMAN AND EUROPEAN STUDIES
General Editor: Rebecca Wittmann

Nietzsche, Freud, Benn, and the Azure Spell of Liguria

MARTINA KOLB

UNIVERSITY OF TORONTO PRESS
Toronto Buffalo London

© University of Toronto Press 2013
Toronto Buffalo London
www.utppublishing.com
Printed in Canada

ISBN 978-1-4426-4329-1

Printed on acid-free, 100% post-consumer recycled paper with
vegetable-based inks.

German and European Studies

Library and Archives Canada Cataloguing in Publication

Kolb, Martina
Nietzsche, Freud, Benn, and the azure spell of Liguria / Martina Kolb.

(German and European studies)
Includes bibliographical references and index.
ISBN 978-1-4426-4329-1

1. Nietzsche, Friedrich Wilhelm, 1844–1900 – Homes and haunts – Italy –
Liguria.   2. Freud, Sigmund, 1856–1939 – Homes and haunts – Italy –
Liguria.   3. Benn, Gottfried, 1886–1956 – Homes and haunts – Italy –
Liguria.   4. German literature – Themes, motives.   5. Liguria (Italy) – In
literature.   6. Geography in literature.   7. Geographical perception in
literature.   8. Displacement (Psychology) in literature.   9. Liguria (Italy) –
Intellectual life.   I. Title.   II. Series: German and European studies

PN56.G48K64 2013   830.9'324518   c2012-906823-3

University of Toronto Press acknowledges the financial assistance to its
publishing program of the Canada Council for the Arts and the Ontario Arts
Council.

Canada Council   Conseil des Arts
for the Arts   du Canada

ONTARIO ARTS COUNCIL
CONSEIL DES ARTS DE L'ONTARIO
50 YEARS OF ONTARIO GOVERNMENT SUPPORT OF THE ARTS
50 ANS DE SOUTIEN DU GOUVERNEMENT DE L'ONTARIO AUX ARTS

University of Toronto Press acknowledges the financial support of the
Government of Canada through the Canada Book Fund for its publishing
activities.

To the memory of my grandfather Karl Weiler,
who taught me the word
for "window" in French.

Contents

Illustrations

Acknowledgments

Research for this book was made possible by grants from Penn State's Institute for the Arts and Humanities, the Maria and Goffredo Bellonci Foundation, Yale Beinecke Library, and the Giles Whiting Foundation.

My cordial thanks are intended to strike a balance between Friedrich Hölderlin's "Wem sonst als Dir?" (To whom if not you?) in *Hyperion* and John Cage's "To whom it may concern" in *Silence*. They go to the following supportive and inspiring friends, family, colleagues, curators, and librarians, who best know the precise reasons: Rolena Adorno, Massimo Bacigalupo, Thomas Beebee, Harold Bloom, Brady Bowman, Peter Brooks, Francesca Cadel, Maureen Carr, Keith Davies, Fran Devlin, Ernestina Drera, Andreas Gerold, Karsten Harries, Kristen Hylenski, Carrie Jackson, Djelal Kadir, İpek Kismet, Ingrid Kussmaul, Nancy Locke, Cinzia Manusardi, María Rosa Menocal, Erdmann von Wilamowitz-Moellendorff, Yasemin Mohammad, Bénédicte Monicat, Tamara Olivari, Mary de Rachewiltz, Fridrun Rinner, Annamaria Riposati, Giuliana and Riccardo Roscini, Jeffrey Sammons, Willa Silverman, Marica Tacconi, Jennifer Trost, Maria Truglio, İlker Tufan, Paolo Valesio, Hülya Yilmaz and Ursula Ziebarth, to Valerie Sebestyen for cartography as well as to the press's readers and evaluators of my manuscript.

That *The Azure Spell of Liguria* is published by the University of Toronto Press is, geopoetically speaking, a felicitous matter: according to Silke Peust and Stephan Hormes's toponomastic etymologies, "Liguria" means land of shine, gleam, and brilliance, and by extension perhaps of *genius loci* or spirit of place, while the etymological origin of "Toronto" denotes a place of encounter or a point of convergence. I am thoroughly grateful not only for this appropriate synergetic momentum on the geopoetic grounds of my book on Liguria in Friedrich Nietzsche, Sigmund Freud, and Gottfried Benn, but in particular to my editor at the University of Toronto Press, Richard Ratzlaff, who has supported my work with kindness, fine knowledge, invaluable advice, and genuine interest.

Finally, let me express my profound gratitude to Maria and Walter Kolb for their continuous support and provision of what Ezra Pound called *the green world*, and my love and heartfelt thanks to Heinrich Gerold, who with unwavering patience, acts of encouragement, and an exquisite graphic outlook has watched this book evolve, never tiring of wishing me *gute Gedanken*.

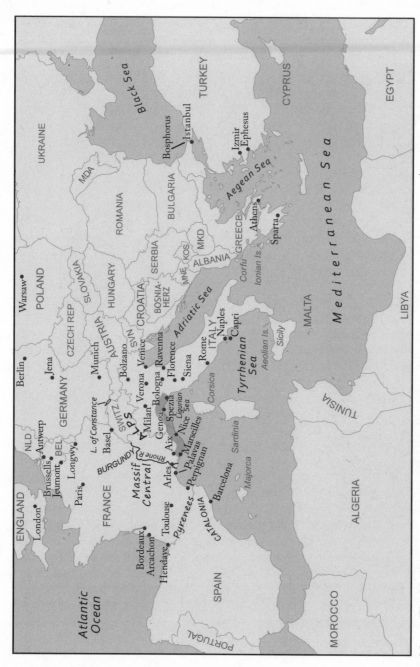

Map 1 The Mediterranean. © 2012 The Pennsylvania State University

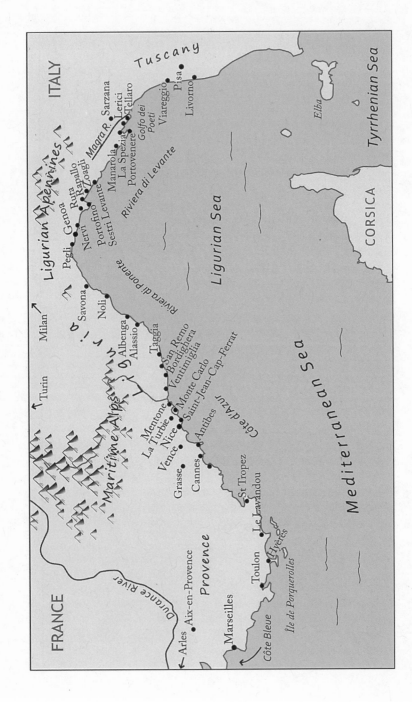

Map 2 Tuscany, Liguria, Côte d'Azur, Provence. © 2012 The Pennsylvania State University

NIETZSCHE, FREUD, BENN,
AND THE AZURE SPELL OF LIGURIA

Ich liebe es ...
Von ferne her mich endlich heimzulocken,
Mich selber zu mir selber – zu verführen.

(I take delight in ...
Luring myself back home from far away,
Seducing myself to revert – to me.)
Friedrich Nietzsche (1844–1900)

An jedem Ort, an den ich komme, stelle ich fest,
daß vor mir schon ein Dichter da war.

(Wherever I go I come to realize
that a poet has already been there before me.)
Sigmund Freud (1856–1934)

... Überbesetzung ... mittels Geographie ...

(... hypercathexis ... via geography ...)
Gottfried Benn (1886–1956)[1]

Preface: Ligurian Geopoetics

... kennst du das Land?
Johann Wolfgang von Goethe

... all forms of landscape are autobiographical.
Charles Wright

... elements of littorality ... shore rhetoric ... coastal writing ... geopoetics.
Kenneth White

Nietzsche, Freud, Benn, and the Azure Spell of Liguria argues that Liguria's smallness, steepness, compactness, and remoteness are qualities reflected in the textual practices and theories of the three authors who are at its core, while others, ranging from the Provençal troubadours and Dante Alighieri to Johann Wolfgang von Goethe, Vincent van Gogh, William Butler Yeats, Ezra Pound, Erika and Klaus Mann, Filippo Tommaso Marinetti, Eugenio Montale, and Italo Calvino (to name only a few), also find their way into the discussion. My reflections on shared form may well be prefigured in those troubadours who called the most complex, condensed, and hermetic of their three kinds of song *trobar clus* (enclosed, remote). Furthermore, my argument is anticipated by Dante and Goethe: in *De vulgari eloquentia* (*On Eloquence in the Vernacular*) and in *Purgatorio* (*Purgatory*), Dante stigmatizes Liguria as the most barren and inaccessible Romance terrain, while Goethe in his *Italienische Reise* (*Italian Journey*) qualifies poetic expression as *steil* (steep, perpendicular), as an augmented intensity, and, as such, opposed to the more extensively viable horizons of epic breadth.

The present study concentrates on Liguria as a borderland located between Italy and France, between the poetically charged regions of Dante's Tuscany and the troubadours' Provence, between sea and sky, and between the Alps and the Mediterranean. This prominent location has, in my judgment, heretofore been underrated in Nietzsche studies (while Nietzsche's creative landscapes – Swiss mountains and Mediterranean Sea – have certainly been examined [by Stephan Günzel, and in word and image by Donald Bates and David Krell], the specificity of Liguria as intensely coded intersection of these has not yet come to the fore), neglected altogether in Freud scholarship, and, in spite of Benn's hardly uncertain terms, by and large generalized into imprecision in interpretations of his unambiguously declared *ligurische Komplexe* (Ligurian complexes) as his first and foremost poetic challenge.

Based on an understanding of literary comparison as a cross-disciplinary and creative principle grounded in difference as much as in likeness, *The Azure Spell of Liguria* primarily draws on comparative energies present in two realms: in the cultural landscape of Liguria on the one hand and in a geopoetic approach to creative life and letters on the other. Adrian Room in *Placenames of the World* and Silke Peust and Stephan Hormes in *Atlas of True Names* etymologically unveil Liguria as the land of *Lugus*: of shine, glow, gleam, brilliance, and perhaps of *genius loci*. As a toponym, Liguria embodies the idea of geopoetics *in nuce*: the name of the place, its etymological denotation, its historical implications, and its cultural connotations in which land meets word. Stretching out as the *Riviera* (Latin *riparia*: shore) between the *hinterland* of France's Provence (Latin *provincia*: province, or more accurately land conquered by the Romans, from Latin *vincere*: to defeat) and the *waterland* of Italy's Tuscany (Etruscan *sk*: water), ranging from Marseilles, the *land of spring* in the west (Ligurian *mas*: spring) to Genoa (Celtic *gena*: mouth, or Latin *genu*: knee, but in any case in that corner where the coast almost rectangularly snaps off to the southeast) to La Spezia in the east (Latin *species*: splendour), Liguria is a geographic and poetic presence on whose grounds *The Azure Spell of Liguria* traces a poetics of influence, a confluence of literary forces, and an affluence of cultural materials and Mediterranean affinities as they converge in Nietzsche, Freud, and Benn's œuvres.

Friedrich Nietzsche cherished mountains and shores, water and sunlight – at Lake Silvaplana in the Swiss Engadine (Celtic *enos*: water) as well as in Liguria (Celtic *Lugus*: god of light) around Genoa and Rapallo, on whose coasts he walked, on whose rocks he rested, awaiting dawns and noons, contemplating islands and other circular matters, while fashioning himself as a sun-seeking lizard who, with the liberating creation of *Also sprach Zarathustra* (*Thus Spoke Zarathustra*), rolled a heavy rock off his soul. Sigmund Freud enjoyed the beach, rolling – in his own words – like a marine creature in an Arnold Böcklin painting on Rapallo's carpets of rocks, blissfully immersed in a time warp that surely transcends his journeying and carries over into his post-Nietzschean discoveries about the human mind. Gottfried Benn did not like the sun. He preferred not only plain to peak and precipice but also desks at windows to rocks on sea shores. Rather than rolling rocks off his soul in Nietzschean fashion (not to mention a Freudian rolling on beaches), Benn was sufficiently content to gaze at the horizon from a distance, occasionally admiring rolling billiards during his few brief escapes to the Riviera, in order to *laisser les bons temps rouler.*

The Azure Spell of Liguria examines European writing in the light of what Predrag Matvejević has called "mediterraneity" – a quality neither ethnically defined, nor based on inheritance alone, but rather centred on forms of cultural learning and literary creativity. None of the three writers who are the focus of my study is Ligurian by birth or heritage, and yet all three hold a remarkable affinity with Liguria. *The Azure Spell of Liguria* concentrates on Liguria as the site where Nietzsche, Freud, and Benn's creative lives intersect, demonstrating the crucial role that the cultural geography of Liguria has exercised on their writing. While exploring Nietzsche's legacy with regard to Mediterranean affinity and literary expression, this study traces the geopoetic presence of the Alps and the Mediterranean as cultural landscapes of considerable impact on these three prominent writers of the Modernist era, arguing that places, their cultural increments, and their evocative names are entitled to literal as well as literary dimensions of signification.

The Azure Spell of Liguria explores Nietzsche, Freud, and Benn's German-language writing as it was conceived against a Mediterranean backdrop, showing that any profound reading of imaginative writing is undeniably comparative in nature. After centuries of northern longing for the south (and of German yearning for Italy, in particular), one may well think that the story has become fairly tedious – were it not for such intriguing cases as Benn and Freud. While Freud's intense relationship with the Italian Mediterranean as a site of antiquity that he frequently visited over a span of decades is certainly more straightforward than the one he entertained with Nietzsche's Liguria in particular, Benn's general dealings with the Mediterranean and with Italy are, by contrast, more deeply shrouded in mystery than his explicitly Ligurian poetics. Even if he visited the Côte d'Azur on few occasions in the interwar period, his fascination with the Mediterranean stems from Homer and the Bible as well as from Goethe and Nietzsche, who were likewise educated in Homeric and biblical matters, as was Freud.

Goethe famously inscribed flowering lemon trees of the south in emblematic ways ("das Land, wo die Zitronen blühn," the land where lemon trees bloom), while Nietzsche's predilections were for Dionysian ripe figs (along with their metaphorical potential) as a form of mature *peideia*. Freud praised the citrus and in this as well as innumerable other aspects followed Goethe, whereas Benn zoomed in on the olive. Unlike Goethe and Freud's lemon and orange trees, however, Benn's olive is less a symbol of longing than an emblem of agency: "da geschah ihm die Olive" (then the olive befell him) he writes in one of his *Rönne Novellen* (*Rönne Novellas*) – he (Benn's *alter ego* Dr Werff Rönne) did not visit the olive; the olive visited him.[2] This unlikely visitor became one possible synthesis (or complex) of the Mediterranean for Benn, given that the olive tree is native not only to the eastern Mediterranean (with one possible origin in Libya) but also to the adjacent coastal areas of western Asia and northern Africa.

In that it is committed to place and displacement in ways that go beyond the practice of travel, *The Azure Spell of Liguria* is not strictly speaking a study of travelogues or travel writing. Rather, it is a geopoetic study that focuses on place and displacement as they emerge in exilic and nomadic texts conceived and composed during Nietzsche's Ligurian wanderings (he called himself a "good European" and had serious doubts when it came to being German), Freud's Ligurian whistle-stops, and Benn the onlooker's imaginary Ligurian escapes into an exotically informed inner emigration.

The psychogeographical work that followed the insights of the early Freud and Sándor Ferenczi in the 1920s into what one could roughly summarize as the psychoanalytical variant of landscape symbolism was primarily conducted in the three decades following the Fascist era, that is, in the 1950s, 1960s, and 1970s – as, for instance, in Guy Ernest Debord's situationist or William Guglielmo Niederland's psychogeographic mappings. These situationist and psychogeographic readings of towers and bridges, rivers and borders, peaks and shores have recently been provocatively adopted by long-distance walker Will Self in his enticingly humorous illuminations of the profoundly complex relationship between place, body, and mind (in his 2007 *Psychogeography* he aptly speaks of the enigmatic "modern conundrum of psyche and place," which he sets out to "disentangle" in tragicomical fashion). Even though the geopoetic school with which *The Azure Spell of Liguria* specifically engages is less intrigued by the precise effects of a given geographical environment on human character and comportment than by the poetic facets and literary outcomes of these effects on receptive and creative minds, Will Self's spicy assessment of what he tellingly terms the "Côte of Desire" does play a certain role in the present study's deliberations on body and mind, word and world.

A so-called spatial turn in the humanities was diagnosed in the early 1980s (and has been discerned as an ongoing concern ever since) – a turning point at which a paradigmatic change of inquiry occurred, no longer concentrating nearly exclusively on time and history but focusing increasingly on place and geography (and including simultaneity as a chronotopic perspective). Since this turn, a wide range of publications have appeared on the geopoetic, geophilosophical, geopsychological, geocultural, geocritical, geohistorical, geopolitical, and even geomantic horizons, such as, for example, Joan Brandt's *Geopoetics: The Politics of Mimesis in Poststructuralist French Poetry and Theory* (1997), Stephan Günzel's *Geophilosophie: Nietzsches philosophische Geographie* (2001), Erika Schellenberger-Diederich's *Geopoetik: Studien zur Metaphorik des Gesteins in der Lyrik von Hölderlin bis Celan* (2006), Bertrand Westphal's *La géocritique: Réel, fiction, espace* (2007), Magdalena Marszałek and Sylvia Sasse's *Geopoetiken: Geographische Entwürfe in den mittel- und osteuropäischen Literaturen* (2010), and Merlin Coverley's *Psychogeography* (2010), which focuses on urban spaces (London and Paris), the visionary tradition, and the birth of the flaneur, while taking note of the 1950s situationists as well as Will Self.

The reasons behind the remarkable career that the plethora of geo-approaches has experienced in European literature are numerous. It is, however, evident that the political-geographic refashioning of Europe since 1989 not only fortified literature's increased investment in geography but also allowed for the rich quality of pan-European variants of the spatial turn altogether. It is its ethical and aesthetic commitment to place that puts geopoetics in particular contact with a series of modern literary theories and poetic experiments with genre – with, for instance, travel writing, exilic writing, and nomadic writing such as Nietzsche's, Predrag Matvejević's, or Kenneth White's. Such a geopoetics confirms the potential of literature to perceive, remember, and conceive worlds at home and elsewhere, and is intricately intertwined with questions of aura and territory, place, exile and displacement, de-territorization and re-territorization, as well as with a panoply of ideas about (post-) Goethean world literature and its place-bound ways of literary making (*poiein*).

Even though *Tel Quel* was influenced by a number of drastically innovative writers – among them Friedrich Nietzsche and Sigmund Freud – *The Azure Spell of Liguria* is not based in the French revolutionary poetics of *Tel Quel* or the post-Marxist theories that Joan Brandt engages with. And if my study sporadically touches upon questions surrounding representations of real and imagined spaces in Westphal's geocritical sense, my primary emphasis falls on imaginative writing and subjectively conceived place rather than socioculturally determined space. True, Westphal thoroughly discusses the differentiation between *espace* and *lieu*, as well as mimetic literary forms of geography – he even examines Cuban-Ligurian writer Italo Calvino in the urban space of Paris. However, *La géocritique* is obviously geocritical rather than geopoetic, draws from fictional spaces rather than poetic places, and focuses on postmodern rather than modern writing.

The Azure Spell of Liguria peripherally touches on Stephan Günzel (who takes note of Gilles Deleuze and Félix Guattari's Nietzsche readings, and briefly addresses *Geopoetik*, without, however, engaging with Kenneth White, nor specifically with Provence and Liguria)[3] and his geophilosophical assessment of Nietzsche as a walking thinker – in the context of Nietzsche's muscular consciousness it is worth recalling that philosophy was born as an itinerant, peripatetic discipline. My book also accords to some degree with Erika Schellenberger-Diederich's readings of geologically inspired lyrical maps, Alpine metaphors, and Friedrich Hölderlin's hints at the poetic interest of the earth's *Gestalt*. The actual geopoetic approach of *The Azure Spell of Liguria*, however, relies primarily and explicitly on Kenneth White, who not only coined the term "geopoetics" and is the founder of the Parisian Institut International de Géopoétique (1989), with which the Scottish Centre for Geopoetics (1995) is affiliated, but who in the mid-1950s in Nietzschean nomadic fashion lodged in a wooden shack on the banks of the Isar river in Munich (studying Nietzsche) and in the late 1970s defended his doctoral thesis on the theme of intellectual nomadism.

In that it traces the literary potential of this kind of *poiesis*, which grounds itself in both the relations and proximities as well as the borders and distances between earth and word, self and other, *The Azure Spell of Liguria* places itself in affinity with the kind of geopoetics that has opened up a wide spectrum of literary readings and representations of time-honoured places and commonplaces, as well as of modern displacements. "Place" in this context is obviously located above and beyond the idea of a literary setting, as well as of that of an inspiring ambience. Rather, it is examined in its particularities in a way that may well be reminiscent of Gaston Bachelard's 1958 *La poétique de l'espace*. It is granted that Bachelard's fine application of phenomenology to architecture focuses on human experience of domestic spaces and intimate places rather than of cultural landscapes. However, Bachelard's interest in lived experience, his classification of places according to their connotations, his categorization of vertical metaphors reminiscent of Freud (such as attics and basements), his study of solitude, his reading of the poetic image as psyche *in nuce*, and – last but not least – his implicit appeal to the makers (in his case, architects) to imaginatively ground their work in the experience that it has engendered and that it likely will engender in future dwellers. These facets enable us to discern some affinities between Bachelard's astute observations about domestic space and the present study's commitment to Liguria as a recess and refuge, outlook and vanishing point in the case of Nietzsche, Freud, and Benn's geopoetically inclined choices of places and words.

The Azure Spell of Liguria follows the geopoetic branch of scholarship that pursues points of convergence of "word and world," as Kenneth White puts it. It relies heavily on White's impressive corpus of geopoetic writing in general, and in particular on his *On the Atlantic Edge: A Geopoetics Project* (2006) and the recent receptions of his theoretical and poetic work as it spreads out from one cultural sphere (the Scottish islands and highlands, shores and moors in the north and west) to others (such as the Arabian world in the south and east) – investigations such as Norman Bissell's essays and poems (*Slate, Sea and Sky* of 2007), Tony McManus's *The Radical Field: Kenneth White and Geopoetics* (2007), and Bsaithi Omar's *Land and Mind: Kenneth White's Geopoetics in the Arabian Context* (2008). What *The Azure Spell of Liguria* shares with White's endeavours is that, while heavily relying on Nietzsche, it takes the word "geopoetic" itself at face value: as "world-writing" or "world-making," reverting to Goethe's idea of *Weltliteratur* (world literature) in a kind of writing that according to White "opens space" and "looks beyond the borders," preparing "sensitive grounds, subtle territory," and ongoing encounters of the "earth-thing" with the "mind-thing."

Kenneth White has stressed from the beginning that geopoetics can never lose touch with place, mind, or poetry. Early on he placed heavy emphasis on such figures as Friedrich Nietzsche, Friedrich Hölderlin, Arthur Rimbaud, and Walt Whitman. This point is crucial for *The Azure Spell of Liguria*, which is committed to tracing the concrete, individual steps that Nietzsche, Freud, and Benn have taken in the geopoetic direction, as well as their subjective associations as they determine their ways of writing – the genres they prefer, the images they conceive, the metaphors they coin. By "subjective," "individual," and "associative" I intend the opposite of "objective," "social," and "symbolic." Freud can become extraordinarly tedious when presenting us with his taxonomies of rather rigid dream symbols (jewels as male and jewel boxes as female genitals, and so on), while he is utterly intriguing when he introduces his open concept of free – subjective, individual, irrational, oneiric – association (one can, of course, always discuss how free free association actually is). I contend that it is this kind of free association that is intimately connected to a writer's geopoetic *techne*, while taking a certain distance from psychogeographic classifications such as William Niederland's symbolism.

Even if Freud was heavily drawn to such matters and Benn spoke of the word as "Phallus des Geistes" (phallus of the mind/intellect/ spirit), I doubt that Nietzsche, Freud, and Benn were drawn to Liguria because Liguria's map may resemble a rather twisted sort of phallus (Italy's entire geographic contour has been read as phallic, and one sometimes wonders to what kind of vistas some of us may have been exposed). It is compelling in this context that while engaged with terminologies and definitions (such as geopoetics versus geoculturology), Marszałek and Sasse's study *Geopoetiken* refers to White but includes an emphasis on the symbolic rather than the associative order of geopoetic things, albeit with a subjective rather than an objective mode of geopoetic construction.

Europe's two central cultural landscapes, the Alps and the Mediterranean, coexist precisely within the boundaries of the small, steep, compact, and remote world of Liguria, where the Maritime Alps and Ligurian Apennines sweep down to the Riviera. *The Azure Spell of Liguria* interprets Liguria as a microcosm in which the north-south axis (the Alps and the Mediterranean) and the east-west axis (the Riviera di *Levante* and the Riviera di *Ponente*) intersect at Genoa, while explaining how this intersection becomes relevant for a phenomenon that, in analogy with Kenneth White's "littorality," "atlanticity," and "nordicity," as well as with Predrag Matvejević's "mediterraneity," I have termed "ligurianity." It is revelatory that White should begin and end *On the Atlantic Edge* with Nietzsche (with whom he shares clearly more than an intellectual nomadism) and that in *Mediterranean: A Cultural Landscape*, Matvejević should remind us that it was Nietzsche who "set forth the possibility of acquiring mediterraneity no matter where one is from."

A joyous moment of curiosity and a memorable journey during my last year of school have left me with impressions so distinct that they have had a relevant impact on the writing of this book. I vividly remember my fascination when Edvard Munch's portrait of Nietzsche was projected onto the classroom wall – a large gloomy figure against a solar vertical landscape.

Munch's painting has repeatedly appeared as the cover for various books on Nietzsche, and is indubitably more appropriate than the well-known black-and-white portrait, devoid of any background, showing Nietzsche with the singled-out vacant stare and exaggerated moustache (dearer to his sister than himself) of his last decade of life in illness. I vaguely recall the confusion I felt following my first viewing of Munch's portrait, while we began venturing into some meaningful connection between Munch's *Nietzsche*, Freud's *Die Traumdeutung* (*Interpretation of Dreams*), and the principles of Expressionism as Germany's major contribution to European Modernism. On another occasion I had been initiated into the rebellious Expressionist aesthetics of shock and taboo through Benn's poems of disease, death, and decomposition, which at the time I found no less repulsive than Freud's major claims about mothers and fathers, sons and daughters, and the family romances in which they engage, whether wittingly or not.

In the subsequent summer I travelled to France and Italy: first to Provence and the Côte d'Azur, and then on to eastern Liguria (Lerici/Tellaro), whose almost vertical landscape, whose houses and gardens, vineyards and olive groves nestled in its terraced promontories, whose *trompe l'œil* paintings, tasty pesto, and azure sea provided reason enough for my enjoyment, even though I did not have the faintest idea at the time that Lord Byron had swum where I was swimming (allegedly farther than me), nor that Percy Bysshe Shelley had (unlike me) drowned and been cremated around there. At that moment I was aware neither of the time-honoured concept of *genius loci* nor of any Ligurian passion other than my own.

When I first encountered Benn's phrase "ligurischer Komplex" in the course of my readings for a university seminar on modern German poetry, my mind flew back to Liguria, delving into Benn's challenging poetics, which pervades virtually all of his creative writing and which he himself emphatically and repeatedly places in a post-Nietzschean context (while carefully shunning Freud). Nietzsche's *Morgenröthe* (translatable as *Aurora, Alba, Dawn,* or *Daybreak*), *Die fröhliche Wissenschaft* (*The Gay Science*), and *Also sprach Zarathustra: Ein Buch für Alle und Keinen* (*Thus*

Edvard Munch, *Friedrich Nietzsche* (c.1906) (oil on canvas). © 2012 The Munch Museum/ The Munch-Ellingsen Group/Artists Rights Society (ARS) New York. Used with permission.

Spoke Zarathustra: A Book for All and None) in particular were essential to my comprehension of literary expression, as well as to my reflections on the geopoetic literary territory of Liguria's aura, lure, and lore within the intellectual framework that Modernism offers.

I was soon convinced that Nietzsche the philosopher and Freud the psychoanalyst called for an evaluation not only according to what they said but also, and perhaps more importantly, according to how they said it (Fritz Martini in *Das Wagnis der Sprache,* for instance, places Nietzsche's poetic prose, along with Benn's and others', in that precise context). Their subversive poetic experimentation with language and literature (primarily with metaphor, syntax, punctuation, and genre) demands to be studied alongside the work of poets such as Dante and Goethe, William Butler Yeats and Ezra Pound, Rainer Maria Rilke and Gottfried Benn. This idea might make immediate sense for Nietzsche, who not only philosophized poetically but also wrote a fair amount of "brilliant prose" (Walter Kaufmann) and significant verse, such as the cycles titled *Idyllen aus Messina* (*Messina Idylls*), *Lieder des Prinzen Vogelfrei* (*Songs of Prince Vogelfrei*) – for the most part revisions and an expansion of the *Idylls* – and the ecstatic posthumous *Dionysos-Dithyramben* (*Dionysos-Dithyrambs*), written at the time of *Zarathustra* but already marked by Nietzsche's impending collapse. But what about Freud?

Lesley Chamberlain, who has written so insightfully on the mature Nietzsche in *Nietzsche in Turin* and who named her fascinating book on Freud *The Secret Artist,* provides more than just a hint at an answer regarding Freud as a repressed imaginative writer who, following Nietzsche,

---

Ernest Thiel's idea for Norwegian Symbolist artist Edvard Munch (1863–1944) to create a posthumous portrait of Nietzsche grew out of his admiration for both the poet-philosopher and the painter. A photograph of Nietzsche in the early 1880s was Munch's inspiration for his monumental 1906 painting of the poet of *Thus Spoke Zarathustra* (1883–5) in the midst of a vertical solar landscape (Nietzsche's moustache, eyebrows, and quiff not only frame his face but appear as imitative repetitions of the mountain peaks, almost as if they had taken on the *Gestalt* of their environs). Hans Olde's photographs of Nietzsche after his breakdown assisted Munch, in particular with his conception of Nietzsche's face – a face that seems intimately familiar with *Zarathustra*'s vision of the loneliest (in German, *Gesicht* is not only "face" but also "vision," as in Benn's *Urgesicht / Primal Vision*). Munch himself sojourned repeatedly on the French Riviera, painted in Nice and Monte Carlo (where he also developed a passion for gambling), and rented a villa in Saint-Jean-Cap-Ferrat in 1891, only a few years after Nietzsche's departure from this same coast.

co-created a language we tend to consider ours. We all, it seems, "speak Freud." Harold Bloom has repeatedly pointed to Freud's notions as the sole mythology that intellectuals of our time are able to share, while W.H. Auden in his poetic commemoration of Freud spelled out that Freud "quietly surrounds all our habits of growth," referring to him as "no more a person now but a whole climate of opinion"; and in *Whose Freud* Peter Brooks and Alex Woloch open up a great variety of possible niches for psychoanalysis in contemporary culture. Freud has become an international idiom, a kind of post-Nietzschean *lingua franca*, in which one converses about art and life, literature and culture. But whose language did Freud speak? Which legacy did he rely on? Whose geopoetic paths did he pursue?

Freud was not only an aficionado of literary texts, received the Goethe Prize for his writing, was nominated for the Nobel Prize by Thomas Mann, and wrote case studies that read like well-plotted detective stories; he was also, as Michael Billig argues in *Freudian Repression*, a frustrated poet who was not always successful in balancing repression and expression. Freud was a sensitive and radically innovative reader as well as an energetic gleaner, anxious denier, and guilty forgetter, whose receptive and creative principles manifest themselves in his post-Nietzschean use of an expressive currency coined in Liguria. *The Azure Spell of Liguria* locates Nietzsche as both Freud and Benn's expressive precursor in a variety of Ligurian locations – a philosopher-poet whose major writings are grounded in his Alpine-Mediterranean-Ligurian wanderings of the 1880s, the most prolific period of his life, and provide the thread that guides the reader through the present study's Ligurian topographies. The geopoetics here at stake is "less a question of genre than a question of intensity: it is situated at the extreme limit of prose," to borrow Bsaithi Omar's words on Kenneth White's "nomadic thought."

The emphasis on Freud after Nietzsche has a double motive. The first concerns my understanding of the complex notions of the Mediterranean and "mediterraneity," while the second is related to my approach to the dynamics of literary indebtedness and poetic tradition. *The Azure Spell of Liguria* welcomes the suggestion that thalassologist Predrag Matvejević makes when defining "mediterraneity" as a quality independent of a writer's "place of birth or residence," and thus as something "acquired, not inherited, a decision, not a privilege." Remaining comparative in scope in spite of its leaning towards texts originally written in German, *The Azure Spell of Liguria* combines Matvejević's trailblazing idea (which is, intriguingly, at once erudite and inclusive) with the related claim that T.S. Eliot made in "Tradition and the Individual Talent" (in 1919, the year that Benn launched the "Ligurian complex"): "tradition cannot be inherited, and if you want it you must obtain it with great labour."[4] As a result of my engagement with comparative poetics and my concern with word and place, the emphasis within the Mediterranean context lies on the nature of the image and the image of nature, as well as on the intimate bonds between this image and Freud's central notions of *Verdichtung, Verschiebung,* and *freie Assoziation* (condensation, displacement, and free association).

Although Benn has been described as Germany's Eliot and as the German Ezra Pound (Benn much admired both Anglo-American Modernists, even if his English was minimal at best), he has not enjoyed an international reception comparable to that of Modernists such as Yeats, Eliot, Pound, or German poets with Mediterranean affinities roughly contemporaneous with Benn (for instance, Rilke, the Mann siblings, or Hermann Hesse). Else Lasker-Schüler, however, described Benn as the "singende Oskar Kokoschka" (the singing Oskar Kokoschka) and each and every one of his verses as "Leopardenbiss" (leopard's bite) and "Wildtiersprung" (wild animal's leap), emphasizing the expressive painterly force of Benn's phenomenal nominal constructions. An exiled George Grosz sent coffee from New York to Benn in postwar Berlin, reminding him that he was, indeed, one of the greatest writers of his generation. While Alfred Döblin confirmed this assessment, other émigrés (most notably Klaus Mann) rejected Benn's work on the basis of his reluctance to leave Germany, together with his Expressionist colleagues, for southern France after Adolf Hitler's seizure of power. "Poets don't emigrate, novelists do" – provocatively asserts the author of *Männerphantasien* (*Male Fantasies*), Klaus Theweleit, emphasizing the poet's life within words as Benn himself time and again foregrounded, while focusing not on Benn's decision to stay as an opportunist move in his flirtation with incipient Nazism but rather on the poetic craft's sheer reliance on a poet's native tongue and full immersion in it.[5]

It took the English-speaking world far longer than Germany and France to face seriously Nietzsche's immense influence (and even today in North America, where French Nietzscheans are avidly read, Nietzsche's own presence hardly compares to that in France), whereas in Freud's case it was precisely the massive reception in the English-speaking world that led to his international acclaim. Nietzsche and Freud's œuvres have been translated promptly, completely, and repeatedly into English (notably by Walter Kaufmann and James Strachey, respectively), whereas

Benn's work has received relatively little attention. Beyond E.B. Ashton's 1958 *Primal Vision: Selected Writings of Gottfried Benn* (the volume's title is the English rendering of Benn's 1929 *Urgesicht*) and Volkmar Sander's 1987 *Gottfried Benn: Prose, Essays, Poems*, English translations of Benn are few and far between.[6]

There is hitherto no complete English translation of Benn's collected works, which is perplexing when one considers that he is not only one of Germany's most accomplished and intriguing poets but also a crucial witness to a turbulent period that reaches from Kaiser Wilhelm II to the Federal Republic's first chancellor, Konrad Adenauer, and that encompasses two world wars and two republics, all of which Benn experienced at first hand and about which he wrote creatively, polemically, and continually. The reticent reception of Benn's work in the English-speaking world may be a consequence not only of the poet's brief period of sympathizing with the birth of Hitler's regime but also of the absence of a complete edition of Benn in English – a lacuna that might at the same time be the result of the relatively unenthusiastic reception of Benn in North America in particular. This ellipsis is in any case curious and perhaps also the consequence of the notorious verbal difficulties that Benn's intense texts pose in their unique density of suggestive neologisms, challenging compounds, scientific terminology, medical jargon, mythical allusion, and geopoetic toponomy. Such innovation is a necessary outcome of what Benn calls – first in *Schöpferische Konfession* (*Creative Confession*) in 1919 and frequently after that – the most difficult problem that he faces as a writer: "Südwörter" (southerly words) and "ligurische Komplexe" (Ligurian complexes) as the ongoing challenge to transform experience and awareness into the poetic image: into something akin to what Eliot in "Hamlet and His Problems" (also 1919) termed the "objective correlative."

Minimal (if any) attention has been paid to the specifically Ligurian dimension of Benn's poetics. Hence it is one of my goals in this book to poetically situate Benn internationally, and to place him in the precise context of a Ligurian geopoetics. With the exception of Lia Secci's brief 1960s article, "Il complesso ligure di Gottfried Benn," Benn's "Ligurian complexes" have at best undergone a generalization into sites of the Mediterranean imaginary at large (the idea of the Mediterranean as a cultural construct rather than a physical reality), particularly so within the tradition of the German and British literary fascination with Italy as established by Goethe and the English Romantics. Alternatively, Benn's "Ligurian complexes" have occasionally been reduced to the poetic role that individual southerly words might have assumed in his poetry, as Reinhold Grimm has shown for the word *Blau* (blue) in *Gottfried Benn: Die farbliche Chiffre in der Dichtung*, legitimately (but perhaps too narrowly) focusing on the very *Blau* that Benn himself had called "das Südwort schlechthin" and "de[n] Exponent des ligurischen Komplexes" (the southerly word par excellence, and the exponent of the Ligurian complex).

Benn's poetics, however, is intimately related to Nietzsche's acute sensitivity to place. It is, I contend, specifically Ligurian rather than generally Mediterranean, and it is formally far more complex than the reading of a single poetic word could manifest (even if that word is *Blau*). It is hardly a coincidence that Ernst Bertram's interpretive milestone *Nietzsche: Versuch einer Mythologie* (*Nietzsche: Attempt at a Mythology*), with which Benn was as familiar as Thomas Mann and many others of their generation, was first published in 1918 (one year before Benn coined his notion of the Ligurian complex), and that it dedicates a small but complex chapter to Nietzsche's Ligurian "Portofino" as *Zarathustra*'s quintessential landscape, in which the philosopher's sentences are said to have formally emerged right out of the Ligurian promontory ("Vorgebirgstypus seiner Sätze," or "promontory type of his [Nietzsche's]sentences," as Bertram has felicitously put it).[7]

It is a writer's pursuit of Liguria's lure and deliberate acquisition of "ligurianity" that *The Azure Spell of Liguria* traces. Such a ligurianity allows for a revision of an exclusively native poetic "ligusticità" (the kind that paves the way towards a national dimension, as, for example, when Giorgio Caproni and Giovanni Cattanei in *La Liguria e la poesia italiana del novecento* consider it to be exclusively characteristic of twentieth-century Ligurian writers such as Camillo Sbarbaro or Eugenio Montale) into what one may want to call a geopoetic *opus ligusticum* that sets out to cross such national borders. Ligurianity suggests a geopoetic dimension that "recognizes strangeness" in the sense that Kenneth White has convincingly shown for the geopoetic nordicity at stake in his writings: "beginning with the lie of the land, remaining close to the elements, [geopoetics] opens up space, and it works out a new mindscape. Its basis is a new sense of land in an enlarged mind."

Through this geopoetic lens, *The Azure Spell of Liguria* perceives Nietzsche as Ligurian by choice, Freud as implacably Nietzschean, and Benn's "Ligurian complexes" as a chosen Nietzschean paradigm with unavoidably Freudian implications: a "complex" for Freud (and for pychoanalysts such as Jean Laplanche and Jean-Bertrand Pontalis in

their *Vocabulaire de la psychanalyse*) is an affective organization of free associations and representational devices: "ensemble organisé de représen-
tations e de souvenirs à forte valeur affective."[8] Recalling Goethe, one
might say that ligurianity is a "Wahlverwandtschaft," an "elective affinity"
that transcends any kind of regional kinship or national birthright and
instead implies Nietzsche's solitary battle for self-expression, on which
Freud and Benn drew so extensively. It is with good reason that Edvard
Munch's posthumous portrait of Nietzsche was inspired by *Zarathustra's*
riddle about the "Gesicht des Einsamsten" (face of the loneliest / vision
of the loneliest). In line with wanderer Zarathustra's own geopoetic
expeditions into the province at hand, ligurianity involves geography
rather than politics, philosophy rather than pedigree, inclusive literary
principles rather than exclusive local traditions, courageous solitude
rather than gregarious belonging, an outsider's perceptive perspectivism rather than an insider's granted osmosis.

The Latin suffix -(*i*) *tas* (English -*ty* as in "liberty" or "ligurianity" and
Italian -*tà* as in "*libertà*" or "*ligusticità*")[9] is added to an adjective (sometimes a noun) to form an abstract feminine noun that indicates a state
of being. What occurs when this adjective or noun happens to be a
toponym such as Atlantic or Liguria(n) is felicitously representative of
what geopoetic notions such as atlanticity or ligurianity set out to be. In
these toponymically derived states of being, as it were, the abstraction
that is inherent in the Latin-based suffix is preceded by a very concrete
root: the name of a place. Grammatically speaking, this place is at least
as firmly rooted in its name (*grammatike techne* as the art of letters and
related to *graphein*: to write) as its name is geographically (as written or
represented earth) rooted in its place.

Even if atlanticity is more abstract than the Atlantic, mediterraneity
more abstract than the Mediterranean, and ligurianity more abstract
than Liguria, these abstract nouns do not forfeit what is concrete about
a place and its name (and happily surrender their right to capitalization
for that matter), while gaining much of what geopoetics, according to
Kenneth White, stands for: a "theory-practice" that is committed to a
minute observation of phenomena as well as a transcendence of boundaries and an expansion of one's horizons: "think[ing] in terms of world
doesn't mean neglecting or forgetting the local. On the contrary. World,
open world begins where one is. Every territory, while maintaining its
presence and compactness, is open, if one knows how to read it."[10]

In his geopoetic approach to nordicity or northernness from a Scottish
point of view, but with "potential extrapolations to other areas" and the

"necessary look beyond the border" in mind, Kenneth White points to the innumerable significations that the word "north" has, while reminding us that he "put a lot of meaning into that word 'Atlantic.'"[11] White stresses the range of such meaning, reaching from a "sheer geophysical space" to a "wave-and-wind philosophy," and on to the "threshold of geopoetics"[12] that he calls atlanticity. Invested as I have been in revisiting mediterraneity and southernness, including the innumerable sites and significations that the words "Mediterranean" and "south" themselves have assumed over time, my geopoetic approach to the threshold of ligurianity in Nietzsche, Freud, and Benn's writing necessarily perceives the study of geopoetic literature as the study of place and word.

"What would Key West be without its name?" asks J. Hillis Miller in the introduction to *Topographies*. Well, "nomen" may well be "omen" – and Liguria is one such (n)omen for a variety of dreams and realities (geopoetic ones included). In the process of deploying and yet transcending the paronomastic dimensions of the toponym by moving between the historical and the visionary, the geographic and the poetic, the literal and the literary – that is to say, in the process of unveiling the land itself as bordering on the literal, of bringing the fascinating locus of the Ligurian littoral in contact with the Ligurian literal (Liguria's spell, Liguria's letters in the literal and literary sense) – I put a lot of meaning into that word "Liguria."

PART I

'Twixt Halcyon and Marathon: Azure Spell and Difficult Beauty

> … a word carries far, very far.
> Joseph Conrad

> … l'Azur! l'Azur! l'Azur! l'Azur!
> Stéphane Mallarmé

> … se allora mi avessero domandato che forma ha il mondo avrei detto che è in pendenza.

> (… had they asked me back then what form the world had I would have said that it was an incline.)
> Italo Calvino

Riviera Existence

> ... mixing memory and desire.
>
> T.S. Eliot

Liguria's lure may well be legendary. More than one poet dived into its sea – Byron swam, Shelley drowned. Not unlike the legends surrounding these poets, albeit hardly as short as their lives, Liguria's is a fairly recent lure, in that its legend's most remote protagonists are, indeed, middle-aged English Romantics sojourning in and around La Spezia in the early nineteenth century, just prior to their premature deaths. About one hundred years after their departures from this shoreline, in 1919, Italian playwright Sem Benelli baptized the Golfo della Spezia the *Golfo dei Poeti* – the same year that the Futurists staged their *Grande mostra nazionale futurista* in Genoa and that Gottfried Benn coined his "ligurischer Komplex" (Ligurian complex).[1] Benelli's act of renaming the easternmost portion of Liguria as a place where various poets have found their horizons was inspired not only by Lord Byron and Percy Bysshe Shelley but also by other (inter)national writers and artists of the nineteenth and early twentieth centuries who had either visited or taken up residence on the eastern Ligurian shore. Among these were George Sand, Arnold Böcklin, Emma Orczy, and D.H. Lawrence, followed by Italians such as Gabriele d'Annunzio, Filippo Tommaso Marinetti, and, more recently, Mario Soldati, to name the most famous. Liguria's lore is familiar with its lure.

Lord Byron journeyed in Portugal, Spain, and Albania and visited Athens, Smyrna (Izmir), and Constantinople (Istanbul). Once he had decided to leave England for good (and with it what he perceived as its hypocrisy, as well as his domestic life – of which he had become even

Lerici – Poesia del mare
(vintage postcard)

more tired than Freud did of his less than a century later), he toured in
Belgium and Switzerland, lived and lodged in Venice, Rome, Ravenna,
Pisa, and Genoa, grew weary of it all, and eventually committed himself
to the cause of Greek independence from the Ottoman Empire. Having
left Genoa for the Ionian Islands, he sailed to Missolonghi in order to
join Alexandros Mavrokordatos and the Greek insurgents, with whom he
planned an attack on Lepanto, in the Gulf of Corinth.

Before they were able to set sail, however, Byron fell ill and died.
Even though he is buried in England, the Greek equivalent of "Byron"
still names a suburb of Athens, while his heart, so the story goes,
remains in Missolonghi. This version of partial burial is reminiscent
of one of Gottfried Benn's favourite composers, Frédéric Chopin, who
spent turbulent times with George Sand in Majorca before continuing
to Barcelona and Marseilles, and whose grave is located in the Parisian
Père Lachaise cemetery, while his heart is kept in an urn in Warsaw's
Holy Cross Church. Such burial also recalls Byron's poet friend Shel-

ley, who drowned in a sudden storm when sailing back from the Tuscan Livorno to the Ligurian Lerici in 1822, in a boat that had been custom-built for him in Genoa.

In an attempt to account for that mysterious incident, it has been surmised that pirates mistook Shelley for the far more controversial Byron. The boat, in any case, was found about ten miles offshore, while Shelley's body was washed ashore and was subsequently cremated on the beach near Viareggio, where Sigmund Freud chose to vacation about a century later. Still in Liguria, Byron witnessed the spectacular scene from a distance, swimming in the Ligurian Sea during the ceremony and subsequently stressing the overpowering impression that the fire on a beach situated between the mountains and the shore made on him, as Shelley's heart was snatched from the pyre for the author of *Frankenstein* (Shelley's wife, Mary Wollstonecraft Shelley) to keep in a jar. Unlike Byron and Chopin's, however, Shelley's heart was buried in England at a later date – together with his son's body. His ashes were interred in Rome and are memorialized with William Shakespeare's famous lines about a sea-change, taken from *The Tempest*, engraved on Shelley's tombstone in Rome's Cimitero Acattolico, occasionally nicknamed the Cemetery of the English. Much later (after a fair amount of resistance and refusal because of Shelley's atheism and Byron's scandalous lifestyle), memorial plaques were installed for both Romantic poets in Westminster Abbey's Poets' Corner. Not surprisingly, most biographical works on Byron, Shelley, and their circle assess their lives and characters as wild, tangled, and rebellious, as mad, eccentric, and adventurous, relating these qualities to the poets' Mediterranean sojourns.[2]

As legendary and uncanny as these Ligurian lives and journeys, ships and shipwrecks, deaths and burials appear, it was an even more uncanny moment for me as a reader to discover in the second chapter of Orhan Pamuk's 1990 Turkish novel *Kara Kitap* (*The Black Book*) that artefacts and accessories, images and idols of lost, scorched, and forgotten people and places ("yakılıp kaybolmuş bazı devlet ve kavimlerin [...] tasvir ve putları"), cadavers, bones, and long-lost skeletons – not only of turbot and swordfish ("kalkan ve kılıç leşleri"), camels and priests ("deve kemikleri" and "papazların iskeletleri"), slave, bandit, and mistress ("köle [...] haydut [...] sevgili [...] iskeletleri") but also of Kaiser Wilhelm ("Kayzer Wilhelm") and the Genoese ("Ceneviz"), the Celts and the Ligurians ("Kelt ve Likyalı iskeletleri") – would come to light when the imaginatively anticipated drying up of the Bosphorus occurred ("Boğaz'ın suları çekildiği zaman").[3]

Byzantines and Ottomans were not the only players on the Bosphorus.

At least three other powers cultivated strong interests in controlling this sea strait: Pisa, Venice, and Genoa. Genoa exercised a strong economic influence in this region and organized its trade routes all the way to the Black Sea. That the only ethnicities Pamuk explicitly mentions should be Celts and Ligurians, rather than, say, Norsemen and Etruscans, or, for that matter, Romans and Greeks, Pisans and Venetians, is on the one hand in line with history, in that it is certainly true that the thalassocratic Genoese fleet appeared in and disappeared from this city's sea strait. On the other hand, however, the image of the marine tomb as readable archive is a product of a literary imaginary that does not revert to history exclusively but inscribes instead the dual nature of the sea in a way reminiscent of Hart Crane's "At Melville's Tomb," a poetic vision in which

> Often beneath the wave, wide from this ledge
> The dice of drowned men's bones he saw bequeath
> An embassy.
> [...]
> The calyx of death's bounty giving back
> A scattered chapter, livid hieroglyph,
> The portent wound in corridors of shells.
> [...]
> High in the azure steeps
> Monody shall not wake the mariner.
> This fabulous shadow only the sea keeps.[4]

Crane and Pamuk's (post-)marine visions of the shelving bottoms of the sea are indeed astonishing, both gloomy and enchanting, in that they intriguingly intertwine the challenges of living and dying with the demands of reading and writing. Pamuk paints an evocative anti-thalassic scene of a new life in a curious deep that once upon a time was celebrated as the attractive Eurasian sea strait of the Bosphorus. Not only is this powerfully imagined scene situated on the shores of the only city traversed and intercontinentally bisected by the sea, as Buket Uzuner repeatedly reminds us in her short fiction of memory and desire *Istanbul Blues*, which is set in the same Mediterranean locale as Pamuk's novel;[5] it is also in line with a vertically inclined Freudian imaginary, in that it creatively inquires into a latent past lying buried (all the while anticipating disinterment) – in the case of Pamuk's scenario underneath the marine surface where the eastern Mediterranean encounters the western Black Sea. Undermining more than just a few of our panoramic assumptions about places of Istanbul's aesthetic and historical calibre, Pamuk's literary dream is nevertheless situated in this city on the Bosphorus while simultaneously excavating its remote past of turmoil, invasion, and conquest and inventing a future perfect that is in thorough accord with the complexities of times only seemingly gone by. Pamuk's anti-diluvian image of the lower depths and the imagined visitor's weaving his way through them offers the reader a challenging perspective on the kind of time-space that is reminiscent not only of Freud's mental and yet Pompeiian archaeologies but of Dante's spine-chilling invention of an awe-inspiring underworld as well.

Whether the Mediterranean even "exist[s] other than in our imagination" is an intriguing question posed "in the South as in the North, in the Levant as in the West," writes Croatian critic Predrag Matvejević in an astute essay on place and memory, word and oblivion.[6] Were we to transpose his fascinating apprehension by selecting from this allegedly imaginary pan-Mediterranean pool a specific geographic region such as the Riviera, we might nonetheless find ourselves confronted with a similarly complex issue: in condensed form, yes, and not entirely unlike Pamuk's vision of the Bosphorus, its geographic situation and cultural potential, its depths and surfaces, its myths and legends, its stories and histories, its pasts, presents, and futures.

Located in southeastern France and northwestern Italy, the "Riviera is the entire French-Italian coastline," while "the Côte d'Azur is its myth," according to Mary Blume's study on the literary invention of what since the late nineteenth century has developed into a grandiose legendary locale of luxury, play, and illusion;[7] while according to François Girard, "la Riviera italienne est la côte de la mer ligurienne qui s'étend sur une longueur de 227 km entre Vintimille à l'Ouest et la Spezia à l'Est, adossée aux Alpes maritimes (Alpi marittime) et aux Appenins liguriens" (the Italian Riviera is the coast of the Ligurian Sea which extends across 227 kilometres between Ventimiglia in the west to La Spezia in the east, leaning against the Maritime Alps and the Ligurian Apennines).[8] In *Placenames of the World*, Adrian Room writes that the Côte d'Azur "is better known to English speakers as the French Riviera, and is the stretch of Mediterranean coastline between Cannes and Menton or Cannes and La Spezia, Italy."[9] Helena Waters, however, declares in *The French and Italian Rivieras* that "LIGURIA is the name of that part of France on the shores of the Mediterranean Sea between Marseilles and La Spezia, commonly called the French and Italian Rivieras."[10] Persuasively showing how the French Riviera was transformed only about a century ago into painterly

Modernism's azure "Elysium," Kenneth Silver submits, in *Making Paradise*, that "Grace Kelly's real-life marriage to Prince Rainier notwithstanding, there is no Côte d'Azur quite as splendid as the one we have long imagined."[11]

Appraisals such as these of one shoreline – its possible extensions, its various toponomastic denominations, its host of connotations, and the array of imaginaries that they have prompted – give rise to a panoply of onomastic questions and their relationships with the re-creation of actual places in the visual arts and in imaginative writing. In this context, acclaimed author-walker Will Self offers a moment of comic relief to a series of serious cultural considerations, hyperbolically empowering our imagination even further than Matvejević's well-placed stimulus, when suggesting that "the Côte d'Azur isn't really a place at all – more a state of mind stretched out over hundreds of kilometers of beaches, headlands, outcrops, fish restaurants, walled villas and foul-tempered chiens." Subsequently, Self mounts a compelling comparison between "this sun-soaked coastline" and "the strap of a bikini, suntan-oiled then teased by the imagination." In the context of his interest in and beyond imitative form, it is amusing to see Self swerve from his psychogeographic precursors who symbolically speak of phallic geographies rather than freely associated bikini straps, zooming in for instance on "Florida's strong resemblance to a limp penis" as related to "Florida as a place of retirement" and "America's siginificant inability [...] to 'project' its power into Cuba."[12]

Subversive though it may be, Self's portrait of the putatively real existence and intrinsic character of place, body, and their complex dealings with psyche relies on both the various degrees of lure indwelling in place names and on the tricks and charms of literary expression, as a result of which embodied minds may well stretch on sandy beaches while narrow strips of marine landscape unveil their family resemblance to the more alluring segments of a bikini. What we tend to forget is that the two-piece itself points to a paradoxically charged place – the Bikini Atoll and the post-Second World War nuclear tests carried out there – a fashionable appellation that may well have emerged in analogy with the dynamic libidinal potential held by bomb and bikini alike.

Granted, Self's stimulating assessment of this Côte as geographically nearly unreal occurs not only four decades after his first stay in Cap d'Antibes as a toddler, and two after his return to the same coast as a young man, but also about a century after Friedrich Nietzsche, Sigmund Freud, and Gottfried Benn's sojourns in a variety of locales on this azure shore. However, Self's chapter is titled "Côte of Desire" and is therefore geopoetically not only in line with the perceptions of Matvejević, Blume, Waters, and Silver but also curiously responsive to Nietzsche, Freud, and Benn's unwavering emphasis on the immense influence that the Mediterranean-Tyrrhenian-Ligurian-Provençal-Côte d'Azurean toponymic-geopoetic spectrum has exercised on their writing.

The space opened up between a place, its name, and a writer's desirous state of mind and imaginative teasing accords well with Self's post-Romantic wordplay on the impure rhyme of the French words *azur* and *désir*, beautifully reflecting Nietzsche, Freud, and Benn's creative and at times anxiously vexed relations with places and place names such as these. Their ingenious Mediterranean affinities are more often than not marked by desires not at all dissimilar to those that Self concisely presents as the dreamlike quality of this coast, while adding a provocative twist to the time-honoured literary *topos* of the classical *genius loci* – the spirit or sense of place nevertheless still dear to a Matvejević and his not entirely unrealistic "dream of a poetic of the Mediterranean where its place [...] seems of primary importance."[13]

Equally intrigued by the golden escarpments of Burgundy (read: his homeland Côte d'Or), and the Mediterranean's azure hues, Stéphen Liégeard, who frequently spent his winters in Cannes (and died there), launched, in his late-nineteenth-century award-winning *La Côte d'Azur*, his suggestive denotation for the coast as we have since imaginatively connoted it. About two years after Nietzsche's completion of the four books of *Thus Spoke Zarathustra* (1883–5), conceived and partially composed on the Riviera (in and around Zoagli, Rapallo, Santa Margherita Ligure, Portofino, Ruta, Genoa, and Nice) less than a decade before Freud initiated his series of Mediterranean journeys, at least two of which took him to the Italian-Ligurian segment of this coast (to Genoa and Rapallo in 1905), and about three decades before Benn embarked on his 1920s interwar tours through France, including the French Mediterranean (Perpignan, Palavas-les-Flots, and Cannes, among others), Liégeard, in 1887, launched the fame of this marine landscape in an intensely hued baptism.

Liégeard poetically liberated the place from its touristic name "French Riviera" that had evolved in analogy with the "Italian Riviera," as the primarily British winter guests at the time had chosen to call the eastern part of the Ligurian coast (which until about 1860 was more popular than the French segment, albeit still on a very small scale),[14] thus modifying "Riviera," which had been around since the Middle Ages. Since then,

Rapallo – Il porto
(vintage postcard)

however, various attempts have been made to feed the imagination with
the less poetic name that promises luxury and beauty: "Riviera," one possible Italian word for coast, has been appropriated not only for cars and
clubs, films and songs, hotels and casinos around the world, but also in
toponyms for various coastal strips, such as the Australian Riviera, the
Chinese Riviera, the Cornish Riviera, the Emerald Riviera, the English
Riviera, the Mayan Riviera, the Russian Riviera, and the Turkish Riviera
– and, hardly marine in nature, the shore of the Swiss Lago di Lugano
has been labelled the Swiss Riviera.[15]

While the French generally refer to the Italian Riviera as "Riviera,"
and to the French Riviera as "Côte d'Azur," the Italians tend to call the
Italian Riviera "Riviera ligure" and the French Riviera "Costa azzurra" – a
rendering that skips the French quantitative expression/genitive *de/d'*
that is partially responsible for the poetic quality of Liégeard's name for
the shore in question, which does not refer to the coast itself as azure,

but rather evokes how the small coastal land takes part in the sum total of its Ligurian sea's azure depths and horizons.

Precisely at the time when Nietzsche took up his nomadic life of a stateless wanderer (as well as various temporary residences in the Alps and on this coast), Liégeard inscribed his conviction that this specific strip of Mediterranean seaside is clearly deserving of a name more potently expressive of its allure than "Riviera," assuring us that "le long de cette plage baignée de rayons mérite notre baptême de CÔTE D'AZUR" (the extension of this beach bathed by the sun's rays deserves our baptism as Côte d'Azur).[16] Withdrawing inland to Brochon, Liégeard not only eagerly anticipated further travels to this coast's azure waters under halcyon skies but also wrote his book from memory, combining future solar perspectives with detailed retrospectives that vividly recall his prior roaming there. Liégeard's performative act of geopoetic naming is intimately bound up with his belief in the close affinity between landscape and longing, memory and expression. This conviction also manifests itself in his attempts to persuade poet-friend Xavier Marmier, an avid traveller and prolific writer in his own right, to join him on the next possible occasion: "O poète ! ... Venez ! ..." (Oh poet, come join me here).[17]

In the 1860 Treaty of Turin, France and Italy agreed (in defiance of Nice-born Giuseppe Garibaldi) that the County of Nice and the Duchy of Savoy should be ceded to France (while Tuscany and the Romagna were annexed to Sardinia). It is particularly compelling to see in this historical context how Liégeard's work captures this land- and seascape of the "Côte" without defining it in terms of the Franco-Italian border in ways as rigid as others would do after him. Albeit for very different reasons, Erika and Klaus Mann in their 1931 *Buch von der Riviera*, for instance – a book that promises to unveil what is not covered in the Baedeker guidebooks – are highly border conscious at a time when Italian Fascism was already in full swing and Hitler's seizure of power, the exodus of exiles from Germany to southern France, and the partisan war in Liguria not too many years ahead.[18]

Rather than being dominated by a nationalistic conception of territorial conquest, Liégeard's *La Côte d'Azur* is permeated by a poet-traveller's enthusiastic mood of enjoyment, as well as by the alluring enchantment of the place. As a poet, Liégeard clearly cares more about Johann Wolfgang von Goethe's passionate Mignon than about the exact location of the national border, which less than three decades previously had undergone that eastward shift in favour of France. Liégeard is committed to this border only in so far as it serves as a vantage point from which to cultivate poetic dreaming, while his contemporary, Nietzsche, who first approached this coast from the Italian side, atmospherically reclaims *Nizza* as an Italian rather than a French city. In contrast to the English language, German to this day deploys the Italian rather than the French version of the toponym: Nizza, not Nice. In any case, the city received its name as a reference to Nike (goddess of victory), which the Greek colonists from Marseilles gave it after they had defeated the Ligurians in the second century B.C.E.

That said, "there is an atmosphere of romance about a frontier," according to Captain Leslie Richardson's 1923 *Things Seen on the Riviera,* "that is not found in other parts."[19] Even though he makes this comment with regard to the western Ligurian Bordighera, he ends up turning Genoa into much more of a frontier than the Franco-Italian border itself. Richardson's concept of the Riviera covers the coast from Marseilles in the west to Genoa in the east. While he characterizes Genoa in a quasi-Nietzschean way as "the city of palaces, old streets, historical associations, and a great commercial harbor," he emphasizes, on the very last page of his book, that "with Sestri Ponente we have reached the eastern limit of the Western Riviera, La Riviera di Ponente, 'Shores of the Setting Sun.' To do justice to Genoa and the Riviera di Levante or 'Shores of the Rising Sun' with all the fairy coast from Nervi, past Rapallo to Spezia, would require another volume" – a rhetorical gesture towards a tome desired, even fancied, but never actually composed.[20]

Neither Liégeard nor Richardson ventured towards La Spezia's eastern Riviera of Shelley and Byron, nor even to the Tigullian Rapallo and Portofino so crucial not only for Nietzsche in the 1880s and for Freud in 1905 but also for Modernists such as William Butler Yeats and Ezra Pound, who took up residence there in the mid-1920s. In stark contrast to Liégeard's vision, however, what Richardson calls a "fairy coast" hardly opens up an imaginative poetic dream-space of desire. Richardson, after all, was a captain in the early twentieth century, and Liégeard a poet of the late nineteenth.

Gradually moving eastward, Liégeard begins his travelogue with a presentation of what is often posited as the westernmost fringe of the Côte d'Azur: Marseilles and its environs. In addition to Toulon, Hyères, Saint-Tropez, and Cannes, among others, his texts revisit isles such as the Île de Porquerolles (memorialized by Joseph Conrad, who set sail from Marseilles and whom Benn admired), as well as Grasse, Vence (where D.H. Lawrence died), and further locales in the hinterland, before proceeding to Antibes, Nice, *La Corniche* (in Liégeard's time one of what were to become three coastal roads), Èze (cherished by Nietzsche), and La Turbie (inscribed by Dante as the westernmost point of the Ligurian shoreline), eventually reaching the principality of Monaco.

Liégeard's continuation to Italian-Ligurian towns such as Ventimiglia, Bordighera, San Remo, Taggia (whose legendary small purple olives– *taggiasche* – Benn praises in his Rönne prose), Alassio, Albenga, Pietra-Ligure, Noli, Savona, Celle-Ligure, Varazze, Pegli, and Genoa is presented in terms as complimentary as those in which he describes stretches of the French coast. And even though Liégeard stylizes his awareness of the border as a perfect viewpoint from which to foster yearning, both French and Italian locations on this coast are presented as one shoreline under the auspices of one poetic title, intended transnationally, with neither the azures nor the waves nor the sun's rays stopping at any such border: *La Côte d'Azur* – "ces filles de la vague et du soleil qui s'appellent Hyères ou Cannes, Nice ou Menton, Bordighera, Pegli ou San-Remo" (these daughters of the wave and of the sun whose names are Hyères or Cannes, Nice or Menton, Bordighera, Pegli or San Remo).[21]

Were we to update Liégeard's eventual salute to an *Italia* which, in becoming a nation, yielded Nice to France, we would face precisely the trajectory from what is currently the French region Provence-Alpes-Côte d'Azur (PACA) in the west (whose capital is Marseilles) to the contemporary Italian region Liguria in the east (whose capital is Genoa) – each one narrowly defined for administrative purposes within the two European countries, rather than more broadly envisioned as time-honoured cultural and auratic territories. Extending from the lower river Rhône to the Italian border, PACA accommodates the former province of Provence, the papal territory of Avignon, the Sardinian-Piedmontese county of Nice (that is: the French Riviera or Côte d'Azur, narrowly defined), and the southeastern portion of the former Alpine province of Dauphiné.

Rather than being inclusive as PACA, present-day Liguria's confines, by contrast, mark not only a substantial territorial compression but also a significant shift that renders Ligurian toponomastics all the more compelling. Mainly with the intention of securing the natural borders of the peninsula, Augustus not only saved Virgil's *Aeneid* against its author's wish but also divided Italia into eleven tribal *regiones* of which Liguria (then termed Regio IX) was one (memorialized in the inscription of the Augustan trophy in La Turbie),[22] while Liguria was also a later Roman province that extended to the river Po and included most of modern Piedmont as well as parts of Lombardy but not the medieval or modern Ligurian region, which was instead incorporated into the Roman province of Alpes Cottiae. Today, the toponym "Liguria" forms a part of the official administrative language, without being assimilated into any vernacular spoken in Ligurian lands.

Literarily removed from territorial considerations of conquest such as these, Liégeard marks his inspiring itinerary by a profound interest in Italia as a fascinating eastward continuation of this coast and its aura (in Kenneth White's sense of territory as an auratic entity) as a place of sentimental longing, assuming a timbre hardly inferior to that of Goethe's intense Mignon, while at the same time putting great emphasis on the fact that the remote has drawn nigh, that distances and differences between French and Italian locations on the panorama that the Côte offers are minimal after all: "D'Hyères a Gênes [...] le trajet est court" (from Hyères to Genoa the distance is short).[23] Liégeard's *Côte d'Azur* is peppered with literary references and allusions, of which that to Italy as "le pays où fleurissent les citronniers et auquel aspirait Mignon: l'*Italia*, dans la langue du *sì*" (the land where the lemon trees bloom and for which Mignon was yearning: *Italia* in the language of *sì*) is a single but crucial example.[24]

It comes as no surprise that Liégeard's *Côte d'Azur* combines an escapist post-Goethean reverie with an erudite hint at Dante's *De vulgari eloquentia*, in which the exiled poet introduced Italian as the Romance "lingua del sì"– the language, that is, which deploys *sì* when it intends *yes*, as opposed to other Romance variations of affirmation, such as *oc* and *oïl*: "bel paese là dove 'l *sì* suona" (fair land where *sì* is heard), writes Dante in the *Inferno*.[25] In Liégeard's work, this reference appears in the textual company of quotations from sources as diverse as Dante's *Inferno*, tributes to Lord Byron's hill in Albaro (a suburb of Genoa), the Provençal etymology of the Golfe-Juan as Gourjan (referring to the sea's immense depth), and the work of the Ligurian writer Giovanni Domenico Ruffini from Taggia, who settled in England and whose *Vincenzo, Or Sunken Rocks* of 1863 greatly contributed to a positive attitude towards Italy on the part of the British.

In stark contrast to Liégeard's poetic denomination "La Côte d'Azur," which was relatively late in entering the lexicon, the toponym "Liguria" designates the narrow strip of land in the northwestern Mediterranean and is eponymically based in the ethnicity of the ancient Ligurians, a pre-Indo-Germanic people in Provence – ethnically speaking, the Provençals were Ligurians – the western Alps, and northern Italy, who were oppressed by both the Celts and the Etruscans, confined to the Maritime

Alps and the Apennines, and eventually subjugated by the Roman founders of Aquae Sextiae, modern-day Aix-en-Provence.[26]

Provence as a cultural realm southwest of the Massif Central is, among
other things, known for its medieval lyrics, its lavender fields, and its
Romanesque architecture derived from a strong monastic tradition and
evident in places such as the Abbey of Sénanque. In his *Rambles on the
Riviera*, Francis Miltoun (after Dante) aptly confirms it as "the fair land."[27]
Provence can be considered as the revised name for the Roman Provincia
Gallia Narbonensis, with which it is roughly coextensive. Similar to the
domains of Provence, those of Liguria have also undergone changes. In
ancient times, Liguria extended from northern Italy into southern Gaul
(Gallia Narbonensis, alternatively known as Gallia Transalpina) – a geographic coincidence, quite literally, that suggests a partial congruence of
the regions, provinces, territories, thresholds, frontiers, and shifting borders and borderlands here in question.

Fernand Braudel and Matvejević have written extensively on the Mediterranean, addressing questions of borders and liminal spaces from a
variety of cultural perspectives.[28] While Braudel's historical insights into
the complex personality of the Mediterranean play the lead in his engaging work on this cultural landscape, Matvejević has composed a memorable Mediterranean breviary around the intriguing affinities between a
multifaceted cultural space and the spectrum of literary imaginaries that
it has driven. His compelling geopoetic inquiry surely tempts one to borrow from Dante, whose literary topography of the *Divina Commedia* consistently hovers between geographic fact and poetic form, between what
Goethe later on with regard to autobiographical writing was to debate
as truth and fiction (a revision of the Platonic *logos* and *mythos*), a textual life's journey of which his retrospective Italian travelogue (*Italienische
Reise*) forms a significant part. It might provide at least one preliminary
reply to what Matvejević presents as a ubiquitously posed question: that
of the Mediterranean's actuality vis-à-vis our Mediterranean conceptions
and deceptions, dreams, visions, and visualizations.[29]

On the Ligurian Edge

... in writing, beauty prefers an edge.

Anne Carson

According to Dante in ante-Purgatory, "tra Lerice e Turbìa la più diserta, / la più rotta ruina è una scala, / verso di quella, agevole e aperta" (the loneliest, most jagged promontory that lies between Turbìa and Lerici, compared with it [the purgatorial slope], provides stairs wide and easy). This triplet mounts a potent comparison between the purgatorial geography and that of Liguria, ranging from Turbìa (the French La Turbie) in the west, to Lerice (the Italian Lerici) in the east. Dante's lines about Liguria's "loneliest, most jagged promontory" are framed by a few comments on Plato and Aristotle at the beginning, and pilgrim Dante and his guide Virgil's decision to ascend Mount Purgatory at the end. The steep mountain rising immediately before them makes such an impression on the wanderers that even Liguria's harsh perpendicularity as Dante recalled it from his exilic wanderings through Romance lands seems to provide "stairs wide and easy."[30]

"Vista dall'alto, da chi vola in aeroplano," write Alberto Girani and Cristian Galletti in their slim volume on Liguria (appropriately titled *Una terra fatta a scalini* / A territory made of stairs), "la Liguria collinare sembra, in alcuni suoi punti, un'enorme carta geografica" (Seen from above, by someone flying in an airplane, some spots of hilly Liguria give the impression of an enorme map). That, seen from the hawk's perspective, Liguria's vineyards, olive groves, and orchards wrap around the hills as colours, words, and lines wrap around a map's pages and hence give the impression of the land itself as a map,[31] that is to say a representation of itself and its staircase composition, or else already a text whose steeply situated geopoetic lines can be read on location, very much accords with the fact that it can hardly be overstressed that the staircased steep structures of Turbìa and Lerici mentioned by Dante are the names of two actual geographic locations in what are now southeastern France and northwestern Italy and roughly mark the westernmost (La Turbie/ Turbìa close to Nice) and easternmost (Lerici close to Tuscany) points of the Ligurian (Genoese) territory of Dante's time. With the coast from Sarzana to Ventimiglia in possession of the Genoese, medieval Liguria was more extensive than the modern region (covering some of current Provence), while the Provence of the time extended into what is now the region of Languedoc-Roussillon, bordering the northeastern Spanish Catalonia.

Where, then, is Liguria? And when? What then, is Liguria, and what is it not? Why not? "I wake in the night and still have to think: is this France or Italy? (One time it was Baden-Baden.) But I always know straight away: this is not Dublin, this is some other place," writes Christine Dwyer Hickey in the "Bordighera 1933" chapter of her 2009 novel *Last Train from Liguria.* Her title plays with the dynamics of arrival and departure, reminding us, perhaps, of the first trains to Liguria, which enabled a wider and more comfortable access to the region as a tourist destination.[32] In other words, where we are, where we arrive, and from where we depart very much depend upon when, and on when not only in the historical sense (that, too, of course, especially when the year is 1933), but also with reference to day and night, reverie and dream.

Is Liguria a part of France? Had Garibaldi intercepted Helena Waters's earlier mentioned suggestion in this regard, he might well have stirred in his grave. If Liguria is, indeed, a part of France, when, why, and in what sense (as conceived by Nietzsche, Freud, and Benn) is this so? Does the Côte d'Azur extend into Italy as Liégeard submits, and if so, how far, when, and why? What is immediately exposed and what lies dormant in the complex Ligurian realm, if we consider such a realm historically and archaeologically, geographically and culturally, auratically and geopoetically? What kinds of bells have the *nomina propria* of the Mediterranean, the Tyrrhenian, the Riviera, Provence, the Côte d'Azur, and Liguria rung, what kinds of imaginaries have they enticed?

From the eleventh century to the end of the eighteenth, the Superb Republic of Genoa was an independent Ligurian city-state, and in a broader Mediterranean context is related to Galata overlooking the entrance to the Bosphorus. Galata was a Genoese-Ligurian colony from the end of the thirteenth century (Dante's time) to the middle of the fifteenth. In Italian, Galata is related to *calata*: downward slope – an appropriate name, so it seems, for both Liguria's small, steep territory and Galata's location on a hill sloping down to the shore of Istanbul's Haliç (Golden Horn).[33] The Greek language, however, offers us another possible signification with *oligos*: small, on the one hand, and on the other both *galaktos* and *Galat* – the former means milk and speaks well for the area's medieval bucolic pastures, while the latter signifies Celtic in Greek and remembers the Galatians, who camped in Galata in the Hellenistic period, before settling down in the central Anatolian Galatia, literalized later on in Paul's Epistle to the Galatians in the Roman province. Galata is also known as Pera, which originates in the ancient Greek equivalent for the fig field located on the other side, and is a neighbourhood in Istanbul's modern borough of Beyoğlu, alternatively known as Karaköy or black village, with the major panoramic outlooks of the Galata bridge and Galata tower as reminders of Genoese conquest and landmarks of profound Ligurian interest.

When studying the Mediterranean, one finds prehistoric sites in Sardinia, Greek settlements in Sicily, the Romans in Lebanon, the Genoese in Byzantium, and Arabic traces in Spain. Any deep understanding of the Mediterranean cultural landscape presupposes a digging down to the beginnings of civilization, to Maltese megaliths and Egyptian pyramids. It implies – when time is as ripe as it seems to be in Pamuk's fantastic novelistic scenario – not only an encounter with Liguria in Provence-Liguria but also its uncanny return from underneath the opaque waters of the Bosphorus.

The fairly recent vogue of modern Mediterranean studies is characterized by a highly energetic potential and becomes more and more complex and compelling, especially if as a multicultural and crossdisciplinary field of study it takes into account the multifaceted possibilities of geopoetic and geophilosophical approaches to its cultural output, rather than standardizing the objects of its inquiry into the monotonous binary of one European centre and many post-colonial non-European peripheries. Among others, Braudel and Matvejević have contributed significantly to an open discourse that is not only transdisciplinary and intercontinental but also draws rather fine distinctions. Matvejević presents his readers with various profound insights into the Eurocentrism manifest in a great deal of classical Mediterranean studies, which have focused mainly on the Graeco-Roman heritage, frequently excluding both the Levant and Africa from their investigations. If this neglect is not the object of the present study, it is a theme significantly deserving of research that dares to venture above and beyond the postcolonial and postmodernist matrices alone. In this vein, both Braudel and Matvejević in exemplary persistence have covered a wide geographic and historical range, all the while including minutely detailed European views in their larger projects.[34]

It is rewarding to avoid homogenizing the cultures of Europe by neglecting their unsubtle pre-national differences in linguistic and literary terms, but instead to discern that centres have been established at a cost to a variety of peripheries located outside of Europe (as centres in the margins and also as peripheries in the margins) but also within it (as peripheries and margins in the centre): as culturally constructive provinces and foundational premises located, for example, in Ligurian-Provençal lands. Toril Moi's assessment of Norway and her native Norwegian tongue, which she emphatically characterized as "marginal within Europe" and, as such, rather "different from German or French," speaks well to this issue.[35] One could zoom in further and say that within the nations that Moi defines as the centre there are margins as well, especially linguistic ones, to which the plethora of European vernaculars bears witness – some already extinct and others on the verge of extinction.

The southwestern German Swabian for example is a vernacular in which major characteristics of medieval German (Old and Middle-High German) are still preserved (but no longer present in standard German). Swabian deviates from modern standard German (which is actually Low rather than High German in the linguistic classification of historical development) to such an extent that German speakers from other regions tend not to understand it. Modern standard German is encountered north of a linguistic border known as the Benrath Line (named after a section of the city of Düsseldorf and similar to the linguistic north-south divide that the river Loire marks in France), in the lowlands of Germany, rather than to the south of that line in the highlands, where Swabian as one possible manifestation of High German is located.

The standard pronunciation of modern German is most common north of the Benrath line, where traditionally Low German used to be spoken. Major German poets such as Friedrich Hölderlin, Eduard Mörike, Friedrich Schiller, and Ludwig Uhland, however, were natives of Swabia and wrote south of the Benrath line – some of them at least partially in the vernacular (particularly Uhland), whereas others interspersed their writing with idiomatic expressions, provincial toponyms, and grammatical constructions derived from the vernacular (as well as, especially in Hölderlin's case, from the Greek). It is therefore not surprising that on many occasions their marginal tongue as a language that carries physical weight compares more easily to the Provençal idiom than to the northern Hanseatic German of, say, a Thomas Mann, at times interspersed with *Platt*, or Low German.

Vernaculars reaffirm time and again their idiomatic potential vis-à-vis forcefully formalized languages for the sake of nation formation. What Dante understood about the superannuated suitability of Latin for a contemporary poetry that is alive is likewise applicable to the politically assigned national languages – an assignment that led to a sort of vernacular aphasia for the sake of an artificially determined national genius of language. But it is precisely the literary use of regionally coloured tongues that offers the space for a creative drift from the normative powers of a rather rigidly defined mainstream.

The southern French Provence, its rich medieval landscape, and the old Provençal language as the *koine* of its troubadour poetry are examples of such a culture – one that, after coming into full flower in the Middle Ages, was long suppressed in favour of the northern French national language (the equivalent of Dante's language of *oïl*), before being rehabilitated as a local language and regional performance in an ethnic turnabout during the last decades of the past century. It seems crucial in this context of revived regionalism that even if he never excludes local detail from his deliberations, Kenneth White puts great emphasis on the continuities as well as the vicissitudes of tradition, reminding us that "regional complacency" and "couthy localism" are diametrically opposed to the geopoetic approach, for "real living, real intellectual endeavour, real aesthetic realisation has little or nothing to do with identity (even less with a fixed collective identity), and everything to do with a field of energy." This approach, however, does not equal a "neglecting or forgetting the local."[36]

It is remarkable that at the end of the nineteenth century, as well as at the beginning of the twentieth, Nietzsche and Pound had already rediscovered and rewritten the Provençals' *gai saber* (gay science) and *alba* (dawn song) in the process of their revolutionary experiments with a poetically explosive language. Both Freud and Benn explicitly celebrate Nietzsche's expressive power time and again, and while Freud aims at repressing Nietzsche's Ligurian influence on him, Benn in his exuberant creative misprisions of Nietzsche repeatedly emphasizes the precursing geopoet's Provençal-Ligurian orientation as essential to what he perceives as their shared task: "Nietzsche als Ganzes [...] Reiche der Helle, der Gaia [...] Schule der Genesung [...] man kann es auch geographisch sagen: [...] das Provenzalische und Ligurische" (Nietzsche sum total [...] realms of light, of Gaia [...] school of convalescence [...] one may also express it in geographical terms: [...] the Provençal and the Ligurian).[37]

Granted, radical literary novelties tended to be coined in capitals such as Paris and London from the turn of the century on. Nietzsche and Pound, however, took significant detours through Provençal and Ligurian lands, following the troubadours, who, shortly before Dante and long before Freud, had situated the adulterous and clandestine version of Eros at the core of poetry (as well as of human concerns more broadly), lifting taboos and inaugurating the intimate relationship between love and exile, while celebrating the strictly codified form of the love poem on the one hand and the love poem as cultural locus of adulterous desire on the other (as well as love writing's self-therapeutic potential). "Provence knew," according to Pound, and Eliot contended that Pound was "much more modern" when working with "Italy and Provence, than when [...] deal[ing] with modern life."[38] This productive tension between the old and the new becomes yet more striking if one recalls that Provençal poetry is composed in the vernacular of the same name,[39] which Dante classified as the *langue d'oc*, a rich language he rejected in favour of his own Florentine *lingua del sì*, by which Liégeard was still much intrigued half a millennium later.

Even though Dante raised his native Florentine to the status of the living vernacular most brilliantly suited for Italian poetry after its liberation from an ossified Latin (calling his native language of *sì* the *volgare illustre*), it is significant that he nevertheless classified Provençal *oc* as poetic in nature, while relating French *oïl* to the prosaic genre (not a compliment at the time that Dante wrote). He did not choose the language of the Provençals as the most illustrious, and yet the troubadours' influence on Giacomo da Lentini, Pier della Vigna, and other representatives of the *scuola siciliana* can be traced in no uncertain terms. Through this thirteenth-century Sicilian school, which developed at the court of Swabian Frederic II, a place where various exiled Provençal troubadour poets found refuge, the troubadours' impact on the thirteenth-century *dolce stil novo* (sweet new style) can hardly be overestimated. This new lyric was first mentioned by Dante in *Purgatory*, where the pilgrim is told that as a poet he had managed to create the new genre of the sweet new style, while his famous love poem from *Vita Nuova* is being quoted: "Donne ch'avete intelletto d'amore" (Ladies who have intelligence of love).[40] That this *stilnovismo*'s precursors are found in Provence-Liguria, for instance in the Genoese Lanfranc Cigala, hardly comes as a surprise.

Centuries after Dante, the Florentine tongue was raised to the status of Italy's national language, whereas the *langue d'oc* (the Provençal spoken south of the Loire) was marginalized to the point of extinction, when the *langue d'oïl* (French) became the central linguistic demarcation of national France. And yet, Dante's Romance classification for the pastures of Provence and its vernacular was eventually responsible for the first half of the modern-day toponym of the southwestern French administrative region Languedoc-Roussillon, which is PACA's neighbour towards the west and borders northeastern Spain, where Catalan suffered a suppression similar to that of Provençal in France – both are recognized as regional languages, while neither enjoys official status in either France or Spain, which recognize French and Castilian as their only official languages.

Another peripheral premise in this geographic sphere is the land named after the ancient Ligurians, with its harsh, arid, and demanding landscape, difficult of access and awkward, at times impossible, to traverse – a spit of land pretty much unfabled until Byron's if not Nietzsche's times, a land whose natural and cultural qualities were a far cry from the Graeco-Roman ruins, idyllic landscapes, and classical architectures that many taking the Grand Tour were determined to see. Liguria, however, is one of the oldest settlements in human history. The Balzi Rossi complex of grottos on the French-Italian border provides evidence for this near Ventimiglia ("Balzi Rossi" comes from *baussi russi* which means "red rocks" in the Ventimiglian vernacular), where paleolithic finds were made, for instance of Cro-Magnon burial sites. The Ligurian language is pre-Roman, locatable somewhere between the Italic and the Celtic, and, with the exception of a few proper names, extinct: *melo* for instance is the Ligurian noun for "stone," and has survived as an etymological remnant in place names such as Quiamelius or Ventimiglia.[41]

For reasons of proto-national concerns in the centre and the related Romantic commitment to the sublime, the French Alps and Paris, Rome and its Campagna (which before Goethe posed in it for J.H.W. Tischbein's 1787 painting had been considered desolate and depressing) represented four major points of interest among the extensive migrations of the Grand Tour. Provence and Liguria, by contrast, hardly constituted a part of such programmatic endeavours prescribed by the normative educational itineraries of tours for aristocratic or otherwise privileged male youth.

Following the major vogue of the Grand Tour, there might have been a few exceptions to this rule, even though those concerned part-time residents or temporary settlers rather than touristic travellers, narrowly defined: Aleksandr Puškin, who probably provided the first image of Genoa in Russian literature (in *Bachčisarajskij fontan*); or the nineteenth-century nonsense poet and topographical artist Edward Lear, who travelled widely in and beyond the Mediterranean, chose Rome as a base, but at the same time settled in the Ligurian Villa Tennyson (named after Victorian poet Lord Alfred Tennyson whose verse he illustrated), and died in San Remo; or the nineteenth-century Russian writer Vilhelm Karlovich K'juchel'beker, who spent about half of his life in Siberian exile but who also met Goethe in Weimar, wrote a poem about Lord Byron's sudden death and a poem titled "Nizza," and surprisingly abandoned his intention to see Rome in favour of a sojourn on the Riviera; or the mature Aldous Huxley, who commuted between Florence and the northwestern Tuscan Versilia, bordering with Liguria.[42] Charles Dickens and Henry James were there as well. James dedicated various passages of his *Italian Hours* (1909) to Liguria (for example in "Italy Revisited"), while Dickens took up residence in Genoa for a time and in his *Pictures from Italy* (1845) wrote a chapter on "Genoa and Its Neighbourhoods," stressing his delight in the city's beautiful difficulties, its "noble bay [...] deep blue Mediterranean [...] palaces [...] dotted all about; lofty hills [...] and [...] strong forts perched high up on their craggy sides [...] bold and picturesque rocks on the seashore [...] green vineyards [...] interminable vistas of grapes, trained on a rough trellis-work across the narrow paths. [...] The lizards [...] play in the sun. [...] narrow lanes [...] great villas [...] avenues and terraces, and orange-trees, and statues, and water in stone basins."[43]

Dickens characterized the remote beauty and discomforting travail inseparable from the charm and beauty of the place, aptly referring to it as a "sequestered spot," whereas James in his assessment of a few Ligurian locales – including an anecdotal account of an unnamed but prototypically inscribed "picturesque old city upon a mountain-top" and its "circling mountains" and "road dipping downward among chestnuts and olives" as well as La Spezia and Lerici – provides us with an acute sense of Genoa's breath-taking verticality, splendid density, and sombrely yawning dimensions:

> Genoa is the tightest topographic tangle in the world, which even a second visit helps you little to straighten out. In the wonderful crooked, twisting, climbing, soaring, burrowing Genoese alleys the traveller is really up to his neck in the old Italian sketchability. The pride of the place [...] is a port

of great capacity [...]. Genoa [...] is the crookedest [...] of cities; tossed about on the sides and crests of a dozen hills, it is seamed with gullies and ravines that bristle with those innumerable palaces for which we have heard from our earliest years that the place is celebrated. These great structures, with their mottled and faded complexions, lift their big ornamental cornices to a tremendous height in the air, where, in a certain indescribably forlorn and desolate fashion, overtopping each other, they seem to reflect the twinkle and glitter of the warm Mediterranean. Down about the basements, in the close crepuscular alleys, the people are for ever moving to and fro or standing in their cavernous doorways and their dusky, crowded shops, calling, chattering, laughing, lamenting, living their lives in the conversational Italian fashion.[44]

Beyond exceptions such as these, however, Liguria, unlike most other places on the Italian peninsula, was generally not appreciated as an artistically worthwhile landscape by foreign travellers. With the exception of poet-philosopher Nietzsche, who chose to withdraw and take up residence there to inaugurate his geopoetic endeavours in an array of locales on the Riviera, up to the early twentieth century Liguria had primarily seemed valuable as an infrastructural point of transition, and mainly as a consequence of Genoa's seaport. Before railways were built in Liguria, the port of Genoa was one possible place where one could arrive by sea from abroad, and a significant visual manifestation of *La Superba*'s earlier nautical rule and spirit of conquest, as well as the entire Ligurian region's seagoing tradition, embodied metonymically in the names of its most adventurous mariners and daring citizens: Amerigo Vespucci and Cristoforo Colombo.

"*Sligo in heaven* murmured uncle William / when the mist finally settled down on Tigullio / But Mr Joyce requested sample menus from the leading hotels," writes Pound in his *Pisan Cantos*, remembering how Yeats ("uncle William") had remembered (and relocated) his Celtic past on Ligurian location (in Rapallo and in Pound's presence) by dropping the place name Sligo – the Celtic Sligeach, which names a county and a town, and which means river of shells, referring to the rocky river bed of the Garavogue, laden with the poet's childhood memories about this western Irish locale off the centre, a place of dream and mystery, of allure and imagery so potently present in Yeats's writing.[45] That the Tigullio, which forms a part of the Ligurian province of Genoa, should in that very moment have so much in common with Sligo is a geopoetic matter of imaginative grafting, an admixture of perception and invention, of mind, myth, and memory so crucial for the formation of toponyms and the places and writings they invoke. But it may well be more than merely visionary; it suggests a mnemonic dimension: before their integration after the Roman conquest, Ligurians and Celts had as a matter of fact maintained intricate relations with one another.

Tracing the presence of the Alps and the Mediterranean as Europe's two major cultural landscapes of substantial impact on Nietzsche, Freud, and Benn, the present study examines how these landscapes coexist precisely within the boundaries of the small and compact, steep and remote world of Liguria, where the Maritime Alps and Ligurian Apennines sweep down to the Riviera, leaving scant space for a narrow coastline of sheer beauty on the one hand and significant difficulty on the other.

On the grounds of this Alpine-Mediterranean microcosmic borderland called Liguria, the north-south axis (the Alps and the Mediterranean) and the east-west axis are inscribed along the sun's daily rhythms of *levans* and *ponens*, lending their names to Liguria's eastern sunrise and western sunset, respectively: Riviera di *Levante* and Riviera di *Ponente* (Captain Richardson appropriately put emphasis on such onomastic dimensions). These Ligurian north-south and east-west axes intersect at Genoa – a Ligurian world of which Cuban-Ligurian writer Italo Calvino says the following:

> Chiamasi "opaco" – nel dialetto "ubagu," – la località dove il sole non batte […] mentre è detta "a solatìo," o "aprico," – "abrigu," nel dialetto, – la località soleggiata. Essendo il mondo che sto descrivendo una sorta d'anfiteatro concavo a mezziogiorno e non essendo in esso compresa la faccia convessa dell'anfiteatro, presumibilmente rivolta a mezzanotte, vi si riscontra di conseguenza l'estrema rarità dell'opaco e la più ampia estenzione d'aprico.
>
> (The location unreached by the sun is called "opaque" – in [Ligurian] dialect "ubago," – whereas the sunny side is termed "solar" or "sunkissed" – in dialect "abrigu." Since the world that I am describing is a sort of concave amphitheater toward the south [noon] which does not comprise the convex face which is probably oriented toward the north [midnight], it is, therefore, extremely rare that one encounters the opaque, while being widely exposed to the location's solar extension to the south.)[46]

With its concave location on the coast (which is diametrically opposed to the convex positioning of Marseilles), Genoa is a perfectly suited locale to present the geopoetic referentiality between Ligurian place and

Ligurian word, as a geographic locale coinciding with a literary entity. This implies more than a sense of surface; it significantly also provides the sense of a concave inward curve, a deeper structure of remoteness, and a geologically and archaeologically informed verticality in accordance with Freud's notion of archaeology as psychology, as well as with Calvino's sense of a post-Nietzschean perspectivist, theatrical, even geometrically inclined approach to the Ligurian arch, wavering between the enclosed and the exposed, between land and sea, between farmer and sailor. Calvino's perspectives are pervaded by local knowledge and offer a vantage point from which to consider Liguria's visual oscillation between obvious open airy spaces and enclosed opaque compartments, precluding a permanent and dependable localization: "D'int'ubagu,' dal fondo dell'opaco io scrivo" (I write from the opaque, from the depths of the opaque), concludes Calvino.[47]

Etymology may well visualize these intentions further. The Turkish noun *kıta* denotes both poetic stanza and geographic continent (island of the world). In that it visualizes and energizes the dynamics of a shared form between an actual place and a literary text, *kıta* might be the most succinct summary of the geopoetic ventures of *The Azure Spell of Liguria*, which argues that Liguria's smallness and compactness, steepness and remoteness are qualities mirrored in the texts and theories of the three modern canonical writers discussed here. The semantic dimension of *kıta* reflects any geopoetic effort in joining the littoral with the literal on a basis that transcends the homophonic quality of these terms of shores on the one hand and letters on the other. In a similar vein, the English noun "stanza" that denotes a structural unit of a poem, derives from the Italian noun *stanza*, wich means both "room" and "stanza" (or strophe).

In partial accordance with the idea of *kıta*, "developed area" translates into German as *erschlossenes Gebiet*, that is to say: "unlocked area," a turn of phrase, in other words, that illustrates well the parallels between place and text as encoded, enclosed entities difficult of access, which are then disclosed and read – be it in composition or interpretation, landscape or travel, architecture or agriculture. The English words "landlocked" and "deadlocked" rely on similar place-bound semantics, throwing further light on the implications of the practically landlocked marine space of the Mediterranean and the sheer spectrum of imaginaries that it has triggered. Further, the Arabic-derived word *kıta*, as a matter of fact, is significant not only in terms of geography and poetry but also with regard to geometry (in that it refers to a section) and geology and archaeology (in that the related *kat* refers to a segment, storey of a building, or buried layer). Word and place are less present in their horizontal than in their vertical dimensions, as Samuel Beckett's Estragon in a discussion with Vladimir about places, memory, and recognition exclaims, while "pointing to the ground with both hands," colouring his speech with a typically macabre touch in the second act of *Waiting for Godot*: "You and your landscapes! Tell me about the worms!"[48]

This coincidence of word and place, etymology/toponymy, and geology/archaeology, which manifests itself in Nietzsche, Freud, and Benn's texts as geopoetic entities marked by distinct geolocational properties, puts form to matter in an Aristotelian sense, providing the exquisite admixture of Alpine and Mediterranean increments in the Ligurian landscape with a concrete identity, definitive essence, or *quidditas*. Liguria is the only region in Italy that is entirely framed by natural borders: the mountains in the north form a gigantic amphitheatre facing the marine stage to the south. In this vein, Ernst Bertram's *Nietzsche: Attempt at a Mythology* not only follows Goethe's visual interests (the book's epigraph quotes Goethe on drawing) but, significantly, also dedicates a small chapter to Nietzsche's Ligurian "Portofino" as Zarathustra's most characteristic landscape, in which the philosopher's syntax is said to have formally emerged right out of the Ligurian promontory – one more way of saying *kıta*:

> Ein Lieblingstypus Nietzsches ist die Satzform, welche den ebenmäßigen Grat des Gedankens über seinen scheinbaren Abschluß hinaus zu einem überraschenden Vorgebirge verlängert und umbiegt, zu einem Kap, das jählings eine neue Fernschau bietet, das zu neuen Küsten wie ein erster Brückenpfeiler hinüberweist – und sich zugleich schon zur Fläche des Schweigens hinunterfallen läßt. Diesem Vorgebirgstypus seiner Sätze begegnet man durchgehend.
>
> (One of Nietzsche's favorite [syntactic] forms is the sentence that extends and turns the balanced spine of thought beyond its apparent conclusion toward a cape that abruptly affords a new perspective pointing toward new coasts like the first pier of a bridge – and already simultaneously slopes down toward the surface of silence. One encounters this promontory type of sentence [of his] everywhere.)[49]

It is unfortunate that Robert Norton's translation not only renders "Fläche" (plain) as surface (which would be "Oberfläche") but entirely skips Bertram's phrase "zu einem überraschenden Vorgebirge verlängert" (extends towards a surprising promontory). It is precisely the sudden emergence of this very Ligurian promontory and its phenom-

Portofino
(vintage postcard)

enological affinity not only with words such as "cape," "perspective,"
and "coast" but also with Nietzsche's highly poetic "promontory type of
sentence" that stresses this affinity, the form that Bertram so distinctly
discerns as shared between Liguria's landscape and Nietzsche's ways
of constructing thought and its expression in a very specific variant of
hypotactic (rather than paratactic) German syntax.

    Predrag Matvejević mentions the Mediterranean qualities of central
European cities such as Salzburg or Prague. The Mann siblings perceive the Côte d'Azur as a combination of France, Italy, and Africa. And
while Nietzsche characterizes the Swiss Engadine as a place where Italy
meets Finland, the Ligurian Portofino was to him, among other things,
an auratic territory (in Kenneth White's sense) from which to envision
not only the Ionian Islands (identifying with Lord Byron's embarkation)
but also Brazil and Africa. In light of such concoctions, it is probably as

"difficult to explain the repeated impulse to piece the Mediterranean mosaic together, to make yet another catalogue of its components, verify the meaning [...] and the value of each with respect to the other"[50] as it is to accept Dante's decisive clarity in passing sentence on the precipitously hazardous qualities of the Ligurian landscape. This seemingly impenetrable, peripheral strip of at times almost perpendicular land – the fully vertical is rare in nature – remote and eccentric in the truest sense, comes not only to classify toponymically but also to embody geopoetically significant passages of Nietzsche, Freud, and Benn's hardly mainstream creative realizations.

Liguria incarnates the three writers' expressive and compositional convictions, and their writings, in turn, formally and thematically manifest precisely the qualities of the Ligurian locality – as small, dry and dense, hard, clear and bright, as their aesthetics of the small and intense form, of a poetic image, an aphorism or other forms of wit – which Liguria presents in its anatomic appearance and physiognomic silhouette. Indeed, rather than a phallus or perhaps a bikini strap, Liguria's contours delineate the shape of a concavely implaced boomerang, determining a point of departure and framing one's perception of the sea on the one hand, while on the other returning to the very point of departure reflecting upon itself, in imaginative accord with Calvino's sense of "forme [...] complesse e nello stesso tempo [...] semplici in quanto tutte contenute [...] da quel mondo di linee spezzate ed oblique tra cui l'orizzonte è l'unica retta continua" (complex and at the same time simple forms in that they all are encompassed by that world of interrupted and oblique lines of which the horizon is the only continuous one),[51] as well as with Roman Jakobson's definition of the "poetic function" as the one out of six possible functions in verbal communication that is primarily in touch with its own message *in situ*. While Calvino points to the horizon as the only dependable straight line in his geopoetic world that is the Ligurian poetic landscape, he very much also stresses Liguria's various vertical lines and dimensions (for instance of palm trees or highly poised houses). Likewise, Jakobson plays off the horizontal and the vertical, relating his elaborations upon the metaphorical dimension of poetic language to the vertical axis of selection rather than the horizontal axis of narrative-metonymic combination, which he eventually coordinates with Freud's notions of "Verdichtung" (condensation) and "Verschiebung" (displacement) as the major proto-poetic aspects of dream work.[52]

As a consequence of a dynamic geological history, the most conspicuous formal features of the Ligurian Mediterranean are massive mountains pressing upon narrow shores, a close juxtaposition of summit and abyss on a precise threshold of land and sea. The rocky skeleton of the Ligurian landscape offers both a maximal surface and a maximal density on minimal ground covered by the alluring mantle of Mediterranean flora. Liguria's almost vertical steepness and quasi-hermetic enclosure are qualities that the locale shares with poetic writing, in that these two aesthetic characteristics – steepness and enclosure – are not merely descriptive of the land's brusque topography but also constitute two distinct literary references: to Goethe's "steil" (steep) on the one hand, and to the troubadour poetics called "clus" (enclosed) on the other.

In his *Italienische Reise* (*Italian Journey*), the seaborne Goethe clearly differentiates between the coordinates of vertical poetic writing and those of horizontal prose: "Einbildung und Gegenwart verhalten sich wie Poesie und Prosa, jene wird die Gegenstände mächtig und steil denken, diese sich immer in die Fläche verbreiten" (Imagination is to reality what poetry is to prose: the former will always think of objects as massive and vertical, the latter will always try to extend them horizontally).[53] This generic assessment follows Goethe's psychological deliberations on why Scylla and Charybdis (he is on a boat close to Sicily at the time) are in present nature much farther apart than in the epic rendering of this legendarily uncertain passage.

This assessment immediately precedes the epistolary entry titled "Naples: An Herder," where Goethe diaristically deliberates on how his being in an actual Mediterranean location has brought *The Odyssey* to life for him. While Goethe thus associates poetic composition with imagination and steepness, the most poetic subgenre of troubadour song has been classified, in contradistinction to *trobar leu* and *trobar ric* as *trobar clus*. Unlike *ric*, which is concerned with a rich style created somewhat for its own sake, *clus* transcends "rich" in that it is committed to shared form, combining the psychological with the poetic and the geographical, presenting itself as the most elaborately enclosed, most highly inventive, rhetorically most complex, and psychologically most enigmatic among the three forms of *trobar*, relying on aura and territory as surrogates for emotion while inscribing the hermetic equally generically as Goethe defines the steep.[54]

Medieval Provence thus revises the spontaneous emotional pleasure of perceiving the easily accessible light song (*trobar leu*) and soft picturesque setting into something akin to the "difficult beauty" elaborated on by Pound – the kind of Modernist beauty that matters greatly in Nietzsche, in Freud, and in Benn, a beauty that is aware of and even construes the hidden vagaries of Liguria's anatomy despite its well-known Mediterranean components of sun, sea, and sky: "vento ligure, veni [sic]," writes Pound, "'beauty is difficult' sd / Mr Beardsley [...] beauty is difficult [...] beauty is difficult [...] beauty is difficult [...] beauty is difficult [...] Beauty is difficult ... the plain ground / precedes the colors. [...] and that certain images be formed in the mind / to remain there / [...] La beauté, 'Beauty is difficult, Yeats' said Aubrey Beardsley [...] / So very difficult, Yeats, beauty so difficult." This somewhat obsessive act of repetition (underlined further by my non-accidental omissions, to recall Marianne Moore) is immediately preceded by an incantation of the Ligurian wind as poetic inspiration on Tuscan location, as well as being juxtaposed with Pound's favourite lines taken from Guido Cavalcanti's love poem "Donna me prega" (A lady asks me), which Pound had earlier translated as *Canto XXXVI*, and which he later consistently remembered in the *Pisan Cantos* of which this segment on "difficult beauty" forms a crucial part.[55]

As a captive in Pisa at the time, Pound remembers not only the Ligurian wind but also the conversations he had there about artists, writers, places, and memories while out walking around Rapallo with William Butler Yeats. The more complex intellectual pleasure in unlocking this kind of demanding beauty as a potential epiphany is not drawn from reliably halcyon shores or bucolic pastures alone; rather, it is laboriously developed as a product of astute perception and reflection. If one stops tending to the demands of a Ligurian geopoetics, its fragile equilibrium begins to dissolve.

However steep and enclosed it may be, however incongruent with our ideas of conventional beauty and stereotypical Mediterranean imaginaries, Liguria exists as a precise geography that helps to complicate a frequently homogenized picture of the European Mediterranean. I insist on Liguria's existence as a distinctly marked actual land, as well as a toponym for this geography in the northwesternmost part of the Italian and the southeasternmost part of the French Mediterranean of our time, eponymically derived from the ancient Ligurian ethnicity and situated precisely between two regions, which, in their own right, developed into *topoi* of significant poetic impact: Provence with its troubadours in the northwest and Tuscany with Dante and the *stilnovismo* in the southeast.

Much in the sense of Matvejević's stimulant doubt about the Mediterranean's existence (or definition) beyond our imagination (and simultaneously as the precise basis for its geopoetic potential), the Mediterranean is, of course, a real place made of many real places; it is also, however, a time-honoured commonplace of classical canonization, of iconic locales and blessed isles, of Arcadia and Utopia, as well as of excluded and neglected areas outside and inside of Europe. Held vis-à-vis this scenario and the question that Matvejević poses in regard to it, the Ligurian land runs not only perpendicular to the Ligurian Sea – it also runs counter to the many imagined horizons of our extensive and at times elaborate Mediterranean mindscaping.

Liguria's nature between Genoa and La Spezia can achieve an almost vertical inclination (for instance around Genoa, Portofino, and Rapallo, in the Cinque Terre, and around Lerici and Tellaro). Its cliffs and slopes are steep, and its art and architecture, culture, and agriculture have adapted to and adopted, extended, reconstructed, and repeated these givens, appropriately reconfiguring the landscape towards practical ends, thus translating the place into a very specific cultural landscape whose cultivation occurs hazardously on man-made terraces precariously poised between laboriously constructed and seemingly endless drystone walls. Constructed landscapes are an agrarian necessity on this demanding territory facing the Genoese and Provençal shoreline. "*I mundi sun veggi* (i monti sono vecchi)"(the mountains are old) is an expression that Ligurian farmers have long used to indicate the age and barrenness of their mountains and the various demands that agricultural activity has posed on them for generations.[56] The cultural heritage of the Cinque Terre, five steep and secluded villages, three of them medieval, and two dating back to Roman settlements, castled upon rock spurs, located between Punta Mesco and Punta Nero – Monterosso, Vernazza, Corniglia, Manarola, and Riogmaggiore – superbly exemplifies this craft of traditional Ligurian landscaping.

It is intriguing in this context of terraced cultivation that, unlike the subterranean infernal circles and niches or, for that matter, the hovering heavens and spheres panoramically viewed from the amphitheatrically constructed paradisal rose, the topographic architecture of Dante's *Purgatorio* is subdivided into "terraces." In ante-purgatory there are spurs, in purgatory terraces, reached by stairs carved out of rock: the Italian *cornice* suggestively implies both frame and ledge (reminding us of the first picturesque Côte d'Azurean coastal road or *Corniche* that Liégeard panoramically celebrated), with the seventh and final purgatorial terrace located at the summit, bordering the *paradiso terrestre* (earthly paradise).

While it is self-evident why the open-air terrace cannot make an appearance in the subterranean landscape of Dante's *Inferno*, it is striking that

Manarola, a Cinque Terre village
(Photograph by the author)

the terrace is explicitly mentioned only once in the *Paradiso* (and on this single occasion it refers back to the previous purgatorial leg of the journey, where it comes far more frequently to the fore).[57] While there are nine circles in the *Inferno*, there are nine terraces on Mount Purgatory, and nine spheres in *Paradise*. Related to "territory," which Kenneth White prefers to "region" (for the former has the "aura" which the latter as "purely administrative term" lacks),[58] the word "terrace" is related to territory and is literally a heap of earth, a level indentation, an element of layered landscape where nature meets culture, reminiscent, indeed, of the carefully landscaped Ligurian terraces that time and again create additional land by way of dramatic architectonic and agricultural means that keep constructing stages, frames, and ledges against the forces of time, wind, and erosion. While Nietzsche's *Gay Science* is a borrowing from the Provençal discipline of *gaya scienza*, it seems worth venturing into the phrase's proximity not only to the auratic and poetic territory of

Provence and its lyric craft but to *Gaia* as the earth itself – a step that geo-poetically combines the "earth-thing" with the "mind-thing," as Kenneth White has it, thus transcending the borders of the place that is more concretely in question here.

Dante's *Divina Commedia* not only presents a geopoetic cartographer's minute construction of a precise literary map of early fourteenth-century Italy, permeated by geographically verifiable places and landscapes, but does so in the form of a vertical archi-texture rather than a map's plane projection. Mount Purgatory practically appears as a reverse image of the infernal funnel, a pit turned upside down and inside out, as it were, with the vertical immensities of high and low approaching each other in meaning (in a sense similar to what Freud suggested in his analysis of pri-meval words: "Urworte").[59] It is in this intermediate *Purgatorio*, the mid-dle *cantica* of the *Commedia*, located between the *Inferno* and the *Paradiso*, that Liguria suddenly enters Dante's arena. It does so not as the birth-place of yet another inimical shade or friendly acquaintance but rather as a *tertium comparationis cum grano salis*, so to speak, when on the journey from the shore to the island base of Mount Purgatory the inclination seems so inaccessibly steep and extraordinarily grand that the actual landscape of Liguria is remembered as something that might present the lesser evil, had the pilgrim not been on a fixed itinerary but free to choose the steep slopes, narrow paths, and rocky stairs of his wanderings.

Throughout the minutely constructed and gradually developed land-scapes of the three canticles of his *Divina Commedia*, Dante consistently relies on intermediate places, which in their existence between actual and mythopoetic geography are of great relevance to the present geo-poetic reflections on Liguria as a literary and expressive landscape in Nietzsche, Freud, and Benn. Similar to his deployment of both mythi-cal and actual figures, Dante's toponymy covers lands and lakes, moun-tains and regions, rivers and cities, while moving swiftly from Babylon, Cyprus, Venice, and Siena, to Morocco, Majorca, Florence, and the Maremma. Dante does not explicitly mention Liguria in his poem, but as is appropriate for his time, refers to the Ligurian terrain metonymically as Genoese.[60] The *Inferno* abounds with landscape vocabulary, mostly of the vertical and hermetic kind (Goethe's "steil" and the troubadours' "clus"), ranging from barren slopes to enclosed passages, from towers, gates, and blocked-off roads, to tombs, chasms, and abysses, from ravines and thickets to fortresses, castles, and canyons. Comparisons to the Alps are legion in the *Divina Commedia*'s rendering of jagged rocks and stairs, bridges and fosses. Lake Garda and Peschiera are mentioned, as well as the Trentino, Brescia, and Verona.[61]

Illustrator Barry Moser has provided an imaginative map of the Mediterranean. It is aptly inserted in Allen Mandelbaum's bilingual presentation of *Paradiso*, precisely between Dante's earthward gaze and the
celestial hierarchy. Moreover, Dante directly refers to the shores of Lig-
uria-Provence, when in the paradisal Heaven of Venus, Folco of Marseilles, one of the troubadours whom he praises earlier in his *De vulgari
eloquentia*, addresses the Mediterranean mnemonically and intercontinentally (almost foreshadowing Orhan Pamuk):

> la maggior valle in che l'acqua si spanda, / [...] / 'fuor di quel mar che
> la terra inghirlanda, / tra ' discordanti liti contra 'l sole / tanto sen va, che
> fa meridïano / là dove l'orizzonte pria far suole. / Di quella valle fu' io
> litorano / tra Ebro e Macra, che per cammin corto / parte lo Genovese dal
> Toscano. / Ad un occaso quasi e ad un orto / Buggea siede e la terra ond'
> io fui.
>
> (the widest valley into which the waters spread from the sea that girds
> the world, between discrepant shores, extends eastward so far against the
> sun, that when those waters end at the meridian, that point – when they
> began – was the horizon. I lived along the shoreline of that valley between
> the Ebro and the Magra, whose brief course divides the Genoese and Tus-
> cans. Beneath the same sunset, the same sunrise, lie both Bougie and my
> own city.)[62]

Importantly, the Mediterranean is here presented as the largest sea in
the hemisphere of land, extending, as a unity, between the Provençal-
Azurean-Ligurian coast of Europe (Marseilles and Genoa) and that of
Africa (Bougie), while the other hemisphere contains the world-girding
ocean with isle Mount Purgatory and its terraced lands as the only body
of land.

Turbìa, finally, of which Dante makes mention in the *Purgatorio* as the
western endpoint of Genoese territory, is a small town in the contemporary French region of PACA, in the vicinity of Nice, while Lerici, the
other actual place name that Dante writes about on this occasion, refers
to the Ligurian seaport near La Spezia where Shelley drowned about five
centuries later. In his three ante-purgatorial verses of poetic landscaping
("tra Lerice e Turbìa …"), Dante makes comparative use of the entire
Ligurian arch, whose coast, at least in the east, is indeed defined by "le
leggi d'abisso" (the laws of the abyss),[63] by steep, rugged mountains that
sublimely rise and dramatically drop off into the clefts of the Mar Ligure-
Tirreno-Mediterraneo as an intermediate realm that consists of a basin

Renato Guttuso, *L'alba / Dawn* (*Shore of Purgatory*) (1970). © 2012 Artists Rights
Society (ARS) New York/SIAE Rome. Used with permission.

Renato Guttuso (1911–87) was a post-Expressionist painter who was most
fascinated by the intense light of his native Sicily. Even though primarily known

defined by its various littorals, portals, and passages, hydrographically
and topographically represented in the way a room is demarcated by its
walls, doors, and windows, calling into nearly landlocked existence what
would otherwise have remained an indistinct and unfathomable aquatic,
terraqueous, or aerial space.

It is noteworthy that in *Purgatorio* Dante calls upon another actual
Ligurian town, located on the Gulf of Genoa: Noli, which, like various

---

for landscapes (inspired by citrus and olive groves, Sicily's almost mythical
insularity, the Gulf of Palermo, the cliffs of Aspra, and the Vucciria market) and
social commentary, he was introduced to the English-speaking world through
his illustrations of Elizabeth David's 1954 *Italian Food.*

Guttuso's *L'alba* demonstrates his commitment to light and colour, while
perfectly visualizing what Dante describes as an "isoletta" (a small and likely
solitary island) on whose shores the sun rises, showing Dante and Virgil upon
their early morning arrival by "miglior acque" (more kindly waters) how with
some effort, beauty and direction can be gained in this steep, remote, purgatorial locale. The painting's hard morning light attests to the time of dawn where
infernal darkness is left behind for the first time.

In *Il Dante di Guttuso* as well as in *Images of the Journey in Dante's Divine Comedy*,
Guttuso's *L'alba* is accompanied by the following verses from the first canto of
Dante's *Purgatory:* "Dolce color d'oriental zaffiro, / che s'accoglieva nel sereno
aspetto / del mezzo, puro infino al primo giro, / a li occhi miei ricominciò
diletto, / tosto ch'io usci' fuor de l'aura morta / che m'avea contristati li occhi
e 'l petto. [...] L'alba vinceva l'ora mattutina / che fuggia innanzi, sì che di
lontano / conobbi il tremolar de la marina" (The gentle hue of oriental sapphire / in which the sky's serenity was steeped— / its aspect pure as far as the
horizon— / brought back my joy in seeing just as soon / as I had left behind
the air of death / that had afflicted both my sight and breast. [...] Daybreak
was vanquishing the dark's last hour, / which fled before it; in the distance, I
/ could recognize the trembling of the sea). Allen Mandelbaum's translation
beautifully captures the intensity of colour when saying that the *sky* was *steeped*
in *sapphire* (which recalls Hart Crane's *High in the Azure Steeps*).

This morning image of the small solitary island may be reminiscent of
Nietzsche as well, not only for the shared interest in dawn, but for the inspiration for Zarathustra's observations on smallness, where various actual islands
play a significant role, among them the Venetian as well as San Michele, Capri,
and Isoletta (the miniature island in Lake Sils in the Swiss Engadine).

other Ligurian places in Dante's times (and a few of them still, such as San Fruttuoso), could only be reached by boat, or else by climbing down the steep cliffs that rise immediately behind them. Once again Dante deploys this place along with three other steep locales on Italian territory as points of comparison for the purgatorial landscape as he invents it: "Vassi in Sanleo e discendesi in Noli, / montasi su in Bismantova e 'n Cacume, / con esso i piè; ma qui convien ch'om voli; / dico con l'ale snelle e con le piume / del gran disio, di retro a quel condotto / che speranza mi dava e facea lume" (San Leo can be climbed, one can descend to Noli and ascend Cacume and Bismantova by foot alone, but here I had to fly: I mean with rapid wings and pinions of immense desire, behind the guide who gave me hope and was my light).[64] Dante's insistent representation of the journey as driven by desire, and of Liguria as inaccessible and barren, as a rough, dangerous, and thoroughly unrefined belt of land, is in accordance with the first known depictions of it as uncultivated woodland, without even olive groves and vineyards.[65]

The reprise and quotability of vegetation runs parallel to that of words. We may well classify various elements as Mediterranean when, as a matter of fact and origin, they are not. Apart from olive groves and vineyards we need to speak of imports: citrus from the Far East; cactus, agave, and aloe from the American West; the Greek-named eucalyptus from Down Under; the cypress from the Middle East; and peaches from the Orient. In this vein, Pound scholar Hugh Kenner reflects geopoetically on the idea, and the practice, of "rhyming climates" by way of grafting the eucalyptus, for instance, which in Pound's Pisan writing, synecdochically stands for memory in the way that lilacs do for Walt Whitman and rosemary does for Shakespeare's Ophelia. "In the late 19th century," writes Kenner with regard to Pound's landscape at Rapallo, "Australia's climate reminded someone of Italy's, and today the gum trees grow here and there by the Mediterranean. A rhymer of climates planted one on a hillside above Rapallo [...]. Its material, like that of most artifacts, is local: Italian water and Italian air, clasped in a cellulose tension network of which the patterned integrity alone is Australian."[66] That "rhyme" rhymes with "clime" may be part of such a tension.

It is of interest to recall Francis Miltoun's discussion of Èze and La Turbie in this context – the former is a Saracen fortress crowning a pinnacle in the vicinity of Nice, while the latter is famous for its Augustan trophy of "Doric order" – a discussion he bases to some extent on the fact that in both cases the construction "material [was ...] close at hand," while perceiving Èze "quite like a scene from Dante's masterpiece, or, if not that like the fabled spectral Brocken."[67] Granted, Nietzsche was not in accord with Saint Walpurga and things of that order; he was, however, thoroughly fond of Èze's dramatic poise and the rough and harsh qualities of the Ligurian-Provençal landscape that underpin and surround it. Miltoun's association of such upward twisting and turning with Dante is important here, since while Dante and Nietzsche characterize this landscape very similarly (as steep and rough, harsh and demanding), they evaluate these characteristics very differently: Nietzsche adores and cheerfully inscribes the very asperity that Dante's *dolce stil* depicted but abhorred, assigning a positive value to to the same symptom.

Reminiscent of this borrowed existence through cultural appropriation and exoticism is the observation that the Riviera di Levante in particular shares certain visual qualities, for example, with the southwestern shore of Lago di Garda (the lake that, following Virgil, Goethe called marine in aspect: "Benace marino"),[68] as well as with Sicily or the Amalfi Coast – and Manarola and Riomaggiore with Amalfi and Positano. At times, the Mediterranean seems to quote and imitate itself. And yet there are reasons why Nietzsche moves to Genoa, Rapallo, and Nice rather than to Sirmione, Taormina, and Amalfi; reasons why Freud chooses Rapallo's beach as a particularly suitable refuge from the stressful constraints of his Viennese domesticism and professionalism; reasons, finally, why Benn most probably circumvents the Italian Riviera in favour of France, while writing of a Ligurian rather than a Lombardian, Tuscan, Campanian, Sicilian, French, or pan-Mediterranean complex, into which his explicitly Ligurian complex has been so consistently generalized without further ado. Had Benn called his poetics Tuscan or Sicilian rather than Ligurian, it would likely have had a better chance of being read literally and with geographical precision, if only because these former toponyms have undergone a signifcantly wider circulation than the more mysterious name of Liguria.

A Liguria that historically, geographically, and culturally transcends the confines of the current Italian region of the same name but that nonetheless remains a local paradigm is the place with which Nietzsche, Freud, and Benn's expressive writing is highly engaged and in which it is deeply steeped (to recall once more Hart Crane's powerful phrase for sounding the marine deep). The cutting edges of Liguria's physiognomy conjure up the three writers' literary visions. The access to the land that Dante describes as "agevole e aperta" appeared so only in this late-medieval comparison with the enormous purgatorial mountain, a nearly vertical ascent, vis-à-vis which, in retrospect, Liguria re-emerges in

Dante's precise memory as a surprisingly rewarding passage. Dante's arid and remote "ruina," which marks the *Inferno* as well as the *Purgatorio* (but not the *Paradiso*) as critical condition and precipitous overhang, makes Liguria seem a wide and inviting flight of stairs.

It is with a certain degree of potentially unnecessary pathos that, in at least partial agreement with Dante's provocative confrontation of the risky purgatorial with the perilous Ligurian landscape, one could claim that compared to the seagirt mountain-isle *Purgatorio*, Liguria's laborious landslide seems paradise, whereas associated with *Paradiso*, its promontorial demands seem infernally steep, enclosed, and difficult. Another way of expressing this comparative geopoetic dimension would be to recall the mythical *locus amoenus* as it is opposed and yet defined in its very opposition to the *locus terribilis*, or else, perhaps, a place suspended between a promised and a waste land.

In *De vulgari eloquentia*, a work that clearly stands out as the first known act of Romance philology, Dante expresses no real appreciation for any vernacular that is not Tuscan (Florentine), and certainly not for the Ligurian-Genoese variants, of which he observes the following: "si per oblivionem Ianuenses ammicterent z licteram, vel mutire totaliter eos vel novam reparare oporteret loquelam. Est enim z maxima pars eorum locutionis; que quidem lictera non sine multa rigiditate profertur" (if the Genoese were to lose by forgetfulness the sound z, they would have to become completely dumb or to invent a whole new language; for z is the greater part of their speech, and it is a letter that cannot be pronounced without much harshness).[69] This verdict goes hand in hand with the serious judgment he passes on the Genoese people in the penultimate canto of the *Inferno*: "Ahi Genovesi, uomini diversi / d'ogne costume e pien d'ogne magagna, / perché non siete voi del mondo spersi?" (Ah, Genoese, a people strange to every constraint of custom, full of all corruption, why have you not been driven from the world?).[70]

In his *Epistles* and *Eclogues* Dante confirms his unequivocal invectives against the Genoese as barbaric, broadly hinting at Liguria as the frontier at which political interests in Italy must clearly end in favour of Tuscany.[71] Already before Dante, others had referred to the Ligurians as a tough, wild, and barbaric lot – terms, in other words, that reflect the slant of ancient Greek ethnography (ranging from *barbaroi* to *tyrrhenoi*). And not only Greek, but also Roman. Marcus Porcius Cato, for instance, saw the Ligurians as illiterate liars. Diodorus Siculus, by contrast, lauded them as audacious and dexterous, and Strabo as fearless, while celebrating the strength of Ligurian women in particular. Cicero and Virgil also stressed the toughness in both the Ligurian land and the Ligurian character but decided to read these qualities in a different manner from Dante, largely motivated by respect and admiration for the Ligurians' legendary courage, strength, and tenacity. "The Ligurians," declares Cicero, "are a hardy and rustic tribe. The land itself taught them to be so by producing nothing which was not extracted from it by skilful cultivation, and by great labour." And in his glorifying work on Italian regions, people, and agriculture, titled *Georgics* (poetry about farming), Virgil writes of the Ligurians as "inured to trouble."[72]

Liguria's topographical verticality and exposure to wind and erosion, as well as its geographic seclusion and entrapment between the mountains and the bay, present its physiognomic *Gestalt* as a part of the phenomenology of the Mediterranean as a place both real and imagined. Liguria is the name of this *Gestalt*, which stages Nietzsche, Freud, and Benn's expressive paradigms and embodies the geopoetic prism of the present comparative endeavour. Without effortlessly presenting or plainly offering the expected, but equally without entirely opposing or effacing the various realities of the Mediterranean as a cultural landscape, Liguria stands for one paradigmatic, vertical Mediterranean *poiein*, providing a literary profile or relief in more than one sense. Such an assessment includes the *topos* of Mediterranean beauty but specifies it as a complex and difficult beauty, and in this sense is strictly related to Matvejević's compelling paradox between, on the one hand, a Mediterranean imaginary that at times threatens to efface the actuality of place and, on the other, the cultural desirability of a Mediterranean poetics grounded in the specificities and individual manifestations of the sheer variety of locales in the Mediterranean cultural land- and seascapes at large.

"Jedes Fenster," writes Hans-Jürgen Heinrichs, "das man zur Welt zu öffnen versucht, will auch den Blick auf das innere Ausland, wie Freud die Seele nannte, freigeben" (Every window that one tries to open towards the world also intends to clear one's view upon the inner land abroad, as Freud called the human mind).[73] And John Banville joins in with a passage from his novel *Shroud* (which culminates in a Ligurian death), provoking with an "as if place meant something": "What do I care for mere topography? The topography of the mind, now, that is a different matter ... *The topography of the mind* – do I really say such things out loud, for people to hear?"[74] Such questions about the supposed dual character of place are pertinent in that they emphasize that caring for topography as topography of the mind is what is necessarily at stake, since mere topography is as difficult to contemplate as landscape would be without an individual's mind and senses to conceive and perceive it. After all, the beholder is necessary for both the aesthetic moment on location as well as its subsequent literary rendering.

"Wer das Dichten will verstehen, / Muss ins Land der Dichtung gehen; / Wer den Dichter will verstehen / Muss in Dichters Lande gehen" (Who wants to understand the art of poetry, must travel to the land of poetry; who wants to understand the poet, must travel to the poet's land), comments Goethe.[75] His lines about text and writer, land and reader, run remarkably parallel, and yet "Land der Dichtung" (land of poetry) begs for further attention. While "the poet's land" is a straightforward *genetivus subjectivus*, "the land of poetry" presents the abstract collective noun *Dichtung* (poetry; fiction; imaginative writing) together with a genitive that may be read either subjectively or objectively (*genetivus objectivus*) – a grammatical structure, in other words, that leads to the following questions: Is the land of imaginative writing a land that belongs to or is made as well as owned by specific literary genres? Or is it, rather, a land that inspires writers, their dreams, and their works? Or is the text itself a land, that is to say a generic area of topographic interest, a territory with an aura, a place with a genius, a field of topophilic inscription, a landscape of the mind? Is geopoetic writing inspired by the place, does it come out of the place, carry the name of the place, or evoke the place? Is it about the place, like the place, or of the place? Does it represent the place, imitate the place, resemble the place, describe the place, remember the place, face the place, or turn its back on the actual place to open up new horizons?

Liguria's geopoetic presence in Nietzsche, Freud, and Benn is certainly grounded in both, a literary land made by the text and a land – on the northern Mediterranean shore and on the French-Italian map – that makes the text, so that the land engenders the writing and the writing the land. Geographic place and human nature interact, thus becoming aesthetic in nature – a form of individual perception and experience of the land (rather than a time-honoured *topos*), located between internal psychology and external geography, between autobiography and topography. Influencing one another, place and text hence grow into a complex relationship of intricate interdependence, as well as into one of uncanny resemblance – mimic rather than mimetic, an expressive manifestation rather than a simple mirror reflection. This Liguria is neither soft nor gentle, nor is it tame. It is an austere and demanding landscape that houses strong-boned mountains, with rolling breakers crashing against its rugged cliffs.

Instead of representing the place with proto-scientific exactitude, Nietzsche, Freud, and Benn's Ligurian texts seize upon actual compositional elements of the Ligurian terrain, configuring their energy as well as the reader's, while condensing visual, formal, and atmospheric characteristics such as flora and fauna, geology and climate, ideas and associations, and more narrowly aesthetic, existential, and experiential qualities such as heights and depths, colours and thresholds into their literary imaginary. Nietzsche, Freud, and Benn select and omit, heighten and alter their details, each on his own terms approaching Liguria's geopoetic inclines and inclinations.

Nietzsche's ground-breaking work *Also sprach Zarathustra* originates in two inspirational walks in Liguria, where the philosopher, escaping the cold and windy climate of the north, spends the better part of his eccentric life in the winters, contemplating the tidal movements in Rapallo, where his notion of the eternal recurrence ("ewige Wiederkunft")[76] begins to take the shape of a poetic philosophy in which the originality of place reigns supreme over time's ongoing repetitiveness, as well as over space's unfathomable uncertainty. In his autobiographical work *Ecce Homo: Wie man wird was man ist* (*Ecce Homo: How One Becomes What One Is*), Nietzsche retrospectively emphasizes how profoundly both *Zarathustra* the book and Zarathustra the character are a geopoetic inscription of place, inaugurated and completed on Ligurian walks and in the Genoese attic to which Nietzsche had chosen to withdraw. He lived, in his own words, in Rapallo's "anmutig stille Bucht" (charming quiet bay), from where he daily took two extensive walks, one up the hills towards Zoagli, where one has a splendid view of the Ligurian Sea, and another one in the bay towards Santa Margherita and Portofino. Nietzsche shared in retrospect (in his autobiographical *Ecce Homo*) that it was precisely on these two walks that the first book of *Thus Spoke Zarathustra* gradually (literally, while walking or taking steps) came into being, and that further, it was exactly there, in the environs of Rapallo, that the figure of Zarathustra himself, or Zarathustra as a type, occurred to him, overtook him – befell him (as the olive befell Benn/Rönne about three decades later): "*er* [Zarathustra] überfiel mich ..."[77]

In Nietzsche's philosophy the names and images of Alpine and maritime landscapes, of mountainous and coastal *topoi* and motifs, biblical peaks and valleys, Swiss lakes and Franco-Italian shores play crucial roles in elevating what is imagined to the plane of the sublime timelessness of highest summits and deepest seabeds: "alles Tiefe soll hinauf zu meiner Höhe!" (anything deep shall rise to my heights).[78] Nietzsche's mostly vertical and frequently insular landscapes consist of fleeting sea views opening up and closing in, of rising and falling hills, of clefts and abysses so typical of the Ligurian terraces that are dramatically embedded between land and sea, mountains and shore ("the area where land and water encounter each other" is the most compelling, to recall Kenneth White).[79] Nietzsche inscribes slopes, winding paths, mountains, and skies, with mountain tops as an obvious point of view into potential epiphanies, reminiscent of biblical images of exiles sitting by shores, living in deserts, or ascending mountains, be it for executions or the delivery of speeches. They find their counterparts in Nietzsche's geopoetics, on which White elaborates in his observations about "our terraqueous globe," citing from an old Gaelic text which calls the shore where land meets water a time-honoured "place of revelation for the poets" and "the point of greatest interest."[80]

Already in his proto-Ligurian period of wandering, wavering between, on the one hand, the climate of the Venetian lagoon leading into states of physical inertia and mental depression, and, on the other, that of the Alps conducive to psychosomatic excitement and geopoetic output, Nietzsche repeatedly makes mention of the influence exercised by the Mediterranean cultural landscape with which he as a prime philologist is familiar not only through his commitment to ancient Greek and Latin texts and their translations but also through his acquisition of an intimate knowledge of it on his extensive hikes up and down the Ligurian foothills, through gardens above shores and on mule tracks through olives and vines, pines, lemons, and figs: "Ein Nordwind bin ich reifen Feigen" (a northerly am I to ripe figs).[81]

Beyond his poetics of "Ligurian complexes" (frequently rooted in his prose, scenes, and essayistic writings), Benn poetically associates based on geopoetic triggers that toponyms such as Mediterranean, Tyrrhenian, Riviera, Côte d'Azur, Provence, and Liguria provide. In his poem "Mittelmeerisch" ("Mediterranean"), for instance, he classifies the rhyme itself as Mediterranean; in "Kleines süßes Gesicht" ("Small Sweet Face") he writes of the "Blau der Traubenhyacinthe, / die ligurische / die bisamartig duftet" (the blue of the Ligurian grape hyacinth whose scent is musky), while in the poem "Englisches Café" he points to the Tyrrhenian Sea's "frevelhaftes Blau" (sacrilegious blue).[82]

Freud, in his letter from Rapallo, not only catches himself assessing the place and its effect on him as Böcklinesque but, significantly, also remarks that one cannot speak of Liguria without being a poet or quoting one: "Vom Land kann man nicht reden, ohne ein Dichter zu sein oder andere zu zitieren."[83] As an expert on dreams, desires, and the intricacies and vicissitudes of time and place, Freud understands how the land relies on the poets (foreshadowing Kenneth Silver's observations about how the painters turned the French Riviera into a myth), and further insinuates the possibility of quoting these poets (without actually doing so beyond an allusion to the palm trees in Goethe's *Wahlverwandtschaften / Elective Affinities*) if one does not happen to be a poet oneself. It is crucial to discern how Freud does not expect these poets in charge of Ligurian expression necessarily to be or have been on location. Rather, in a moment of extramarital bliss on Rapallo's shore, Freud alludes to the necessity of metaphors and other vehicles capable of transporting the appropriately expressive language to climes and their increments that are hardly quotidian and inhabit an extraordinary literary function.

In the course of his residence in the "Zaubermuschel Venedig" (magic shell of Venice),[84] Nietzsche expressed an urgent need for specific books: one on eccentric Lord Byron, swimmer not only in Ligurian bays but also in the Venetian Grand Canal; another on the French Riviera, where Nietzsche was destined to live soon after (in Nice); and a third on the Greek islands, a connection to the philosopher's philological background as well as his insular inclinations, and perhaps to Byron's escape to the Ionian Islands as well. Even if in Venice Nietzsche inhabits a room with a view onto the cemetery-island San Michele, his actual view onto what Jürgen Heinrichs calls the Freudian inner land abroad is only found in his later Ligurian hermitage, in which Nietzsche liberates himself and his expression as a writer in direct confrontation with himself. External and internal lands abroad criss-cross each other in his Venetian scenes, as well as in the philosopher's waves of depression, upon which he leaves Venice for Genoa, judging the lagoon to be a thoroughly inappropriate location for his much-desired quotidian walking: "Venedig hat den Fehler, keine Stadt für einen Spaziergänger zu sein – ich brauche meine 6–8 Stunden Wegs in freier Natur" (Venice's disadvantage is that it is not a walker's city – I need my 6 to 8 hours of walking in open nature).[85] The otherwise decidedly anti-Socratic Nietzsche has a precursor in the truest sense of the term, in that Socrates is the founder of the philosophical walk through the olive groves of the *akademeia*, while Aristotle's peripatetic followers practised philosophical discourse in the partially wooded pastures of the *lyceum*.[86] Even though Nietzsche's walks exclude conversation and are strictly solitary, they embody an early turn to a small territory off the centre, outside of the city walls. With every step the vertical walker not only engages in a conversation with himself but also literally covers ground, touches base.

Does Pound, the other determined walker, leave Venice for Liguria for the same reason as Nietzsche? Pound and Nietzsche both walk extensively before, in, and after visiting Venice, in Provence, Switzerland, and eventually Liguria, the peripheral region to which they both move in order to withdraw into the inner emigration of focused work. Nietzsche goes so far as to stress the necessity of absolute isolation for the sake of self-preservation: "der Conservirung halber [s]ich zu verlöthen, wie eine Büchse," dreaming of monastic silence and absolute solitude ("stiller Convent") among trustworthy friends on an otherwise perfectly secluded southern island – or else discovering for himself the anonymity of the most thoroughly strategized *incognito* lived in the attic ("die unbekannteste Dachstuben-Existenz").[87]

For a life in retirement such as this, Liguria conveniently becomes Nietzsche's hidden home abroad, accommodating with great ease many a quirk of the hermit's highly eccentric career. Like Provence, Liguria also has a strong monastic tradition and thus a rich monastic topography – one of the region's characteristics that anticipates exactly what the idea of the monastic cell has in common with a writer's seclusion. Benn makes repeated mention of such cells as perfect places to work in solitude, concentration, and frugality, while Kenneth White is drawn to the "intellectual vigour of the monastery" as a part of his geopoetic deliberations, admiring the monastery's "organizational structure" and "pelagian inspiration" while excluding any "transcendental belief." Geopoetics, he writes, is "of this world," and Nietzsche, Freud, and Benn would likely agree.[88]

In as much as Nietzsche's Ligurian life in the attic is the consequence of a decisive act of self-protection and liberation into his solitary concentration in a Franco-Italian, Provençal-Ligurian borderland of seas, mountains, and skies, *Zarathustra*, the "*Non plus ultra*" and most unfettered of his productions ("das losgebundenste [s]einer Erzeugnisse"), is a work of late self-expression, self-liberation, and at least momentary self-cure. Nietzsche refers to it as very small, but his best book, within which he rolled a heavy rock off his soul ("ein ganz kleines Buch" and "mein Bestes, ich habe einen schweren Stein mir damit von der Seele gewälzt"), an explosion of forces, accumulated over decades: "eine Explosion von Kräften, die Jahrzehende lang sich angehäuft haben." It is with *Zarathustra* that the philosopher becomes a geopoetic creative writer in the truest sense of these terms, breaking the burden of enlightened rationality by

setting free repressed energies and seemingly forgotten urges. In retrospect, Nietzsche tells of the book's genesis as follows:

> Das Ganze ist somit genau im Verlaufe eines Jahrs entstanden [...] Die
> letzten zwei Wochen waren die glücklichsten meines Lebens: ich bin nie
> mit solchen Segeln über ein solches Meer gefahren; und der ungeheure
> Übermuth dieser ganzen Seefahrer-Geschichte [...] kam auf seinen Gipfel.
> [...] Ich habe nicht umsonst Jahrelang in der Stadt des Columbus gelebt.
>
> (Hence the entire thing came into existence in the course of one year.
> The last two weeks were the happiest of my life: never have I sailed with
> such canvas over such a sea; and the enormously high spirits of this entire
> seafarer's story came to their very peak. Not in vain did I live for years in the
> city of Columbus.)[89]

Captain Gonzalo Fernandez de Oviedo characterized Columbus as "a
learned man well read in the science of cosmography," who "set out to
make a fresh discovery of the islands," who was "a native of the province
of Liguria, in which lies the city and lordship of Genoa" (some claim of
Genoa, others of Savona), and who "left Italy for the Levant and travelled over the greater part of the Mediterranean" before leaving "these
restricted waters" in order "to see the great ocean" from the shores of
Portugal and Spain, slowly beginning his adventures to allegedly undiscovered countries.[90] Benn in his 1918 novella *Querschnitt* (*Cross-section*)
poeticizes Granada, the last Moorish city in Spain, under whose auspices
Columbus was dispatched: "Immer stehe ich, ein Maure, vertrieben,
das Gesicht nach Granada. [...] Doch was ist Granada?" (As a Moor, an
exile, I keep standing with my face turned to Granada [...] But what is
Granada?).[91]
In "The Philosopher at Sea," Karsten Harries reads Nietzsche in his
own exuberant terms, wavering, as Nietzsche does, between a blissful
attic-stasis under halcyon skies and an adventurous kind of Genoese
seafaring as a "seafaring discoverer, a new Columbus," further extending this image even to Nietzsche's audience: "[a]s he likens himself to a
seafaring explorer, Nietzsche likens his perfect reader to a sailor," eventually addressing "The Shipwreck" by mounting a very fine connection
to Dante's *Inferno*, where seafarer Ulysses sets sail for "the landlocked
Mediterranean."[92]
Nietzsche's Ligurian liberation of the self in a language expressive of
a concrete place results in what Benn refers to as his own era's earthquake precisely in the land where Nietzsche travels, which is also the

German language that he gradually turns askew, heightening, deepening, and diversifying its imaginative potential while wittily stretching its creative capacities to their very limits: "[Nietzsche] ist [...] der weitreichende Gigant der nachgoetheschen Epoche," according to Benn, and for Benn's generation "das Erdbeben der Epoche und seit Luther das größte deutsche Sprachgenie" (Nietzsche is the most far-reaching giant of the post-Goethean era, the earthquake of the era and since Luther the greatest genius of the German language).[93] Indeed, Nietzsche believed himself to have taken the German language to its expressive completion, having remained a poet in every sense and to every extent of that word: "Ich bilde mir ein, mit diesem Zarathustra die deutsche Sprache zu ihrer Vollendung gebracht zu haben. [... Ich bin] Dichter bis zu jeder Grenze des Begriffs geblieben" (I have the sense that with this Zarathustra I have taken the German language to its completion. I have remained a poet in every sense and to every extent of that word).[94]

Zarathustra as a prophetic type, as an ancient Persian, an eastern Mediterranean religious figure, seizes (overtakes) the wandering philosopher, serving as an *alter ego* during the entire process of writing *Zarathustra*'s four books. Nietzsche's title refers to the powerful transmigration of souls in Zoroastrianism, a theology in which the literary theory of place seems to find its foundation on location: "Ich bin ein Wanderer und ein Bergsteiger [...] ich liebe die Ebenen nicht [...] ich laufe dorthin, wo der Wind stille steht, zum Sonnen-Winkel meines Ölbergs [...] Ein Versuchen und Fragen war all mein Gehen" (I am a wanderer and mountain climber, I am not fond of the plains, I run to where the wind stands still, to the sunny corner of my olive grove, all my walking has been a questing and a questioning).[95]

A shelter from the wind, a sunny corner in the midst of winter, an olive grove overlooking the sea – such is the place to which this wanderer withdraws to conceive his writing in seclusion, under strictly Ligurian auspices. This scene is highly reminiscent of the myth of Halcyon, the mythical bird of grief (*penthos*), often identified as the bright blue kingfisher and said to breed at sea during the winter solstice when the gods bring the winds and waves to a halt. In a brief dialogue titled *Halcyon* (the manuscript names both Plato and Lucian as authors, but there is evidence that it was penned by neither), Socrates relates the myth of the daughter of Aeolus, god of the winds, Alcyone, who, widowed, threw herself into the sea and was transformed into a bird, endlessly searching the seas in lament. Halcyon days, *alkyonides hemerai*, has come to mean the short period around the winter solstice when no gale occurs, when

both air and time have come to a standstill so that the bird can peace-
fully breed in a nest floating on calm seas (according to both Virgil and
Ovid).⁹⁶ The etymology of "halcyon" is enlightening in this respect (*hals*:
sea/salt, reminiscent of brine, and *kyein*: to conceive, reminiscent of
poiein).

Nietzsche, the classical philologist and northern German pastor's son,
travels to the Alps and the French and Italian Mediterranean (from summers in Sils-Maria and Silvaplana in the Swiss Engadine to winters in
Genoa, San Remo, Rapallo, and Nice on the Ligurian coast), drawing,
in Goethean manner, the Hellenic world closer onto Italian soil, writing
and looking for peace of mind in an ideal climate, in order to counteract
his various psychosomatic agonies. Nietzsche ends up in Liguria. He does
not follow the route of any Grand Tour, nor does he duplicate Goethe's
or anticipate Freud's Austrian-Italian itinerary. Despite his profound
admiration for Sallustus, Nietzsche disliked Rome as whole-heartedly as
Goethe and Freud adored it. The philosopher is a modern rambler who
freed himself from the bonds of formal Apollonian restraint to traverse
the newly forged, post-tragic pastures of an eccentric wanderer's ecstatic
Dionysian terrain.

In his discussion of geopoetic Nietzschean dimensions such as these,
Predrag Matvejević provides an excellent passage on "mediterraneity"
as a qualitative principle based on, but hardly constrained to, Mediterranean locations. It depends on a slightly revised understanding of
Nietzsche's Apollonian and Dionysian principles. Matvejević points out
that:

> [i]f we understand the Apollonian principle to represent form and rules,
> restraint and reason in the individual or society, that is, discipline and order,
> and the Dionysian principle to represent individuality and originality rather
> than the commonly invoked inclination to impulsiveness and ecstasy, then
> Mediterranean cultures partake of both [...]. Nietzsche [...] sets forth the
> possibility of acquiring or inheriting Mediterraneity no matter where one
> is from, citing Goethe and Winckelmann and defining the transparency of
> Mozart's music as "a belief in the South." Zarathustra's admirer wants us to
> seek the meanings behind the mysterious cry "Great Pan is dead!" heard as
> the ship with the Egyptian Thamous at the rudder sailed past the island of
> Paxos [...]. The Mediterranean is made up of such riddles.⁹⁷

In that the qualities of land, air, sky, and wind are not only proper to
a specific locale but provide the actual ingredients of art and memory,

Hugh Kenner's rhymed climates and Matvejević's Nietzschean assessment of mediterraneity are reminiscent not only of Dante but also of Gertrude Stein. While Dante stresses the correspondence between the sound of vernaculars and the quality of the landscapes in which they are spoken, likening them to people's characters as well (such as Liguria's, the Ligurians', and their vernacular's harshness), Stein repeats this organic approach from a Modernist's post-Nietzschean perspective, intimately intertwining mind and nature on geopoetic grounds, stating that one's land is where one is – be it at home or abroad:

> After all anybody is as their land and air is.
> Anybody is as the sky is low or high,
>
> the air heavy or clear
> and anybody is as there is wind or no wind there.
>
> It is that which makes them and the arts they make
> and the work they do and the way they eat
>
> and the way they drink   .
>
> and the way they learn and everything.[98]

As an American writing in Paris, Stein was thoroughly committed to the impact of place on literary writing – she went so far as to develop a concept of drama as landscape. Envisioning a Mediterranean poetics of place in Matvejević's sense implies such a Steinean understanding of land and air, sky and wind, not as tied to one's homeland alone but rather as a potential affinity that results from one's actual being and writing in (and occasionally about) one place instead of another. Edward Casey's philosophy of place emphasizes a similar Nietzschean actuality of place:

> Whatever is true for space and time, this much is true for place: we are immersed in it and could not do without it. To be at all – to exist in any way – is to be somewhere, and to be somewhere is to be in some kind of place. Place is as requisite as the air we breathe, the ground on which we stand, the bodies we have. We are surrounded by places. We walk over and through them. We live in places, relate to others in them, die in them. Nothing we do is unplaced. How could it be otherwise? How could we fail to recognize this primal fact? Aristotle recognized it.[99]

That Zarathustra's journey into freedom (as well as Nietzsche's into the intellectual and emotional placement of what Matvejević astutely diagnoses as his mediterraneity) should be so tightly bound to the formal and atmospheric qualities of the Ligurian land in which it quite literally takes place is reminiscent of Geoffrey Hartman's insights in his essay on the *genius loci*: "the spirit of liberty [...] is part of the spirit of place."[100] Freeing oneself means facing place, and facing place means coming to terms with oneself. Goethe, too, embarks on his journey to Italy in order to get to know himself better by way of a direct confrontation with the objects: "Ich mache diese wunderbare Reise nicht, um mich selbst zu betriegen," he writes, "sondern um mich an den Gegenständen kennen zu lernen" (My purpose in making this wonderful journey is not to delude myself but to discover myself in the objects I see).[101] A thus approachable self, however, as well as the objects in question, are collected, recollected, and transported elsewhere and become graftable entities not entirely dissimilar to Hugh Kenner's eucalyptus landmark grounded in place but not bound to it alone, or Nietzsche's "Engadin-Charakter" and "nizzahafte Reinheit und Leuchtkraft der Farben" (Engadine-character and Nice-like purity of air and luminosity of colours) mnemonically ascribed to his last Italian residence in Turin.[102]

Nietzsche's many topophilias and topophobias, mountainous ascents and marine immersions, as well as Francesco Petrarca's climb of the Provençal Mont Ventoux and his praise of the Ligurian coast and its wine and vineyards (he dedicated his *Africa* to the Riviera di Levante), provide vistas that hardly impede a focus on the inner imaginative life. Rather, they foster an elevation of the mind beyond merely physical concerns.[103] Such views are not far from Freud, who has supremely demonstrated how witnessing and experiencing things in place does not necessarily render their presentation (or oneself, for that matter) less imaginative, does not mean, in other words, a thinning down of the literary increments of one's writing. Freud owned two editions of Goethe's complete works, was familiar with Goethe's œuvre, and knew the *Italienische Reise*, *Venezianische Epigramme*, and *Römische Elegien* especially well. He quoted Goethe not only in his psychoanalytic writings but also in his letters and, after thorough travel preparations (by reading Victor Hehn's *Italien* for instance)[104] and at times procrastinations (particularly with regard to Rome), partially followed Goethe's itinerary in Italy.

Close to Goethe in more ways than one, Freud is in thorough accord with his revered precursor's metaphor of the poem as land (and the land as poem), and sees the human mind as that inner foreign country or largely unknown land abroad, powerfully hinting at the ever-present possibilities and necessities of an inner landscape in its intimate relationship with a cultural territory in which the vertical *axis mundi* of Dante's late medieval world undergoes a significant change: the lofty may well go underground while the highly sublime becomes deeply repressed – a turn of the axis comprised in Freud's etymologically grounded presentation of primeval words.

Freud repeatedly likens the human mind not only to the topographies of various types of multi-storey dwellings but to the geology of ancient excavation sites as well, locating subterranean archaeological layers, situating reliefs, analysing fragments. For Freud (as for Dante), both literal (real, actual) and metaphorical (oneiric, literary) forms of travel are equally existential: into visions and visualizations, into poems and dreams as eye-openers for an understanding of the vertical structures and metaphorical textures of the mind. Nietzsche's design of an archaic antiquity (from which Benn borrows as thoroughly as he does from Goethe's scientific writings) and Freud's archaeological methods in approaching the psychic apparatus visually demonstrate the impact of the past upon Modernist writing.

This psychological-archaeological revelation takes place as locally as the Ligurian text, on the threshold of life and land, on the border of territories, on the cusp of consciousness. In *Poets in a Landscape*, Gilbert Highet presents a taxonomy of genre and its *raison d'être*, claiming that

> the world is full of patriots. But few of them, surprisingly few, have been able to describe the charm of their own land – at least in words. Artists have done so in paint. [...] Some have conveyed it very well in music [...]. Scarcely any have made their love of their actual country, of its physical presence, clear through a work of prose fiction: there are many novels of patriotic feeling, few of landscape. Poets have been the most successful in conveying the love of country.[105]

Even though literary writing, and poetry in particular, belongs more to languages and territories than to countries and nations, and even if Nietzsche, Freud, and Benn had all been exceptionally patriotic (Nietzsche and Freud were not, while Dante and Benn were), it would nevertheless be hard to claim that they wrote about their love of their own countries. They are writers who learnt from European and Mediterranean culture at large, including the classics and the ruins, the myths and the poems, the Bible and the visual arts. They are writers who oriented themselves and their writing imagistically and geopoetically, knowing well the landscapes of painters, studying thoroughly the impact of sculpture and architecture (both ruined and intact), conveying the love of a country not theirs by birth, but theirs by elective affinity, extensively reading their sources, attentively walking in particular places, contemplatively resting in other places, in landscapes and libraries, museums and galleries, at home and elsewhere.

From the era of the Attic tragedy on, place has been classified as a vital part of any aesthetic setting, be it in one's own lands or in those of others. In combination, place and travel, dream and text open up a new space, make for a new genre, which joins literary invention with cultural history and autobiographical memory, with travelogues and philosophies, theatres and landscapes, taking place regionally and yet internationally, in synchronicity, contemporaneously, only seemingly anachronistically signalling a dramatic coexistence of different temporalities in one place. Le Corbusier said that Freud's "Pompeii [...] constitutes the single true museum worthy of the name,"[106] and I suggest Pamuk's post-thalassic scene of a dried-up Bosphorus and Hart Crane's marine tomb steeped in azure as further qualified candidates for such an outlook on the spirit of place and memory. The Greek *mouseion* is the shrine of the Muses as well as a place of study and learning, and that the French *muser* (to muse) is so felicitously homophonic with the Greek root for what we know as the museum strikes one as a particularly fine coincidence, while recalling Freud's leisurely *otium* and yet instructive stays in Mediterranean locations, or, for that matter, Benn's inspiring strolls through Berlin museums and art galleries.

Pompeii more than any other place functions as Freud's principal spatial metaphor for the mind, whilst remaining a very concrete cultural place in southern Italy, to which Freud enthusiastically travelled in 1902, informing his readers more than once and in great detail about his love of the place. He was intensely attracted by the scene that Pompeii presents, and was thoroughly intrigued by Pompeii's fatal burial and subsequent excavation as an ideal visualization of the psychic burial that is carried out in repression (and its subsequent psychoanalytic excavation). What Pompeii is to Freud is not entirely unlike what the imagined dried-up Bosphorus is to Orhan Pamuk, Rome to Goethe, and Liguria to Nietzsche, Freud, and Benn: a visual representation of a realm that is located between an actual and an imagined place, a visualizing agency or illustrative auxiliary located between a literal land, its literary traditions, and its cultural metaphors, an image that has the potency to confront the subjective with the objective and perception with memory, as well as to weave experience into writing in such a way that sights become sites, landscapes stages, and places texts.

If books and texts occupy one end on the scale of evidence, and voices of writers or those who have known them the other, I would geopoetically situate place as an aesthetic manifestation of cultural memory, literary tradition, and natural confirmation as located between written matter on the one hand and living person on the other: while sharing qualities of both, it is neither. The book is an object: it is static and reliable, conserved in a library, an archive, or a display case. The person, by contrast, is a subject: (s)he is dynamic, vulnerable, and by definition one who undergoes change. In one sense, place is objective, while in another it is dynamic, exposed, influenced, partially man-made, and likewise vulnerable. Even though it is subject to seasonal and more violent changes, such as disfigurations beyond recognition in times of war or in natural catastrophes, it is fundamentally there as a presence, immobile, embedded somewhere between the relativities of time and space (which Benn calls a curse and Calvino a landslide). When place undergoes changes, it is altered, divided, developed anew, but on its own foundation, perceivable as its own premise, in its quasi-palimpsestic life on location, in its basic earthly qualities not altogether perishable, not altogether displaceable, guarding some of its deeper identity even under daunting topographic metamorphoses.

Liguria is one such place: a dramatic landscape, a Mediterranean seascape, and a geopoetic mindscape. Not only does it have a real existence on the globe and a representational one on the map; it also has a life and a culture that continue inscribing its geographic existence, its topographic nature, and its imaginative making. Its biography is placed in its culture and agriculture, and in the land of texts and textures that either originate there (as is the case with writers such as Italo Calvino, Eugenio Montale, and Camillo Sbarbaro), are grown and remembered there (as is the case with wanderer Nietzsche, who resides and writes there, and to some degree with Freud, who joyfully travels and represses his precursor Nietzsche there), or are conjured up elsewhere (as is the case with inner émigré Benn, who works towards his Nietzschean-Ligurian poetics of Freudian projection). All three writers are founders of their own geopoetic Ligurian text-places, while their readers are voyagers in the Ligurian lands and seas co-authored by them.

Liguria is the writer's land as well as Goethe's land of imaginative writing. It is also Freud's inner land abroad, which can be observed from real as well as imagined vistas. It is an actual geographic as well as an intellectual place, in which a certain density of literary writing can be found in peripheral concentration. Literary Rapallo with its various circles of writers, as well as the *Golfo dei Poeti* (La Spezia) so crucial for Byron, Shelley, and others after them, are possible toponyms to evoke this marginally situated and at the same time internationally engaged aggregation of artists and intellectuals. Max Beerbohm was there, as were Basil Bunting, Gerhart Hauptmann, Ernest Hemingway, Hermann Hesse, Hugo von Hofmannsthal, Robert Lowell, Ezra Pound, Rainer Maria Rilke, Franz Werfel, and William Butler Yeats – some of them brief visitors, others residents for months, years, or even decades.

Writing about modern visual art and its relationship with the French Riviera, Kenneth Silver persuasively shows how art "transformed the Riviera from a physical place into a site of the imagination [...] turn[ing] geography into myth."[107] Kenneth White on the other hand repeatedly points to the shifts with regard to centres and margins in view of what one might call a geopoetic absence of myth. "Pytheas's Marseilles was a Greek colony," he writes, "which added to the intellectuality of Greece the advantages of being on the edge, at the limits, away out there in the Western Mediterranean."[108] It is intriguing that this coast, even if we were to maximally define it beyond Silver's intention as extending from Marseilles in the west to La Spezia (rather than Mentone) in the east, was visited by domestic as well as foreign writers, painters, and travellers, but in comparison with other points on the Italian and French maps, only intermittently before the end of the nineteenth century.

It is all the more intriguing to witness how the western (French) part of this coast initially (from the second half of the nineteenth century onward) almost exclusively attracted painters, while its eastern (Ligurian, narrowly defined) segment became a location primarily for writers – beginning with Byron and Shelley and developing more fully into a colony of authors at the time of Yeats, Hemingway, and Pound, with painters Arnold Böcklin (whom Freud exuberantly remembers in Rapallo), Wassily Kandinsky, and Oskar Kokoschka as noteworthy exceptions in an otherwise extremely writerly scene.[109] The point being that while the French coast is light and open, accessible and convex, compliant and horizontal – in short, a painterly paradise – the Italian-Ligurian coast (and increasingly more so the farther east one ventures) is, by contrast, concave and opaque, terraced and enclosed, difficult and vertical – in short, a writerly scene, a demanding refuge, and a poetic challenge.

Painters who either sojourned or resided on the French Côte d'Azur were Pierre Bonnard, Georges Braque, George Grosz, Wassily Kandinsky, Paul Klee, Henri Matisse, Edvard Munch, and Pablo Picasso, to name only the most famous. Paul Cézanne, Provençal by birth, and Vincent van Gogh, resident of the yellow house at Place Lamartine in the Provençal Arles (and next to Nietzsche and Joseph Conrad one of Benn's most relevant Ligurian affinities), did not venture east or south to work on the coast directly but preferred painting inland, whereas Claude Monet and Auguste Renoir, rather like Byron and Shelley in eastern Liguria earlier in the same century, were pioneers in travelling to both the French and the Italian Rivieras prior to Liégeard's coining of the coast's alluring name.

To phrase things differently: mainly visual artists created what Kenneth Silver characterizes as the mythical dreamscape of the French "Côte," while it was the Italian coast east of Genoa in particular (Riviera di Levante) that became a port of arrival and a refuge for the poets. Because of a lack of infrastructure and a difficulty of access that until at least the middle of the nineteenth century was not that different from what Dante described in the fourteenth, neither segment of the coast was part of the Grand Tour's traditional itinerary.[110] The French as well as the eastern Ligurian stretch became more magnetic only in the later nineteenth century, towards the end of which railways gradually began to make these regions more accessible – and, later on, luxuriously so, for instance with *Le Train Bleu,* which was the nickname for the navy-coloured Calais-Mediterranean sleeper express train that from 1922 to 1938 carried the wealthy from the north of France to the Riviera (among them Winston Churchill and King Edward VIII) – reaching, in the case of the French coast, an overwhelming fame certainly no later than the first decades of the twentieth century. Erika and Klaus Mann, for instance, rhetorically interrogate and at times expertly inform their readers about this locale, while at others they address places such as France, Italy, Europe, and Africa in terms of the German self and the Mediterranean other:

> Woher hat diese blaue Küste ihren großen Ruhm? Warum bleibt die Côte d'Azur durch verschiedene Jahrzehnte der Vergnügungs- und Erholungsstrand des Kontinents, der Welt? The Coast of Pleasure – Die Riviera: Legende von Luxus, Glanz, rollender Kugel, Hermelinpelz und Champagnerseligkeit. [...] Gesegnetes Frankreich, mit Paris als Hauptstadt und dieser Mittelmeerküste als Badestrand! Der französische Künstler, der aus dem perlgrauen Licht von Paris sich keine neuen Inspirationen mehr holen zu können glaubt, besteigt den D-Zug und ist nach einer Nachtfahrt dort unten, wo das Licht härter und heißer, zugleich satter, blühender und trock-

ener ist; italienisch, aber manchmal schon mit einem afrikanisch dürren Einschlag; und dieser Einschlag wiederum französisch gemildert, gleichsam durchzivilisiert, zarter, zärtlicher gemacht.

(Whence springs this blue coast's great fame? Why has the Côte d'Azur remained for various decades the beach of pleasure and recreation for the entire continent, if not the entire world? "The Coast of Pleasure" – The Riviera: legend of luxury, glamour, rolling billiard balls, ermine fur and champagne bliss. [...] Blessed France, with Paris as her capital and this Mediterranean shore as her lido! The French artist who no longer believes [herself/himself] to be capable of drawing any kind of new inspiration from the pearl-grey light of Paris boards the express train and arrives down there after a one-night trip, down there, where the light is harder and hotter, at the same time more replete, more flourishing and also drier; Italian, but at times already with a hint of African aridity; but this hint is rendered French, milder, more sophisticated as it were, more delicate, more tender.)[111]

Captain Richardson and the Manns were not alone in wondering why they all came to this coast. And, depending on one's perspective, the west-east extension of this coast can vary, especially with regard to the Franco-Italian border, where for some the Côte ends and Italy begins, while for others the Côte simply carries on, at least till Genoa and its environs. Writers, however, have tended to sojourn or reside on the Italian rather than the French segment of the Ligurian coast, and more precisely in places east of Genoa (Portofino, Rapallo, La Spezia, Lerici). Why? I contend that the radical steepness and pronounced isolation of the Riviera di Levante are markers intricately intertwined with the challenges of writing, whereas the horizon and especially the quality of colour and light in the west have certainly mattered more to the painters. In fact, various Parisian painters escaped the grey light of the city, jumped on the blue night train, and anticipated inspiration by the solar landscape of their Côte of choice.

Sharing their travel observations about Côte d'Azurean places, customs, and people (mainly artist friends and celebrities), promenades, markets, and cafés between Marseilles in the west and La Spezia in the east, the unambiguously Francophile Mann siblings, after an extensive and enthusiastic salute to southeastern France, certainly mark the passage from France to Italy as a decisive one, referring to Mentone as the last French town "aber schon halb italienisch" (but already half Italian), almost playfully offering that it is perhaps for that very reason that their affection for the place is not reliable.[112] Their book's comparatively tiny section on *Die italienische Riviera* is divided into *Riviera di Ponente, Genoa,* and *Riviera di Levante.* They not only admit to not really taking the Italian Riviera seriously but even go so far as to suggest that the world does not either.

True, the Manns characterize Liguria in ways that would clearly not appeal to the tourist of their time; it would, however, most certainly attract the Nietzsche-type (they explicitly mention Nietzsche as well as his Zarathustra, for instance, while elaborating on Liguria's "erholsame Öde," restful dreariness).[113] Even if there are moments when the Mann travellers have to face the fact that in a variety of places in western Liguria one might well confuse the Italian with the French Côte, they generally firmly stand by their impression that in spite of a potential family resemblance, it is no longer the real thing: "Die Küste könnte manchmal mit der Côte d'Azur verwechselt werden. Aber es ist nicht mehr *das.* Nein, *das* ist es nicht mehr" (Sometimes one may confuse this coast with the Côte d'Azur. But it is no longer the real thing. No, the real thing it is no longer).[114] Why not? And: what is this real thing, this *das,* this *je-ne-sais-quoi,* which, according to the Manns, Liguria is not?

It is absolutely crucial for Nietzsche, Freud, and Benn's affinities with Liguria to witness how the Manns astutely characterize the Ligurian landscape as altogether "kahler" (barer) and "felsiger" (rockier), presenting Genoa itself appropriately as "steil" (steep), "finster" (gloomy), "verwunschen" (enchanted), "mystisch" (mystic), "gravitätisch" (solemn) – and in all that very unlike Marseilles. Like Dante, the Manns hardly consider such qualities a plus. Nietzsche, however, certainly did, not only because of Genoa's "große europäische Tradition" (grand European tradition), but also precisely because of the qualities most characteristic of the Ligurian landscape (steep, enclosed, enchanted).[115] In this vein, the Manns' *Buch von der Riviera* aptly emphasizes the Ligurian landscape's barrenness and ruggedness, its rocky and steep, mystic, dark, even accursed aspects, while cultivating a nostalgia for the previously visited French Côte, its celebrities and lifestyle, luxury and play, elegance and light.

Benn, who will have far more serious issues to face in to his exchange with the exile Klaus Mann, who left Germany for southern France after Hitler's seizure of power (while Benn did not), literarily transformed Nietzsche's geopoetic Ligurian landscape into various acts of steep and enclosed poetic expression (precisely in the sense of Dante, Goethe, and the troubadours).[116] However, he was also the one to temporarily indulge, on his brief interwar journeys to France, in the very southern

French luxury that the Manns were to cherish as *das* only few years later. Neither Benn nor the Manns express much interest in the Ligurian landscape's mnemonic dimensions. For all we know, Benn never visited the Italian portion of the Ligurian shore, while Erika and Klaus Mann travel there but find Nietzsche's Rapallo to be an uninspiring place of nothing beyond "schöne Erinnerung" (beautiful memory) rather than present enjoyment, referring, as Freud does, to Arnold Böcklin and, as Nietzsche does, to Lord Byron when they write of Rapallo's "Byron-Böcklin-Stimmung" (Byron-Böcklin-atmosphere) [117] as suitable for retirement and as such radically opposed to the French coast's excitement of cars and *routes*, billiards, ermines, and champagne.

According to the Manns – and not exclusively the Manns – this coast has not only been blessed with halcyon skies and the presence of the famous. It is not only entertaining and relaxing but is significantly situated on the edge of Europe. This border position implies two things for them: European off-centredness on the one hand, and a tempting proximity to Africa on the other. Its air and light are dazzling, hot, dry, and intense, which is what the Manns tend to think of as exotic and Italian-African rather than what they call civilized French. In his brilliant retrospective almost a century later, Kenneth Silver classifies the French coast as "the single most celebrated resort area of the twentieth century," stressing that it is primarily two things that render it so special: "150 miles of inhabitable coastline" – an assessment much in line with the phrase the Manns use for the French coast's compliant nature: "eine nachgiebige Küste." [118]

The *sinus ligusticus* and *ligusticum mare* (Ligurian shore and Ligurian Sea) have formed integral parts of the Mediterranean world since antiquity. On the one hand, Liguria is part of the Mediterranean and its spirit of place, its rich repertoire of traditional and at times clichéd landscape images (imagined primarily by [post-]Goethean writers native to northern climes), its artistic and cultural requisites, and an elaborate fabric of literary reference, ranging from the ancient and medieval epic to a rich variety of Romantic and Modernist quests, in which the spirit of place and its images are stored and remembered but also frequently generalized into imprecision.

Liguria, however, has neither been canonized like Venice and Florence, Rome and Naples, nor achieved what Kenneth Silver, in his study on the French Côte d'Azur, perceives as its mythical dimension. Unlike Rome or Athens, Liguria is not a prototype for the cultural centre of times past. Incidentally, even Rome became the travellers' central myth only at the time when Jerusalem and Santiago di Compostela began to be considered no longer the only destination that mattered. As secular pilgrimage into Italian antiquity became more common, journeying to Rome gradually evolved as any serious traveller's central dream. It meant visiting Venice and Florence on the way and was frequently rounded off by a final escape to Naples, Pompeii, and Sicily. It did not, however, imply laying eyes on Liguria, which because of its isolated situation and demanding terrain was almost completely disregarded even by through traffic.

Luring Onomastics

... what would Key West be without its name?

J. Hillis Miller

Liguria provides one possible access to Predrag Matvejević's dream of a Mediterranean poetics in which its place as precise cultural geography matters as much as a writer's poetic affinities with it. In other words, Liguria presents itself as a borderland that invites a redefinition of time-honoured Mediterranean imageries into something denser and harder, drier and steeper than Goethe or the Manns would have dreamt of – the Goethe, that is, who with his "Lied der Mignon" (1782–3) as something like a primeval text of yearning and a textual referent for an elsewhere established the German literary desire for Mediterranean faring in the genres of travel and fascination. Goethe's suggestive lines about the land of lemons and oranges are easily among the most famous lyrical sequences composed in the German language. The poem's adolescent and likely androgynous singer is Mignon, who poses her well-versed question in the legendary song of romantic love and sentimental longing that Goethe wrote more than three years before he actually embarked, at night and incognito, on his journey to Italy. Almost a decade after the traveller's return to Weimar in 1788, Mignon's song found its way into Goethe's second novel, *Wilhelm Meisters Lehrjahre* (*Wilhelm Meister's Apprenticeship*), which is generally regarded as the first and still, perhaps, most prominent example of a genre intensely debated in world literature: the "Bildungsroman" (novel of formation or coming-of-age novel).

Mignon's passionate lines of yearning open the third book of *Wilhelm Meister*, where Mignon initially tenderly invites and eventually urgently begs Wilhelm to take her with him to the gentler climes of Italy – should he plan to visit. Even though the song is printed in German in Goethe's text, Mignon presumably sings her song in Italian (she is Italian), potently expressing Goethe's as yet unsatisfied longing for Italy, which is presented in images of an eroticized and luring geopoetic landscape. Freud is not alone in quoting from Goethe's "Lied der Mignon" in his correspondence from Sorrento, reverting to his precursor's elusive dream of Italy:

> Kennst du das Land, wo die Zitronen blühn,
> Im dunkeln Laub die Goldorangen glühn,
> Ein sanfter Wind vom blauen Himmel weht,
> Die Myrte still und hoch der Lorbeer steht?
> Kennst du es wohl? Dahin!
> Dahin möcht' ich mit dir,
> O mein Geliebter, ziehn.
> [...]
> Kennst du [...] Dahin! Dahin [...]
> [...]
> Kennst du [...] Dahin! Dahin [...]

> (Know you the land where lemon blossoms blow,
> And through dark leaves the golden oranges glow,
> A gentle breeze wafts from an azure sky,
> The myrtle's still, the laurel tree grows high –
> You know it, yes? Oh there, oh there
> With you, O my beloved, would I fare.
> [...]
> You know it, yes? Oh there, oh there
> [...]
> You know it, yes? Oh there, oh there [...])[119]

While Goethe's blooming lemon trees and golden oranges glowing out of their dark foliage are miraculously united with myrtle and laurel under soft winds and blue skies, auratically enriched by the southern architecture of columns and marble, as well as sublimely situated in a site of rocks and mountains, caves and tides, one must not overlook the possibility that this poem's refrained inquiry "Kennst du das Land?"

(Do you know [of] the land?) might initially provoke a negative reply, since the speaker ironically describes the lures of this land in a way that seems to thoroughly exclude any sort of precise local knowledge. Without explicitly saying "Italy," the singer describes its allure in an image that simultaneously presents blossoms and fruit of lemons and oranges. On the one hand, such a juxtaposition may suggest an out-of-synchrony poetic positing that veils what could be a more precise form of botanic knowledge – if one were to assume that lemon trees blossom in the spring, whereas orange fruits ripen in later summer. On the other hand, however, various varieties of the citrus, and the orange in particular, are special in this respect: as Theophrastus already observed, under favourable climatic conditions, orange trees tend to blossom and bear fruit simultaneously and all year round.

Laurel and myrtle in Goethe's poem suggest a related issue, in that on the one hand they are actual plants that may readily be present in any given Mediterranean landscape, while on the other hand they are more strongly codified as symbols of love and poetry, glory and memory than as dominant botanic components of a seasonal setting. Hardly geared towards a demonstration of the sort of geopoetic awareness that the wandering troubadours of medieval Provence (and Nietzsche and Pound who literally followed in their footsteps) had of the seasons, conditions, and ways of the place, Goethe, who as a consequence of his committed studies of Italy's art and geography, climate and botany, was certainly acutely aware of such detail, nonetheless chose to auratically poise lemon blossoms and golden orange fruits in harmony with myrtle and laurel as the most memorable requisites for his lyrical act of Italian landscaping. It is compelling that the first substantial lemon cultivation in Europe took place in fifteenth-century Liguria (in the environs of Genoa) from where Columbus brought lemon seeds to Hispaniola – a stretch of land unvisited by Goethe.

One way of visualizing the complexity of Liguria through a geopoetic lens is to mount a comparison between Liguria and "Orplid" on the one hand and Liguria and Arcadia on the other. This distinction is decisive for an understanding of Liguria as an alluring landscape from which Nietzsche, Freud, and Benn took much more than mere inspiration. In 1831, Eduard Mörike, Romantic poet of dreamscapes, together with Ludwig Bauer, his student friend at the University of Tübingen, created a place called "Orplid." Orplid is a conjured mythical island protected by divine Weyla, a far-away and blessed land full of imaginative prospects, at once psychologically real and geographically unreal:

Du bist Orplid, mein Land!
Das ferne leuchtet;
Vom Meere dampfet dein besonnter Strand
Den Nebel, so der Götter Wange feuchtet.
Uralte Wasser steigen
Verjüngt um deine Hüften, Kind!
Vor deiner Gottheit beugen
Sich Könige, die deine Wärter sind.

(Thou art Orplede, my land
Remotely gleaming;
The mist arises from thy sun-bright strand
To where the faces of the gods are beaming.
Primeval rivers spring renewed
Thy silver girdle weaving, child!
Before the godhead bow subdued
Kings, thy worshipers and watchers mild.)[120]

The poem's first stanza addresses the distant island, its sea, sun, and foggy shore, while the second stanza sings of rising primeval waters. Not only does the speaker take possession of a far-away sea-girt land called Orplid – Mörike went so far as subsequently to design maps for Orplid's invented insular dreamscape, which in spite of its stressing the mental reality-value of thus created lands confers an almost comical twist to the more popular version of artistically altering the actual charting of a real land's geography. Benn was not at all fond of this poem by Mörike, and in his own writing inserts phrases hinting at the invented place's non-sensical non-existence: "kein Orplid" and "nichts von Orplid" (no Orplede and no hint of Orplede / away with Orplede).[121]

Arid Arcadia, by contrast, is so much closer to Nietzsche, Freud, and Benn's program – as a consequence of their respective receptions of the ancients and of Goethe (and Freud and Benn's of Nietzsche). Arcadia: the difficult actual stretch of land enclosed in the mountainous Greek Peloponnese, established as the *topos* of pastoral and Arcadian myth-making by the Roman poet Virgil, who transplanted the Sicilian farm life that Theocritus had idealized in the *Eidyllia* to the Greek Arcadia, which to Virgil was the land in which poets and poetry were born – a kind of imaginary idyllic, pastoral, harmonious homeland of any poet, one that Jacopo Sannazaro in *Arcadia* (1502) poetically consolidated as thoroughly as did Sir Philip Sidney, in prose, in *The Countess of Pembroke's*

Arcadia (generally known as *Arcadia* or *Old Arcadia*).

It is curious indeed not only that this Arcadian *topos* portrays the exact opposite of the terrain's actual qualities but that it has been transmitted so consistently that we are more familiar with the invented bucolic dimension than we are with Arcadia's actual properties – if we know of its geographical challenges at all. "Arcadia" and "Liguria" are not only words defined by the same rhythmic (and partially the same sound) pattern but are actual lands equally unlike the soft pastoral lures and legends surrounding them. Even though Arcadia is cool (too cold for the olive, in fact, although according to Fernand Braudel the Mediterranean is coextensive with the cultivation of the olive) and located inland, whereas Liguria has both a warm coastal land and a rough Alpine hinterland (the latter likewise lacking olives), it is essential for the present geopoetic readings of literary topography that both landscapes are actual, both are hermetic, and both are challenging – and that these geographic facts revise the highly stylized images that we have tended to cultivate of Mediterranean locales such as these.

"Siamo in un mondo che s'allunga e contorce come una lucertola in modo d'offrire al sole il massimo della sua superficie […] tendendo a far coincidere l'aprico con l'esistenza del mondo," writes Cuban-born Italo Calvino of his Ligurian world (We are in a world that stretches and twists like a lizard so as to offer the largest possible surface area to the sun […] to have the sunny coincidence with the existence of the world).[122] Granted, "Liguria" is definitely less well-known as a Mediterranean toponym and hence, as a name, clearly enjoys less popularity than "Riviera" or "Côte d'Azur." It is, however, a place name that nonetheless evokes blue seas and the even bluer skies that are surely typical of its situation and that for many have become synonymous with an enchanting and mystifying south. The shore, however, is only the coastal section of this landscape, and as such only one side of Liguria's Janus-faced terrain, beautifully suspended[123] between the mountains and the sea, with wide sandy beaches and flower gardens on the Riviera di Ponente, but harsh and steep rocks and condensed colourful villages on the Riviera di Levante, and caves, hills, and valleys in its hinterland, locally called the *entroterra*.

The traces that keep forming the Mediterranean as the cradle of more than Europe rely on continuous acts of cultural reminiscence and literary transmission which allow for the construction of the places and commonplaces that have surrounded the various shores, borders, and boundaries of the Mediterranean basin for much longer than its more recent name would lead us to believe. The Mediterranean is a multicultural mosaic on whose shores Europe was conceived. However, it is "not merely geography [...] not merely history [...] not merely belonging [...and its] cultures are not merely national cultures [but ... – it is a place] whose boundaries are drawn in neither space nor time."[124] Liguria as one small but striking segment of this Mediterranean – as a steep landscape, an isolated terrain – might lend itself more readily to more concrete geopoetic rapprochements: beyond mere geography, beyond mere history, beyond mere belonging, and beyond nationalism (to recall Predreag Matvejević's fine assessment). Such a movement towards definition, however, becomes increasingly complex with Liguria's admission to the topical mindscapes that Nietzsche, Freud, and Benn inscribe in their Ligurian variations.

Dante declassifies the Ligurian land as among the most unrefined and literally outlandish in the Romance territory. And indeed, its coastline is a harshly weathered relief rather than a smooth profile of beauty. The land is small and as such ideal for Nietzsche, Freud, and Benn on their way towards a small world and a large self. This small land, however, entertains an immense relationship with the sea. Predrag Matvejević's question whether the Mediterranean is "a sea surrounded by land or land by a sea"[125] might be posed with regard to Liguria as well, a land whose compositional nature lends itself well to a visualization of the characteristics of the writing here in question, and also, perhaps, in the sense of a *mise-en-abîme*, which, according to Paul de Man's reference to Walter Benjamin's writings on Friedrich Hölderlin, is "the kind of structure by means of which it is clear that the text becomes itself an example of what it exemplifies."[126] Liguria's razor-sharp silhouette approaches such a congruence with the literary text and its poetic edges. It is akin to such wording, which unveils its own etymology, to such writing, which manifests its own genesis, in something like a critical, if not a psychoanalytical, edition of itself, located between Benjamin's psychoanalysis of things and Freud's psychoanalysis of minds – and suggestive of the eerie post-thalassic depths conjured up in Orhan Pamuk's *Black Book*.

Nietzsche wrote enthusiastically of mountains and seas, boats and isles. He was fond of water and ships, sailing and ports, of Genoese power and pride, parks and palaces – and of Columbus. Freud not only wrote on a series of water dreams; he actually sailed to Athens with his brother Alexander in 1904, and then went on a voyage to America in 1909 to deliver five lectures on psychoanalysis at Clark University. And Benn was not only a physician drawn to lido, waterfront, and marine horizons in his poetry; when he sailed to New York in 1914, he provided medical treatment to the passengers in the lower decks (as did Döblin). Nietzsche swam. Freud loved the Venetian Lido (and regretted in a macabre way that he was not lucky enough to find a sheep skull there as Goethe had more than a century earlier, something that Wilhelm Fließ had hoped Freud would encounter – a curious twist on the Arcadian *memento mori*, and at the same time of course evidence of Fließ's fierce support of Freud's avid scientism) and various other beaches, including Rapallo's, where he admits to having rolled in the sand like a Böcklin-esque sea monster (it is known that Freud had visited a Böcklin exhibition in Munich's Schack Galerie, and *Im Spiel der Wellen* has been part of the collection in Munich's Neue Pinakothek since 1888). Benn, who became seasick on his voyage to New York, was content to gaze at the water and also adored postwar popular songs (performed by Lonny Kellner and René Carol, among others) that sentimentally told of Mediterranean taverns in the Ligurian San Remo and the Sicilian Palermo, and of Mediterranean ports such as the Greek Piraeus or the Italian Adano.[127]

Despite their different but genuine passions for the Mediterranean in general and for Liguria in particular, Nietzsche, Freud, and especially Benn seem unlikely candidates as beach boys and as what Kenneth Silver calls the "Cannes type" or the "Marseilles kind of guy," or as what the Manns in analogy with the guests at the magic mountain in the novel of the same title penned by their father (*Der Zauberberg / The Magic Mountain*) call a "Riviera-Existenz" (Riviera creature).[128] Nevertheless, the Beach Boys might need to enter this Ligurian scene after all, for their "Kokomo" song and an Internet exchange about its setting are revelant to the theme of this discussion. A place called Kokomo? No place called Kokomo? And Liguria? Would a song with that title spur a similar kind of debate, since its name is hardly as well known as those of the Riviera and the Côte d'Azur, even though its individual towns, beaches, and bars have in the meantime become equally popular?

The lyrics of the "Kokomo" song include not only Aruba, Jamaica, Bermuda, the Bahamas, Key Largo, Montego, Martinique, Monserrat, and Port au Prince but also "a place called Kokomo," which this song boldly locates "off the Florida Keys," where on maps it cannot be found. On a website for British expatriates, incidentally, the following attempts at questions and answers regarding the Kokomo hit have made their appearance.[129] The online discussants wonder "where the Beach Boys' place is," given that one has "trouble finding Kokomo on the map." One commentator assumes that "they made it up," while another feels that "it does not matter." One thinks that "it's all in their minds," while another challenges this assumption, suggesting that it does matter to "the people in Kokomo, Indiana" – a proposal that meets with much resistance, since it removes the Caribbean dream aspect of the place in all its alluring promise: "That's most certainly not the Kokomo in the song," someone snaps, while another claims to have seen "what appeared to be a Kokomo Florida Hard Rock Cafe shirt," which is then read as evidence that "there was indeed a Kokomo in Florida." However, "there may not have been a Kokomo in Florida before the song was released." True, and then the general surprise that "they haven't named or re-named some location in Florida Kokomo" is certainly reminiscent of the legion of proper names deploying the toponym "Riviera" to their advantage. "The kinds of images the song invokes are found roughly between Key Largo and Marathon," a further voice assserts, while another adds: "and Bermuda and Aruba."[130]

And what of Liguria and all that is associated with its alluring name? Liguria and fantasies of regression, of escape, of Ur, of what Romain Rolland called the "oceanic feeling" – one of the concepts that Freud happily adopted while elaborating on our uneasiness in culture?[131] I contend that regardless of whether their existence is actual or merely fictional, in each one of these toponyms and *topoi* (Arcadia, Orplid, Kokomo, Liguria) dwells an in-betweenness, a tension between the familiar and the unfamiliar (a secret familiarity as in Freud's definition of the uncanny) that reconciles geography and geographic representation with the imaginative potential of poetic vision and portrays life as longing. The "Kokomo" song envisions the Caribbean as a sort of Mediterranean – that is to say, as a sea that, much like the Afro-Asian-European Mediterranean, runs between islands and continents. "Kokomo" also makes mention of the actual Monserrat in the Lesser Antilles as "Monserrat mystique," where Will Self, incidentally, vividly remembers "painterly strokes of field terraces" and a "rendez-vous with the volcano."[132]

Beyond its obvious cultivation of exotic-erotic fantasies of yearned-for escape to well-rhymed climes and alluring places, the "Kokomo" song is also about placing the lyric in real geography, instilling the desire to anchor the text in actual reality. "Kokomo" is, after all, the only fictional toponym in the song and thus promotes the desire to try and find this place of fantasy in the midst of the actual insular world. Such an attempt is not entirely unlike Mörike's drawing of dream maps of Orplid: A place called Orplid? No place called Orplid? "Kokomo" is not unlike the medieval Provençal lyric either, even if such songs convey the joy of remembered love rather than a projected erotic encounter. Grounded as it appears to be in place, "Kokomo" sets up a prospective journey towards love, including a withdrawal from daily routine and ordinary life, while extravagant twelfth-century troubadour Peire Vidal's "Proensa" (Provence) practises not only an homage to local air in ways that foreshadow Nietzsche and Gertrude Stein but also a personification of place and a concomitant sublimation of eroticism into poetry via the Provençal *gai saber* / *gaya scienza*. Such joyful science is a talent that enables growth as a perfect combination of joy and effort, while illustrating emotions in images as poetic surrogates for clandestine loves, discreetly concealing the lady within an image of the land (similarly, Catullus's Lesbia is a pseudonym for Clodia and really refers to Lesbos, which is Sappho's Greek island). In light of the troubadours' geopoetic achievements, one may well be tempted to prefer them to the metaphysical poets favoured by T.S. Eliot as the actual inventors of the "objective correlative," since, long before the proclaimed deaths of authors and subjects, the troubadours inscribed their understanding of emotional intelligence in a way that has affected major forms of Western writing (and geopoetic writing in particular) ever since.

In that it localizes a desire for love in a celebration of place and toponym rather than person and eponym (even though the lady is clearly looming in the background), Vidal's high medieval "Proensa" song may well unveil some affinity with geopoetic places such as the Beach Boys' Kokomo, Mörike's Orplid, and Nietzsche, Freud, and Benn's Liguria:

I
Ab l'alen tire vas ma l'aire
Qu'ieu sen venir de Proensa;
To quant es e lai m'agensa,
Si que, quan n'aug ben retraire,
Ieu m'o escout en rizan
E·n deman per un mot cen:
Tan m'es bel quan n'aug ben dire.
II
Qu'om no sap tan dous repaire
Cum de Rozer tro c'a Vensa,
Si cum clau mars e Durensa,
Ni on tant fins jois s'esclaire.
Per qu'entre la franca gen
Ai laissat mon cor jauzen
Ab lieis que fa·ls iratz rire.

III
Qu'om no pot lo jorn mal traire
Qu'aja de lieis sovinensa,
Qu'en liei nais jois e comensa.
E qui qu'en sia lauzaire,
De ben qu'en diga, no·i men;
Que·l mielher es ses conten
E·l genser qu'el mon se mire.
IV
E s'ieu sai ren dir ni faire,
Ilh n'aia·l grat, que sciensa
M'a donat e conoissensa,
Per qu'ieu sui gais e chantaire.
E tot quan fauc d'avinen
Ai del sieu bell cors plazen,
Neis quan de bon cor consire.

(I
With my breath I inhale the air
which I feel blowing towards me from Provence;
everything from there so delights me,
that when I hear good things spoken of it,
I listen to it all laughing
and demand one hundred times more words:
it is so sweet to my ears to hear good of it.
II
There is no sweeter dwelling place
than that which lies between the Rhône and Vence,
enclosed between the sea and the Durance,
nor one where more perfect joy shines forth.
And so I have happily left my heart
amongst that noble company,
with her who brings laughter out of sadness.
III
It is impossible to be afflicted
when one thinks of her,
for in her joy is born and has its beginning.
Whoever should praise her cannot lie,
no matter how much good he says of her;
without doubt she is the best
and most noble woman in the world.

IV
If I am able to do or say anything well,
it is thanks to her, for she
has given me knowledge and talent,
my gaiety and my song.
All my most pleasant deeds,
the best imaginings of my heart
come from her beautiful presence.)[133]

While Fraser aptly renders "repaire" as "dwelling place," it is worth mentioning that the coincidence of the Latin *reparare*, to repair or to mend, with the Latin *repatriare*, to repair or to return to one's place, in the Provençal *repaire* is rather felicitous, for it points to the therapeutic dimension of Vidal's words of Eros as mnemonically embedded in and ennobled by the worthy topos that is Provence (which at the same time becomes the locus for a poetic talking cure *avant la lettre*). A variant of the song concludes with the line "qu'en Provensa me retira," putting even greater emphasis on the place as extraordinary retreat and respite (if no longer as a physical retreat, then even more as a mental respite).[134] The place of this proto-Freudian act of poetic sublimation is precisely presented as the geography of Provence, defined by the rivers Rhône and Durance, the community of Vence (between Nice and Antibes), and the Mediterranean Sea, to which Vidal pays homage. The integration of this precise locale and the anonymous lady into one geopoetic entity (the third-person singular pronoun "lieis" is deliberately ambiguous, simultaneously referring to the lover and to Provence) is presented as intimately connected with the singer's regional inspiration by Provençal winds and the lady's thus recalled erotic breath, which the wind imitatively repeats in ways that are both soothing and inspiring for a poet aiming for "mot cen," a hundred further words. If wind is a commonplace in poetic matters, Vidal's emphasis on wind and breath also recalls Kenneth White's stress on a territory's aura when it comes to fruitfully combining word and world in the field of geopoetics: while aura generally refers to a subtle emanation or radiation that somewhat mysteriously surrounds a person or a thing, the Greek and Latin *aura* means air or breeze, and as such speaks to Vidal's geopoetically sublimated winds of passion.

Subversive though he may have been, Vidal never questioned the actual existence of Provence as a place; nor did he write of Alazais de Rocamartina's bikini straps. His amorous synthesis of place and body, however, is nonetheless suggestive of Will Self's assessment of the Provençal Côte, in that it attractively embodies desire while leaving room for humour, all the while relying on the intrinsic allure of place names such as Provence or Côte d'Azur, as well as on the tricks of the geopoetic trade. Toponyms may be fictional – like Kokomo and Orplid – or a combination of actual and fictional, such as appears to be the case with Self's "Côte of Desire" as well as with Provence, Arcadia, Sligo, the Bosphorus, and Liguria: even though their materialities themselves betray their poetic valence, these places nevertheless thoroughly rely on an imaginary vista spurred primarily by intensely alluring names that reveal novel glimpses and open up new horizons. In this vein, Guillaume Apollinaire writes in "Les fenêtres" ("Windows"):

Et maintenant voilà que s'ouvre la fenêtre
[...]
Vancouver
Où le train blanc de neige et de feux nocturnes fuit l'hiver
O Paris
[...]
Paris Vancouver Hyères Maintenon New York et les Antilles
La fenêtre s'ouvre comme une orange
Le beau fruit de la lumière

(And now look at the window opening
[...]
Vancouver
Where the train white with snow and fires of the night flees the winter
O Paris
[...]
Paris Vancouver Hyères Maintenon New York and the Antilles
The window opens like an orange
Lovely fruit of light)[135]

Such poetic dreaming over maps may be further enlightened by philological considerations about etymological and cultural origins. The complementary colour of orange is azure, and the word "azure" originates in the Persian *lāzhward* and the Arabic *lāzaward*. It refers to a place, the Afghan province Badakhstan, which in ancient times was the main source of the rare semi-precious stone lapis lazuli, highly prized for its intense azure colour. *Lazheward* was adopted into French at the time of the troubadours, when the initial consonant "l" was understood as the noun's article: *l'azur*.

Marathon, too, has enticed dreamings over maps – the Greek Marathon looks back on a longer history of associations than the Marathon in Florida that seems so close to the Beach Boys' fantastic Kokomo. While the city of Marathon in southeastern Greece is named after a nearby plain (Greek *marathron*: fennel), it most famously refers to an endurance race whose name originates in the battlefield of Marathon in Greece. Pheidippides, so the legend goes, was sent from Marathon to Athens to proclaim the Persian defeat and collapsed from exhaustion right after his report of the Greek victory.[136] It is crucial to take into consideration the fact that there were at least two roads from Marathon to Athens. In spite of various doubts with regard to the historical accuracy of the Marathon legend – a legend dismantled by none other than Herodotus, who claims that the messenger ran from Athens to Sparta rather than from Marathon to Athens and did so in order to seek aid rather than to proclaim victory – it is generally assumed that the less strenuous of the two roads was the one not taken, and that the messenger chose to face the challenge of the more mountainous route via the pass of Thracian Dionysus, to which Nietzsche would most likely have given his enthusiastic approval.

While Marathon is hardly Halcyon (and not only because one is a toponym, the other an eponym), Liguria holds a share in both. Suspended as it is between the two legendary ideas that Marathon and Halcyon have come to embody, Liguria is situated between its Côte's halcyon azure calms and creative charms on the one hand and strenuous mountainous travails on the other. Its difficult beauty embodies these characteristics in an intermediate realm in which Liguria's geo-poetic dimensions (including Alps, sea, and shore) record more than just one resemblance with Dante's purgatorial landscape compared to the Ligurian Lerici and Turbìa. They also accord well with Freud's notion of the intermediate realm of transference and are reminiscent of what Goethe refers to in his retrospective travelogue *Italian Journey* as an admixture of truth and lie out of which the successful poet forms a third representational realm, combining a proto-mimetic "Beobachtungsgeist" (spirit of observation) with a creative "Welterschaffung" (making of a world).[137]

It is upon his arrival in Vicenza that Goethe studies architect Andrea Palladio's perspectivism, saying that "es ist wirklich etwas Göttliches in seinen Anlagen, völlig wie die Force des großen Dichters, der aus Wahrheit und Lüge ein Drittes bildet, dessen erborgtes Dasein uns bezaubert" (there is something divine about his talent, something comparable to the power of a great poet who, out of truth and falsehood, creates a third [realm] whose borrowed existence enchants us).[138] It is worth remarking that W.H. Auden and Elizabeth Mayer's translation chooses "talent" for the German *Anlage*. While this is one possible correct reading of the original, it misses the ambiguous dimension of Goethe's expression: rather than referring to the architect's talent and genius alone, the German *Anlage* in this context may also translate as "arrangement," "construction," or "installation," readings that would refer to the architectonic complex itself that Andrea Palladio's talent was able to create, and would as such conjure up an intimate, and crucial, connection between mind and matter. Goethe's formation of the third realm as an instance of borrowed existence could then be better understood as an aesthetic experience that geopoetically transcends not only metaphysics and idealism (and their tendency to reduce matter to mind) but also physics and materialism (and their inclination to reduce mind to matter).

It is not only Liguria's hovering suspension in this kind of third realm but also its verticality, concavity, and proto-insularity that one must not neglect in a context of *mythos* and *logos*. Unlike convex Marseilles and the more level lands of the French Côte d'Azur east of Marseilles, the various Ligurias that make up Liguria as a whole climb up and curve inward: "tante Ligurie verticali e parallele constituite dai singoli centri costieri e dai loro retroterra" (so many vertical and parallel Ligurias which are constituted by single coastal centres and their respective hinterlands) notes Giovanni Assereto, while Bruno Gabrielli goes so far as to suggest that Liguria is best defined as a multitude of vertical sectors that form something akin to Ligurian islands: "per capire la Liguria, occorre analizzarla come insieme di settori o spicchi verticali: i sistemi di valle hanno sempre determinato le diverse 'isole' liguri" (in order to understand Liguria properly, it is necessary to analyse it as an agglomeration of sectors or vertical segments: the systems of the valleys have always determined the various Ligurian "islands").[139]

Edward Casey asks rhetorically whether it might not be time "to *face place* – to confront it, take off its veil, and see its full face? Is it not time to face up to place? Or even to give it a new face, so that we can at last find *it*, and thus our own ineluctably implaced selves, once again?"[140] In a similar vein to Nietzsche's vision of the future as a new dawn, as well as to Predrag Matvejević's concept of "mediterraneity," Casey's attention to the "new face" of place does not simply suggest that we engage in a place debate, contributing to the ongoing spatial turn, as it were. Rather, he proposes an intensely personalized kind of vis-à-vis with place, the very kind that Kenneth White geopoetically engages with and that Nietzsche,

Freud, and Benn practised, each on his own non-native Ligurian terms. All three writers faced Liguria as a place of geopoetic concentration, transforming it into a vanishing point that defines the imaginative goal of their journeys of lure and longing, as well as the formal and structural characteristics (or *Gestalt*) of their textual compositions.

Nietzsche nomadically weathered the storm in various places in Liguria (notably Genoa, Rapallo, and Portofino); Freud revisited Rapallo about two decades after Nietzsche during what was likely an adulterous escape to its late summer shore; and Benn poetically stole away into his Nietzschean-Freudian "Ligurian complexes." All three writers engaged in highly imaginative flights of fantasy, while none of them permanently returned: Nietzsche took further refuge in his mental breakdown, Freud was eventually forced into exile by the National Socialists, and Benn yielded ever more deeply to his controversial inner emigration, while continuing his celebration of post-Liégeardean blues and azures, launching once again the power of Nietzsche and Portofino, of Provence and Liguria, while enlivening a sort of self-perpetuating, self-reflexive multiplication in mathemathical-psychoanalytical terms ("exponent" and "complex") that represent his full immersion in the post-Mallarméan local hue of poetic azure: "Blau. Es ist das Südwort schlechthin, der Exponent des *ligurischen Komplexes*" (Blue. It is the southerly word par excellence, the exponent of the Ligurian complex).[141]

Freud and Benn's endeavours do not follow the pathos of Stopford Brooke's Ligurian bardolatry – "I came to Lerici so long desired / [...] Shelley was here [...] and heard like me" – neither do they much resemble Henry James's intricate ironies about deceptive places and illusive placements of fictional authors – ironies that entertainingly ridicule gregarious touring in putative museums while saying nothing whatsoever about solitary Nietzschean walks through a territory that is as demanding as it is enchanting. Brooke's poem ends with the awakening from a dream of being in Lerici, hearing Shelley speak, and seeing him arise from the very depths in which he had drowned. It is remarkable that Brooke writes "here" (as referring to his own oneiric Lerici), not "there" (the actual eastern Ligurian Lerici where Shelley lived and close to which he died), speaking as if actually in the place rather than oneirically remembering it, thereby precluding a more imaginative momentum in this instance of the Irish chaplain's almost religious poetic pathos.[142]

The principal theme of James's "The Birthplace" is the "whereness" of an enthusiastically located author who is turned into a "personal friend" and a "universal light" by his delusional followers, who reverently touch objects they believe to be his and who eagerly transform a potential *genius loci* into a pathetic pseudo-shrine, confessing that "it's rather a pity [...] that He *isn't* here. I mean as Goethe's at Weimar. For Goethe *is* at Weimar."[143] Like Brooke's speaker, but unlike Nietzsche, James's characters likewise forget about the laws of anamnesis as well as those of deixis.

Were we to invite Nietzsche to momentarily assume a place between Brooke's geopoeticized Shelley and James's fictionalized Goethe, we would then maximally approximate what Nietzsche meant to Freud and Benn – a very real Ligurian precursor who returns in and beyond their creative dreams, and at the same time an overpowering shadow or authorial father whose spatial ubiquity and temporal priority press as strongly on Freud and Benn's ephebian shoulders as the Maritime Alps press on the Ligurian shore. Contrary to Gertrude Stein's observation about Californian Oakland, there is a there there – as Henry James himself witnesses for us in his lines on the "sentimental pilgrimage" that he embarked on upon leaving Genoa, first for La Spezia, then for a "drive among vines and olives, over the hills beside the Mediterranean" to Portovenere, and eventually on a boat to Byron and Shelley's Golfo dei Poeti, listening "to the murmur of the tideless sea at the base of the narrow promontory." James continues, observing the following:

> The place is very lonely – all overwearied with sun and breeze and brine – [...] It is a place where an English-speaking pilgrim himself may very honestly think thoughts and feel moved to lyric utterance. But I must content myself with saying in halting prose that I remember few episodes of Italian travel more sympathetic, as they have it here, that perfect autumn afternoon. [...] Lerici [...] in the fading light, on the vine-decked platform that looked out toward the sunset and the darkening mountains and, far below, upon the quiet sea, beyond which [Shelley's] pale-faced tragic villa stared up at the brightening moon.[144]

Unsurprisingly, James's exercise in understatement vis-à-vis his hardly prosaic talent is persuasively efficient (rather than being its opposite, his allegedly "halting prose" may well be curiously close to "lyric utterance"); it is once again Kenneth White's emphasis on geopoetic intensity over a more traditional generic taxonomy that is at stake here with regard to the vertically inclined viewpoint ("below," "up") adopted by James. And when writing on Nietzsche's rugged and perpendicular Portofino, Ernst Bertram significantly opposes the "Fläche des Schweigens" (the plain of silence)[145] that immediately follows Nietzsche's tough and cut-off promontory-type of sentence, thus putting one last accent on silence as flat and horizontal and on geopoetic words as steep and vertical.[146]

If the hardly Italophile Mann siblings did not venture as far east as Byron, Shelley, and James's Lerici, they surely put great emphasis on the original, the primeval, the authentic, the Ur in the eastern segments of Liguria that they explicitly label as non-French and therefore less civilized. And yet, however hard they tried, and try they did, the Manns could not help acknowledging the sheer authentic presence and rough difficult beauty of Portofino, reminiscing about *Zarathustra* and the impact of Nietzsche's verbal renderings of Portofino on the poetically inclined soul. The Manns foreground the promontory's almost geometrically positioned cuts into the sea, as well as its dramatic perpendicularity and sense of brooding power: "Das Vorgebirge von Portofino liegt eckig ins Meer hinaus gelagert. Es hat felsig abstürzende Ufer, hochtheatralisch, sehr pittoresk. [...] Es ist beinahe zu echt" (Portofino's foothills protrude angularly into the sea. They have rocky declivitous shores, highly theatrical, very picturesque, they are almost too authentic).[147]

Liguria's difficult beauty or austere harmony gives rise to yet another poetic consideration. Until Norbert von Hellingrath's insightful analysis of Friedrich Hölderlin's translations of Sophocles and Pindar appeared in 1911, Hölderlin's mature verse had generally been considered as a product of the poet's fall into madness rather than a fine instance of an unconventional, proto-Modernist poetics that the late Hölderlin had adopted from Pindar, the master of what Greek rhetoric would label *armonía austera*. When confronting *armonía austera* with its opposite, *armonía glaphyra*, von Hellingrath avails himself of a set of terms from Hellenic rhetoric (the terms are Dionysius Halicarn's), providing his German rendering of these Greek terms as "harte Fügung" (*armonía austera*) and "glatte Fügung" (*armonía glaphyra*), which is to say "rough and tough" as opposed to "soft and smooth" composition. "Smooth" implies here that the individual word forms an interconnected part of a larger construction and is thus absorbed in a sentence, thought, line, or phrase, whereas the individual word in a so-called tough composition sets out to draw attention first and foremost to its own insular presence, its own immediate beginning, its own cut-off ending, its own maximal surface and density, and its own sharp circumference, rather than becoming an integral part of a larger sentence, thought, line, or phrase. Such words are difficult and beautiful – such "words have edges."[148]

Hellingrath's rendition "harte Fügung" was quickly absorbed into the kind of poetic differentiation between tough and smooth composition that is readily applicable to the lyric beyond Pindar and Hölderlin. This distinctive contrast between harmonies as either tough or smooth, I suggest, can be related to Goethe's aforementioned qualification of poetry as an intense, condensed, metaphorical, and therefore "steil" (steep) genre, as well as to the troubadours' concept of the most exquisite poetry as maximally "clus" (enclosed in and reflective of itself) – either way, an arduous task. In all these cases of tough, steep, and enclosed composition, the stress falls on a highly unconventional, minimally mediated, and thoroughly defamiliarizing presentation of the poetic word as non-quotidian, surprising, provoking, and close to the senses. Nietzsche's poetic, aphoristic, parodic, and neologistic output (and, following in his footsteps, Freud and Benn's poetic styles as well) more often than not belongs to the category of tough rather than smooth composition, thereby reflecting once again the presence of an imitative form between geopoetic word and Ligurian terrain, of a shared form between the lines of a place and the lines of a text, to recall once again the aforementioned Turkish noun *kıta* and what it conveys in highly condensed fashion. Such thoughts seem all the more appropriate when one reconsiders that in aerial perspective the Ligurian territory itself resembles a topographical map as much as it resembles a place; that is to say, Liguria looks as if it were a poetic representation of itself, a mise-en-abîme, a *kıta*, or stanza.

Reminiscent of the double-entendre that the German word *Anlage* provides as previously discussed with regard to Andrea Palladio's talent in designing architectonic installations of the calibre that Goethe enthusiastically describes, the German word *Fügung*, which Hellingrath deployed in his translation of the Greek word for "harmony," provides a similar semantic dimension: *Fügung* may intend accord or composition, in Hellingrath's sense of showing the joints (*Fugen*) between words rather than painting over them by using set pieces or other kinds of conjunctive material; *Fügung*, however, likewise signifies "lot" or "fate" and, as such, accords well with Hölderlin's geopoetic interest in the earth's *Gestalt* and his celebration of geopoetic metaphoricity (as Erika Schellenberger-Diederich has recently demonstrated). In this geopoetic sense, Nietzsche's composition is as tough as his lot: his *amor fati* (love of fate or *Fügung*) is coined on the very basis of what the Manns, too, recognized as an "almost too authentic" terrain.

Nietzsche's discernment of geopoetic laws – ranging from steepness and enclosure, to insularity and exposure, to anamnesis and deixis, and on to tough and smooth composition – is thoroughly intertwined with

his profoundly troubling understanding of the difficulty of finding an
ending that is not silent, not flat, not prosaic – a hybrid kind of ending,
in other words, that does justice to what Calvino fashions as Liguria's
all-encompassing, compact, and nevertheless thoroughly segmented singular engulfment, which continues to break its inner and outer banks.
He writes of

> serie d'insenature e golfi e avvallamenti interni a queste insenature e
> golfi, fino a incontrare promontori che si spingono nel mare più di altri
> promontori delimitando golfi più vasti che comprendono golfi più interni,
> e così via fino a stabilire che questo sistema di golfi interni ad altri golfi,
> dorati al mattino e azzurri la sera verso ponente, verdolini al mattino e grigi
> la sera verso levante, continua così per quanto sono lunghi i mari e le terre,
> tendono a inglobare tutto il mare in un unico golfo [...].
>
> (series of bays and gulfs and basins within these bays and gulfs, until one
> reaches promontories that venture further into the sea than other prom-
> ontories, confining vaster gulfs that comprise bays further inward, and so
> on and so forth, until one comes to the realization that this system of bays
> internal to other bays, golden in the morning and azure in the evening
> toward the west, greenish in the morning and grey in the evening toward
> the east, continues in this fashion for the entire span of the seas and conti-
> nents with a tendency to enclose the entire sea in one single bay [...].)[149]

Had Nietzsche been granted the opportunity to read Calvino's assessment of the Ligurian world (or, perhaps, of his world as Ligurian), that
is, the geopoetic basis on which Calvino insistently deploys those Ligurian locales with which he is intimately familiar, he would most probably
have welcomed the Cuban-Ligurian's minutely cut-out details of sea and
bay, mountain and valley, as well as his geopoetic writing that is so firmly
based in the tough, terraced, and mnemonic composition that is its lot.
    While Stéphen Liégeard envisioned Portofino as located in the lands
of Goethe's Mignon, calling it an "écran violacé" (purplish screen)
prematurely suggestive of Gerardo Dottori's 1935 Futurist painting *Il
Golfo della Spezia*,[150] Nietzsche in *Die fröhliche Wissenschaft* (*The Gay Science*) recalls, and personifies, a vertical Ligurian location (to the east and
yet suggestive of the one Calvino will have had in mind): the proud,
calm promontory of Portofino as it descends "in's Meer [...] dort, wo die
Bucht von Genua ihre Melodie zu Ende singt" (into the very sea, there,
where the bay of Genoa finishes its song).[151]

Gerardo Dottori, *Il Golfo della Spezia* (*The Bay of La Spezia*) (1935). Private collection, Perugia. Used with the permission of Giuliana Roscini and Riccardo Roscini.

In Dottori's *Il Golfo della Spezia* a variety of Modernisms intriguingly intersect, while the scene remains strictly Ligurian. The eastern Ligurian bay of La Spezia is portrayed here as a Modernist vortex that evokes the azure spell of the site's Alpine-Mediterranean land- and seascape, of its prototypical steepness and enclosure, proto-insularity and exposure. In this primordial oneiric vision, Dottori seems to simultaneously celebrate Stéphane Mallarmé's triple *Azur*, Stéphen Liégeard's "écran violacé" (purplish screen), and Futurism's post-Nietzschean addiction to the sea that also fascinated Benn.

Gerardo Dottori (1884–1977) joined the Italian Futurists in 1912, three years after Filippo Tommaso Marinetti's launching of the movement with the *Manifeste du futurisme* in Paris, which had swift effects internationally — Gottfried Benn, whose Modernist (Expressionist) debut likewise occurred in 1912, read it in German. Dottori remained active during Futurism's postwar wave and signed the *Manifesto dell'aeropittura* in Genoa in 1929, focusing his work on the Bay of La Spezia, alternatively known as the *Golfo dei Poeti* (where Shelley drowned).

Dottori's triptych (now lost) *Il Golfo Armato* (*The Bay in Arms*) won the first prize at the *Mostra nazionale di pittura Premio del Golfo* in 1933, the same year that the *Premio nazionale di poesia Golfo della Spezia* was awarded to Marinetti for his *Aeropoema del Golfo della Spezia*, a long poem inspired by this bay and a Futurist vision of its destruction.

The 1935 *Il Golfo della Spezia* (*The Bay of La Spezia*) likewise assembles images of Portovenere in the west, La Spezia in the centre, and Lerici in the east; unlike the triptych, however, *Il Golfo della Spezia* has clear affinities with non-Futurist forms of Modernism. If its wavelets are blade-like, the overall appearance of the bay is non-militaristic and reminiscent of Expressionism, Cubism, and, perhaps, of Robert Delaunay's Orphism, with its strong colours, its geometric shapes, and its experimentation with depth and surface, lightness and luminance. Portovenere and Lerici come to the fore in very specific terms here: Dottori combines Lerici's twelfth-century castle with arcades reminiscent of the architecture of the Palazzo della civiltà in Rome, while extending Portovenere's twelfth-century church of Saint Peter (restored in 1931-1935) into a number of modern high rises. Restoration and commemoration are diametrically opposed to Futurism's core tenets; Dottori, however, celebrates the completion of this restoration in 1935, albeit by lending a Modernist twist to Portovenere's time-honoured site. In his poem *Portovenere*, Ligurian Modernist Eugenio Montale puts it thus: *ed ogni ora prossima è antica* (and every coming hour is ancient); with Nietzsche's cyclical perspective in mind, one might add: and every future past.

As is the case in Dottori's *Il Golfo Armato* and in the 1935 *Aurora sul Golfo* (*The Bay at Dawn*), the perspective of *Il Golfo della Spezia* is aerial as well — a position frequently assumed in Futurism. The beholder's aerial vantage point, however, also accords well with the sort of all-encompassing engulfment which Cuban-Ligurian postmodern writer Italo Calvino has depicted as *inglobare tutto il mare in un unico golfo* (to enclose the entire sea in one single bay), while singling out geometric and geopoetic details of sea and bay, peak and shore. Such a dreamscape combines Dante and Columbus, as it were, in that it hints at breaking free from the known waters of the Mediterranean into the Atlantic Ocean as a perilous endeavour. In spite of the radical clarity of Futurism's many *Manifesti*, Marinetti's own relationship with the past was rather complex. Allegedly, during one of the Futurist evenings held on a Ligurian lido called Colombo, he conducted an imaginary interview with Shelley *redivivo*.

It is the suspiciously authentic, auspicious Ligurian image of Nietzsche the mighty ancestor – framed by this Alpine height, this Mediterranean descent, and this Ligurian bay – that Sigmund Freud and Gottfried Benn were to epigonically assume so shortly after him. When visiting Liguria (Freud) and inaugurating the Ligurian complex (Benn), Freud and Benn might not have been warring against Thebes like the famous Seven; they were, however, anxiously (mis)reading Liguria's azure spell as prefigured by Ligurian nomad, Provençal troubadour, and gay scientist Friedrich Nietzsche.

PART II

Nietzsche, Freud, Benn: A Ligurian Complex

… by indirections find directions out.
William Shakespeare

… examine this region of short distances and definite places.
W.H. Auden

… vedi che si trasforma questo lembo di terra solitario in un crogiuolo.

(… see how this solitary stretch of land's transformed into a crucible.)
Eugenio Montale

Copious Dawns, High Noons, Blessed Isles: Nietzsche's Ligurianity

> ... vivere risolutamente.
>
> (... to live resolutely.)
> Giuseppe Mazzini[1]

> ... il vento ... sconvolge la sintassi.
>
> (... the wind... churns up the syntax.)
> Maria Luisa Spaziani

> ... it's sublime, this perfect solitude of foreign lands.
> Elizabeth Barrett Browning

Nietzsche characterized the Provençal notion *gaya scienza* as an "Einheit von Sänger, Ritter und Freigeist" (unity of singer, knight, and free spirit), claiming that "das Klima des *littoral provençal* (climate of the Provençal coast) was the creative condition for him to complete his *Zarathustra*: "ich hätte den Schlußreim zu meinem *Zarathustra* nur an dieser Küste dichten können, in der Heimat der *gaya scienza*" (I could only have found the final rhyme for my *Zarathustra* on this very coast, the homeland of the *gaya scienza*) – a rhyme of great noon and morning sun.[2]

Nietzsche's belief in art as the only creative justification for human life is inextricably intertwined with his challenging of the foundation of Judaeo-Christian morals in general and Christianity and what he unravels as its celebration of weakness and life-negating pity in particular. His life-affirming, revitalizing philosophy was particularly inspired by Greek serenity on the one hand and Provençal *gai saber* (or *gaya scienza*) on the other, with his early emphasis on ancient culture and Attic tragedy the *Die Geburt der Tragödie aus dem Geiste der Musik* (*The Birth of Tragedy from the Spirit of Music*) (1872) and his later focus on Provence and Liguria in *Dawn* (1881), *The Gay Science* (1882), and *Thus Spoke Zarathustra* (1883–5).

From 1880 until his breakdown in 1889, Nietzsche led the nomadic life of a stateless wanderer (he had given up his Prussian citizenship without adopting Swiss citizenship when he became a professor at the University of Basel). The words "nomadic" (seeking new pastures) and "vogelfrei" (outlawed) entertain significant associations with this period of his life. Kenneth White appropriately deploys the word "nomadic" in his discussion of Nietzsche in particular and intellectual nomadism in general, while Nietzsche himself used the word *vogelfrei* (free as a bird and outlawed) eponymically in his *Songs of Prince Vogelfrei,* added as an appendix to the second edition of *The Gay Science.* Nietzsche's journeys during his most prolific decade would take him perennially to Naumburg, where his mother lived, to Sils-Maria in the Swiss Alps, as well as to the Ligurian seaside and other Italian locales (including Messina, Venice, Sorrento, and Rome).

Nietzsche's pages are pervaded with references to peaks and shores, from which he draws images for hypotaxis as well as his pool of metaphors. After quitting his endowed professorship at the University of Basel at age thirty-five, Nietzsche spent his winters on the Mediterranean, primarily in Genoa and Nice, and his summers in the small Alpine village of Sils-Maria, 1800 metres above sea level, in southeastern Switzerland (Engadine), not far from St Moritz, where Italian winds encounter cooler airs from the north, lending an azure hue to the skies. Nietzsche regarded the place as a perfect combination of Finland and Italy.

Nietzsche's first attempt at an Italian journey ended abruptly in Bergamo, a city whose air he found repulsive and hence instantly left. He despised Rome as whole-heartedly as Goethe and Freud adored it, while his perceptions of Sorrento, Venice, Genoa, Rapallo, Nice, and Turin were, on occasion, somewhat less critical. Nietzsche set foot on Italian soil for the first time in 1876 – in Genoa. The city's name has two possible etymologies: *ianua* (door, gate), and *genu* (knee, turn). They suggest beautifully the new beginning or turning point in his life that Nietzsche was about to embark on. This first Ligurian location became a field of energy for the wandering Nietzsche, in which he gradually assumed what, in line with Kenneth White's definition of *atlanticity* and Pedrag Matvejević's of *mediterraneity*, I call Nietzsche's *ligurianity*. While this first journey was envisioned as an escape into life, Nietzsche arrived there with a migraine that forced him immediately into bed rest. He remained for only a short while, and did not return to Italy until 1880, when he began to gradually discover a variety of landscapes that at least temporarily would accord well with his mind, body, and soul. Many of these locales were on the Riviera, including Genoa, Rapallo, Nice, and their environs.

Nietzsche adored Genoa's verticality and terraced topography, as well as its location right on the Mediterranean Sea, and its port, parks, and palaces.[3] It is in Genoa that his first Ligurian refuge takes shape in the form of a modest attic abode in the Salita delle Battistine, which he famously referred to as his "unbekannteste Dachstubenexistenz" (completely anonymous/incognito existence in the attic). This first extended Genoese sojourn lasted from November 1880 to April 1881. Nietzsche dispatched the manuscript of *Dawn* in January (dawn, January, and Genoa all imply a fresh start), and it appeared in print that year, while he was in his summer retreat in Sils. There, in August, while out walking by the lake and the Alpine Surlej rock, he was struck for the first time by the idea of the eternal recurrence. In October 1881 he returned to Genoa and remained there until spring 1882, when he embarked on his journey to Messina, Sicily, as well as to Rome, and eventually Naumburg. The first edition (books one to four) of *The Gay Science* appeared in the summer of that year.

Nietzsche's attraction to Genoa was due to its climate on the one hand and its time-honoured will to life, egotism, conquest, and survival on the other. Dario Martini and Divo Gori conclude their book on Liguria with a reference that foreshadows Kenneth White's geopoetics (beginning and ending with Nietzsche), as well as Predrag Matvejević's mediterraneity (relying on Nietzsche):

> Nietzsche ha capito la psicologia dei genovesi. Con la *Gaya Scienza* ha voluto darci il senso di una vittoria spirituale sulle avversità dell'esistenza. In fondo, anche nell'accrescerle, queste avversità, lottando contro i loro fratelli, i Della Volta, i Doria, i Grimaldi, gli Spinola, i Fieschi obbedivano ad una legge imposta dal destino alla Liguria, terra di contraddizioni, dove tutto ciò che deve proiettarsi nel futuro – dal seme dell'olivo alla vita delle città – è costretto a conquistare faticosamente il proprio diritto a non soccombere.

(Nietzsche understood the psychology of the Genoese. With the *Gay Science* he wanted to give us the sense of a spiritual victory over the adversities of our existence. At bottom, even by expanding these adversities, fighting against their brothers, the Della Volta, the Doria, the Grimaldi, the Spinola, the Fieschi abided by a law that was imposed upon Liguria by destiny, a land of contradictions, where everything that must project itself into a future – from the olive seed to city life – is constrained to painstakingly conquer its own right not to succumb.)[4]

This variant of the will to life (and survival against all odds) was to become exemplary for Nietzsche's *amor fati* (the love of one's fate regardless of this fate's nature) and for his assessment of art as defying time by its determination to dare and last.

"Ich lag wieder still am Meere, wie eine Eidechse in der Sonne, an den fernen Bergspitzen glänzte zum ersten Male der Schnee" (I was once again quietly lying by the sea, like a lizard in the sun; on the mountain tops the snow was glistening for the first time), writes Nietzsche suggestively in an 1881 letter from Genoa to Heinrich Köselitz, who resided in Venice at the time. In a letter to his mother and sister, written on the same day, he poetically emphasizes the "blaues warmes Wetter" (blue warm weather), while in a third letter of that day, to Franz Overbeck, who was in Basel at the time, Nietzsche confesses that he often thinks of his friend when he "nach Mittag, fast Tag für Tag, auf [s]einem abgeschiedenen Felsen am Meere sitz[t] oder lieg[t], wie die Eidechse in der Sonne ruh[t] und mit den Gedanken auf Abenteuer des Geistes ausgeh[t]" (after lunchtime almost every day sits or lies on his isolated rock by the sea, resting like a lizard in the sun while embarking on adventures of the mind).[5] Nietzsche is Mediterranean in the sense of Matvejević's "mediterraneity": "ein Südländer, dem Glauben nach" (a man of the south in spirit) says Nietzsche, the self-declared "good European," and "Freund Italians" (friend of Italy).[5]

In the winter of 1882, Nietzsche discovered Rapallo, where he composed the first part of *Also sprach Zarathustra*, which he himself and others after him have characterized as his poetically densest, metaphorically most compact, and most esoterically enclosed and challenging work.

Nietzsche spent the summer of 1883 in Sils, where he fondly remembered Rapallo and composed the second part of *Zarathustra*, while for the fall and winter months he returned to Genoa, visited La Spezia, and eventually moved on to Nice, where he met the Viennese scholar Joseph Paneth, a close friend of Freud's (whom Freud also mentions in *Die*

Traumdeutung). Nietzsche remained in Nice until spring 1884, continued his dialogue with Paneth first in person and subsequently in letters, and wrote a portion of the third book of *Zarathustra*. After further trips and dislocations, he travelled to Mentone and then back to Nice for the winter of 1884, where he completed book four of *Zarathustra*. In 1886, Nietzsche spent his fifth summer in Sils, wrote his self-critical preface to *The Birth of Tragedy*, and in the fall moved on to Genoa and Ruta Ligure, where he worked on the second editions of *Dawn* and *The Gay Science*, which were completed that winter, in Nice. These second editions appeared in 1887, including an appendix of poems in the manner of the Provençal troubadours. Both *Dawn* and *The Gay Science* are Provençal borrowings – the generic *alba* and the technical *gaya scienza* – and attract literary attention. The former rubric designates medieval dawn songs, which were erotic poems of frequently adulterous passion, while the latter refers to the technical skill required for poetic composition: *gaya scienza* marks the beginning of European poetry of a type categorized by Pound as "Provence 1200" or more gracefully as "Provence knew." In a proto-Poundian vein, Nietzsche deployed Provence's troubadours' poetic know-how to infuse joy and laughter, dance and lightness into his serious, complex, and defiant thought. In 1888 Nietzsche spent his last winter in Nice, leaving for Turin in April (where he wrote *Ecce Homo*), from where he returned for his last summer in Sils.

Nietzsche is not merely an influential philosopher; he is also an outstanding poet, an expressive stylist in both prose and verse – indeed, his most influential works read more like poems than philosophical prose, as Walter Kaufmann pointed out; in *Also sprach Zarathustra* above all, where loneliness, high noon ("Grosser Mittag"), and blessed isles ("glückselige Inseln") define the tone. Nietzsche's poetic expressiveness is grounded in solitude and existence – he even composed a poem titled "Vereinsamt" (Lonesome) – a profoundly moving expression of turmoil and travail by a man whose message was nonetheless an enthusiastic affirmation of life.

Nietzsche's thorough grasp of the Provençal and Ligurian lands, their character and conditions, shows not only in his borrowing from the Provençals. He also tells us, in his retrospective autobiographical work *Ecce Homo*, that walking in the environs of Rapallo played a crucial role in the composition of *Zarathustra* and the book's major teachings (primarily those of the "overman," the "eternal recurrence," and the "great noon"), and that the idea of his protagonist Zarathustra overcame, overtook, befell, even "assaulted" him while he was hiking the promontory between Portofino and Santa Margherita Ligure (Nietzsche later spoke of Zarathustra as an event: *Zarathustra-Ereignis*). Zarathustra's thoughts on steepness, smallness, and insularity are granted careful attention in this context, as is Nietzsche's conquest of uncharted linguistic territory in intimate connection with Rapallo's landscape:

[Ich Iebte] in jener anmutig stillen Bucht von Rapallo unweit Genua, die sich zwischen Chiavari und dem Vorgebirge Porto fino einschneidet. Meine Gesundheit war nicht die beste; der Winter kalt und über die Maassen regnerisch; ein kleines Albergo [della Posta], unmittelbar am Meer gelegen, so dass die hohe See nachts den Schlaf unmöglich machte, bot ungefähr in Allem das Gegentheil vom Wünschenswerten. Trotzdem und beinahe zum Beweis meines Satzes, dass alles Entscheidende "trotzdem" entsteht, war es dieser Winter und diese Ungunst der Verhältnisse, unter denen mein *Zarathustra* entstand. – Den Vormittag stieg ich in südlicher Richtung auf der herrlichen Strasse nach Zoagli hin in die Höhe, an Pinien vorbei und weitaus das Meer überschauend; des Nachmittags, sooft es nur die Gesundheit erlaubte, umging ich die ganze Bucht von Santa Margherita bis hinter nach Porto fino. Dieser Ort und diese Landschaft ist durch die große Liebe, welche der unvergessliche deutsche Kaiser Friedrich der Dritte für sie fühlte, meinem Herzen noch näher gerückt; [...] – Auf diesen beiden Wegen fiel mir der ganze erste *Zarathustra* ein, vor allem Zarathustra selber, als Typus: richtiger, *er überfiel mich* ...[7]

(I stayed in that charming quiet bay of Rapallo which, not far from Genoa, is cut out between Chiavari and the foothills of Portofino. My health could have been better; the winter was cold and excessively rainy; my small *albergo [della Posta],* situated right at the sea so that the high sea made it impossible to sleep at night, was in just about every way the opposite of what one might wish for. In spite of this and almost in order to prove my proposition that everything decisive comes into being "in spite of," it was that winter and under these unfavorable circumstances that my *Zarathustra* came into being.

Mornings I would walk in a southerly direction on the splendid road to Zoagli, going up past pines with a magnificent view of the sea; in the afternoon, whenever my health permitted it, I walked around the whole bay from Santa Margherita all the way to Portofino. This place and this scenery came even closer to my heart because of the great love that Emperor Frederick III felt for them. [...] – It was on these two walks that the whole of *Zarathustra I* occurred to me, and especially Zarathustra himself as a type: rather, he *overtook me.*)[8]

Both *Morgenröthe* and *Die fröhliche Wissenschaft* precede *Zarathustra*, while showing a similar sensitivity to Ligurian places of spiritual liberation. The geographic and psychic circumstances under which *Die fröhliche Wissenschaft* was written were marked by Nietzsche's friendship with Heinrich Köselitz and his love of Georges Bizet's music in general and *Carmen* in particular (of which Nietzsche attended a performance in Genoa in 1881). It was through Bizet that, after his split with Richard Wagner, Nietzsche was able to continue with what he repeatedly refers to as a "southerly aesthetics" of the kind that Goethe had inscribed before him. In this context Genoa, the city of Columbus, plays a central role precisely for what was absent in Wagner: a Provence-inspired light and gaiety.

Nietzsche's acute sensitivity to place, landscape, and air lives on in his conviction that the effect of one's atmospheric surroundings, of the climate in which one breathes, has a strong bearing one what one thinks and writes (as Gertrude Stein suggested in "Landscape," quoted earlier). Even though Nietzsche was not a tourist in the usual sense of that word, and certainly not in the sense of the Grand Tour, he was not in his native land either but chose instead to take up residence in Liguria. The places in which he chose to live and write are certainly among the most strikingly beautiful in Europe, even though Nietzsche always found a way to discover their despicable aspect as well. The French and Italian Rivieras offered him hospitality during the winter, while the Swiss Alps welcomed him in the summer (spring and autumn having been difficult times of more than just seasonal transition for Nietzsche). However, geographic beauty as difficult beauty forms the basis not only for Nietzsche's poetic expressiveness but also for his ethical considerations and his questioning of time-honoured moralities and thoughts on sin, crime, and guilt, on pity, neighbourliness, and compassion. Nietzsche's acute and yet volatile perceptions of existential qualities of place, pleasure, and pain come to the fore, such as those of Rapallo, Genoa, and Nice, which he calls a very Italian city, admitting to being simultaneously drawn to and repulsed by it. Most of the locales where Nietzsche took up residence in his years of wandering had played no role in the canonical terrain of the Grand Tour.

Unlike Goethe, who fashioned himself into a detached onlooker (for example observing the various street spectacles during the Roman carnival), Nietzsche did not present himself as a stranger to any foreign place. In Genoa he felt Genoese. And from Nice he wrote that one was simply so un-German there. Even though Nietzsche's extended sojourns in Nice were on many accounts good experiences, his complaints about the city are nevertheless legion. Wherever he was, he dreamt of an elsewhere less tortured by certain atmospheres – in the literal meteorological as well as the metaphorical cultural sense of the term. His accounts are intensive as well as extensive, and may quickly take negative or positive turns, but are reliably endowed with those sparks of passion that in *Zarathustra* he neologistically terms "Freuden- und Leidenschaften"[9] (something like "joys and passions," but really untranslatable because the English equivalents are Latin-based rather than Germanic, so the pun does not transfer).

Nietzsche's autobiographical sketches of his dislocations along the Riviera reveal how his touring was more than that – and certainly not aristocratic or "grand" (Benn was fascinated by Nietzsche's ascetic modesty and repeatedly refers to the latter's simple rooms where, in winter, without a stove, he would sit and eat his carefully rationed sausage sandwiches). Nietzsche's frequent sensations of contempt and disgust for his surroundings, however, do not equal disenchantment. Rather, they give rise to explosive antitheses and a courageous lifting of taboos in expressions of physical unease, showing Nietzsche's passion for the dilemma that Liguria (broadly defined and including Nice) represented for him. While Liguria enabled him to climb closer to halcyon skies under which fruitful poetic conception was possible, he simultaneously referred to Nice's luxurious dreadfulness. The tension of such contrary perception conditioned the pleasures and pains that Nietzsche took in his antithetical, aphoristic writing cure in an unconventionally personalized Ligurian-Provençal south.

In the famous passage on *amor fati* (the love of one's fate) in *Die fröhliche Wissenschaft*, Nietzsche begins with a unique New Year's resolution, stating that in 1882 he has decided to approach his creative life differently. He is resolved to dedicate his attention to the necessity of life as beauty, albeit difficult beauty; in other words, *vivere risolutamente*.

> Ich sehe sein [Epikurs] Auge auf ein weites weissliches Meer blicken, über Uferfelsen hin, auf denen die Sonne liegt, während grosses und kleines Gethier in ihrem Lichte spielt, sicher und ruhig wie diess Licht und jenes Auge selber. Solch ein Glück hat nur ein fortwährend Leidender erfinden können, das Glück eines Auges, vor dem das Meer des Daseins stille geworden ist und das nun an seiner Oberfläche und an dieser bunten, zarten, schaudernden Meereshaut sich nicht mehr satt sehen kann; es gab nie zuvor eine solche Bescheidenheit der Wollust.
>
> (What I see is Epicurus's eye directed towards a wide whitish sea, over rocks by the shore on which the sun lies, while small and bigger creatures

are mirrored in its light, certain and calm as this light and this eye itself. Only a man of continuous suffering could have invented such bliss, the bliss of an eye in whose presence the sea of existence calms down and which now can no longer get enough of focusing on that surface, on that colourful, tender and shuddering skin of the sea; never before was there any such modesty in lust.)[10]

This Epicurean bliss is distinctly Genoese – and certainly suggestive of Nietzsche's *Sonnenwinkel* (solar corner) and open sea as the antithesis of *Winkelglück* and oceanity. The kind of *gaya scienza* that Nietzsche pursues from here on in is an admixture of Greek serenity combined with various psycho-poetic Provençalisms. In order to enable oneself to love one's fate and thus free oneself, one needs to revert to an Epicurean attitude and Genoese defiance towards life, and towards perceptive and creative life in particular, while retaining one's openness to experience, even vulnerability, for the sake of life, art, and knowledge.

Supplementing the ideas of Epicurus, Goethe's thoughts on developing an eye for the world and simultaneously for oneself ("ich mache diese Reise, um mich an den Gegenständen kennenzulernen") already in 1882 pave the philosopher's tortured mind's way into a pre-Zarathustrian zone of self-liberation – Nietzsche reread Goethe's *Italienische Reise* while in Genoa, training his post-Goethean spirit of observation on this Ligurian location as a place where Goethe did not tread (reminiscent of Goethe's reading Homer in Italy, which helped him, at the time, to repopulate place and text). Goethe read Homer (almost) on location, whereupon he was inspired by the place and his readings of it to write a new literary life into the locale at hand. An initial reading scene is thus turned into a landscape stage, which allows the poet subsequently to change the genre from read epic to written drama, and to create, in a Mediterranean location, an intensified form of his own verbal art, thus giving in

> dem nach und nach auflebenden Drange [...]: die gegenwärtige herrliche Umgebung, das Meer, die Inseln, die Häfen, durch poetisch würdige Gestalten zu beleben und [mir] auf und aus diesem Lokal eine Komposition zu bilden, [...] wie ich sie noch nicht hervorgebracht. Die Klarheit des Himmels, der Hauch des Meeres, die Düfte, wodurch die Gebirge mit Himmel und Meer gleichsam in ein Element aufgelöst werden, alles dies gab Nahrung meinen Vorsätzen; und indem ich in jenem schönen öffentlichen Garten zwischen blühenden Hecken von Oleander, durch Lauben von

fruchttragenden Orangen- und Zitronenbäumen wandelte [...] fühlte ich den fremden Einfluß auf das allerangenehmste. Ich hatte mir, überzeugt, daß es für mich keinen bessern Kommentar zur "Odyssee" geben könne als eben gerade diese lebendige Umgebung, ein Exemplar verschafft und las es nach meiner Art mit unglaublichem Anteil. Doch wurde ich gar bald zu eigner Produktion angeregt, die [...] mich endlich ganz beschäftigte. Ich ergriff nämlich den Gedanken, den Gegenstand der Nausikaa als Tragödie zu behandeln.

(to the gradually growing impulse to liven up the present wonderful surroundings, the sea, the islands, the ports, by poetically dignified figures, and to form for myself a composition on this place and out of this place, as I have not produced it yet. The clarity of the sky, the breeze of the sea, the scents, through which the mountains together with the sky and the sea are dissolved into one element, all this nourished my ideas; and while strolling through that beautiful public garden between blooming hedges of oleander, through arbors of fruit-bearing lemon and orange trees, I felt the foreign influence in the pleasantest of ways.

Convinced that for me there could not be a better commentary to the Odyssey than precisely these lively surroundings, I had bought myself a copy, which I read in my manner and with an incredible interest. And yet I was quickly inspired to produce my own work, which finally took up my entire time and attention. I had the thought of working the theme of Nausikaa into a tragedy.)[11]

Goethe attests to the enormous influence of the Mediterranean landscape on his creativity as a writer, together with a profound appreciation for the poetic tradition (Homer) that grew out of its soil. Goethe's account was surely attractive to Nietzsche, who, roughly a century after Goethe, found himself inspired and shaped by places such as these, as well as by the writing that takes place, as it were, on their very grounds.

While Nietzsche hardly follows Goethe's Italian itinerary, he follows in his precursor's footsteps in other ways, in that through Goethe's insight he, too, wants to find his way out of abstractions and back to the things themselves as much as they can be grasped with one's senses. In *Die fröhliche Wissenschaft*, Nietzsche speaks of learning to love what is foreign in this context: "das Fremde lieben lernen als ein Wohlgefallen an allen nächsten Dingen," a capacity that enables the writer to continue as a free agent or gay scientist in *Zarathustra*. It is in Genoa, Liguria, that Nietzsche finds self-sufficiency, self-liberation, self-love, and the courage to glorify himself (as he claims the Genoese do in their "unersättliche Selbstsucht" [insatiable egotism or, literally, addiction to oneself] accompanied by the kind of strong will that Nietzsche also admired in Goethe).

Nietzsche celebrates the southern life that he advocates in *Die fröhliche Wissenschaft* in a variety of other writings as well, particularly in his poetry. Once he received the long-desired typewriter in 1882 (soon after his New Year's resolution), Nietzsche embarked on a geopoetic tour. Eight of his poems of this time were published under the title *Idyllen aus Messina* that same year, and six of these eight poems he ended up rewriting under the title *Lieder des Prinzen Vogelfrei*; these were subsequently added to the second edition of *Die fröhliche Wissenschaft*. The German adjective *vogelfrei*, to which Nietzsche grants eponymic status, is tricky, since while it denotes the freedom of a bird to fly about the skies, it somewhat unexpectedly connotes the other side of the coin of such freedom: "outlawed," or deprived of all civil rights and in danger of being shot – the risk, in other words, that accompanies "Gesang, Scherz, und Liederspiel" (song, joke, and songplaying), the celebrated goals of a free creative life. Such a freedom is demanding; it comes at a cost, and is chosen "in spite of," as Nietzsche says. Prinz Vogelfrei has clearly flown the coop (one may even want to relate his initials, P.V. to those of another singer of Provence: Peire Vidal). In spite of Nietzsche's highly enthusiastic literary celebrations of liberation by way of the south, his sense of freedom and his understanding of beauty are, indeed, those of difficult beauty and of freedom based on sacrificing a home for the sake of nomadic, poetic wandering, for a cultivation of strength and stamina, life and joy, courage and energy – *trozdem* (in spite of).

> Das weisse Meer liegt eingeschlafen,
> Und purpurn steht ein Segel drauf.
> Fels, Feigenbäume, Thurm und Hafen,
> Idylle rings, Geblök von Schafen, –
> Unschuld des Südens, nimm mich auf!

> Nur Schritt für Schritt – das ist kein Leben,
> Stets Bein vor Bein macht deutsch und schwer.
> Ich hiess den Wind mich aufwärts heben,
> Ich lernte mit den Vögeln schweben, –
> Nach Süden flog ich über's Meer.

> (The white sea stretches, fast asleep,
> A crimson sail, bucolic scents,

A rock, fig trees, the harbor's sweep,
Idyls around me, bleating sheep:
Accept me, southern innocence!

Step upon step – this heavy stride
Is German, not life – a disease;
To lift me up, I asked the breeze,
And with the birds I learned to glide;
Southward I flew, across the seas.)[12]

With his songs of *Prinz Vogelfrei* and *Im Süden,* Nietzsche introduces himself as a modern troubadour, singing autobiographically of his own
experience and his own passion, whether joyous or risky, the neologistic
"Freudenschaft" or "Leidenschaft" (passion).

While the images of the south as a perfect host for the creative writer
and exilic wanderer appear almost in anticipation of the Imagist aesthetics that Ezra Pound and T.E. Hulme propagated about three decades
later (where the moon is glued to the sky as Nietzsche's crimson sail is
placed onto the surface of the sea), these lines also repeat the colour of
the (Ligurian?) sea as white, as previously when Nietzsche referred to
Epicurus. The Turkish language, incidentally, calls the Mediterranean
Sea *Akdeniz,* which literally means White Sea, in contrast to *Karadeniz* or
Black Sea. Epicurus, who highly recommended freedom from fear and
pain, came from the island of Samos in the Aegean, not far off the Turkish coast; he was a self-taught thinker whose school was called "the garden." Nietzsche was as susceptible to Epicurus's thoughts on happiness,
as he was to Provençal gaiety and Genoese will.

Zarathustra saw many countries and people, as Nietzsche repeatedly points out. His wandering and searching include a sojourn on the
"blessed isles," to which the second book of *Zarathustra* devotes a chapter: "Auf den glückseligen Inseln," where Zarathustra's teachings are
likened to ripe figs ("reife Feigen"), for which the wandering teacher
himself does not seem quite ready yet. There is, however, a later chapter in the same book, "Von großen Ereignissen" (On Great Events), of
which Zarathustra himself is one. In this chapter, Nietzsche describes a
curious insular scene:

Es gibt eine Insel im Meer – unweit den glückseligen Inseln Zarathustras –
auf welcher beständig ein Feuerberg raucht; von der sagt das Volk [...], daß
sie wie ein Felsblock vor das Tor der Unterwelt gestellt sei. [...] Um jene Zeit

nun, als Zarathustra auf den glückseligen Inseln weilte, geschah es, daß ein Schiff an der Insel Anker warf, auf welcher der rauchende Berg steht. [...] Gegen die Stunde des Mittags aber [...] sahen sie [captain and crew] plötzlich durch die Luft einen Mann auf sich zukommen, und eine Stimme sagte deutlich: "Es ist Zeit! Es ist die höchste Zeit!" Wie die Gestalt ihnen aber am nächsten war – sie flog aber schnell gleich einem Schatten vorbei, in der Richtung, wo der Feuerberg lag – da erkannten sie mit größter Bestürzung, daß es Zarathustra sei. [... Es] lief das Gerücht umher, daß Zarathustra verschwunden sei, und als man seine Freunde fragte, erzählten sie, er sei bei Nacht zu Schiff gegangen, ohne zu sagen, wohin er reisen wollte.

(There is an island in the sea – not far from Zarathustra's blessed isles – on which a fiery mountain smokes continually; people say that it was placed like a huge boulder before the gate to the underworld. It was around the time that Zarathustra sojourned on the blessed isles that a ship dropped anchor at the island on which the smoking mountain stands. Toward the hour of noon, however, as the captain and his people were together again, they suddenly saw a man approaching through the air, and a voice said: *It is time! It is high time!* As the figure came closest to them – and it flew past quickly like a shadow in the direction of the fiery mountain – they recognized with the greatest dismay that it was Zarathustra; the rumour was circulating that Zarathustra had disappeared; and his friends, indeed, related how he had departed by ship at night, without saying where he would be travelling.)[13]

What follows this curious admixture of realistic and mythic elements – island, sea, ship, mountain, volcano, crew, versus blessed isles, underworld, shadow, hell, and an old helmsman reminiscent of Charon – is an era of profound doubt and yearning, a time in which it is assumed that the devil had come to summon Zarathustra – or vice versa. After a few days, however, Zarathustra reappears to relate the story of the fire hound as the "earth's ventriloquist" ("Bauchredner"), another volcanic trope (probably for Etna or Vesuvius), and to whom he speaks thus: "Und glaube mir nur, Freund Höllenlärm! Die größten Ereignisse – das sind nicht unsre lautesten, sondern unsre stillsten Stunden." (And just believe me, friend Infernal Racket! The greatest events are not our loudest, but our stillest hours.) While Zarathustra tries his best to mount a parabolic comparison between state, church, and fire hound, his disciples, who are eager to tell their own story about the ship's crew dropping anchor, shooting rabbits, and witnessing a man fly by, turn out to be a less than attentive audience for their teacher.

Zarathustra leaves his home when he is thirty and goes into the mountains, where he remains for ten years. He decides to descend to the townspeople, but then leaves his friends and returns again to the mountains. This is where *Zarathustra* begins. After ten more years of solitude, he once again returns to the world of people, and in the second part of part two he again finds himself on the blessed isles and resumes his teaching. Part two, written in the Swiss Alps and fondly remembering the Ligurian coast, concludes with Zarathustra's retreat into yet another solitude and Nietzsche's move to the French Côte, to Nice, where the better part of *Zarathustra* III would be composed.

In parts one and two, Zarathustra is a teacher, while in parts three and four he is alone. This solitude begins with "Der Wanderer" and is governed by crisis, for while Zarathustra is in the process of becoming a teacher of the eternal return, he himself still has to learn how to tolerate the pain of his own teaching (in an almost Eliotic scene of creative suffering). It is crucial to note that Zarathustra leaves the blessed isles at midnight, hiking over a ridge in order to arrive on the other shore by early morning, where he intends to board a ship. Thus begins part three. It is, however, midday when the flying wanderer's voice announces that it is high time, or high noon, "großer Mittag" (the exact wording of the ending of part four), the time of standstill, a great event, a silent hour, a still life, a vicarious image, an epiphany.

Nietzsche's islands are anything but blank slates or sites of fearful isolation. At least three actual islands are of great significance for the Nietzsche of *Zarathustra* (I mention these despite knowing that the autobiographical dimension of Nietzsche's work, in particular of *Ecce Homo*, has been a locus of great controversy): San Michele, Capri, and Isoletta. The Venetian San Michele is a cemetery, and it has been argued that Zarathustra's "Grablied" in which the island of graves is mentioned, is a reference to this island in the Adriatic lagoon (Nietzsche rented a room facing San Michele, the island of the dead, in 1880). As for Capri: Nietzsche spent the winter of 1876–7 in Sorrento, viewed mount Vesuvius, and visited Capri, where he went on spectacular hikes, winding along the steep cliffs of the island's north side, and descended to the blue grotto, which subsequently appeared in his post-Sorrento notes, in which he stated dramatically how Sorrento allowed him to shake off a decade of moss.

His rejuvenating visit to Capri (as well as the beginning of his illness, which soon followed) coincided with what was going to be the great turning point in his life and thought: he resigned his professorship in 1879. He spent the subsequent winter in Naumburg, but in the following two winters he preferred the gentler climes of Liguria: specifically, Genoa. It was during his sojourn in the city of Columbus that he composed *Die fröhliche Wissenschaft* (1881–2). Enjoying Genoa's cloudless skies (which somewhat anticipate the halcyon skies of Nice), Nietzsche claimed that cloudless skies make for cloudless thoughts as well. Nietzsche adored Genoa for its sunshine and sky, and also for its palaces, parks, and cemeteries. The city takes on the symbolic status of longing for health and adventure, solitude and freedom – all themes that permeate *Die fröhliche Wissenschaft.*

Nietzsche became an exilic wanderer, roamed alone, and embarked on an era of intense expression that lasted for about a decade: "vertrieben bin ich aus Vater- und Mutterländern. So liebe ich allein noch mein Kinder Land, das unentdeckte, im fernsten Meere: nach ihm heiße ich meine Segel suchen und suchen"[14] (exiled am I from father- and motherlands: Thus I love only my children's land, the undiscovered land in the furthest sea: for it I command my sails to seek and seek.) This shows the first outline of Nietzsche's mask as a Ligurian writer: that of seafarer Columbus leaving Genoa. Isoletta, finally, is the little island in Lake Sils in the Swiss Engadine where Nietzsche spent many post-Capri summers, and it has been argued that this miniature island was a major inspiration for Zarathustra's thoughts on smallness.

Besides references to actual islands such as these, Nietzsche also frequently deployed the island as a time-honoured rhetorical device or trope, as in his "verborgene Eilande des Lebens"[15] (hidden islands of life). What I consider most compelling, however, is the fact that besides real islands such as Capri, and rhetorical islands such as the islands of life, there is a third insular species in *Zarathustra*: these are islands as *topoi* or literary commonplaces, such as "die glückseligen Inseln" (blessed isles). "On the Blessed Isles" presents a vicarious Mediterranean image of superabundance: ripe figs fall from the trees, Zarathustra's teachings are said to resemble these figs, and Zarathustra asks his disciples to drink up their juice. Meanwhile, it is afternoon, and one has moved from speaking of god to speaking of overman.

On these isles, Zarathustra also encounters dancing girls, cripples, beggars, and a soothsayer. These isles are Nietzsche's variation on the canonical theme of the Elysian Fields as a final resting place of heroic souls, described in Homer as located at the end of the earth, encircled by Oceanus ("selig" in German is a euphemism for "dead"; it is also the anaphora in the benedictions in the Sermon on the Mount). Is Zarathustra, then, meeting his friends and disciples on an island of the blessed dead? It is essential to note that Elysium was a region in the Greek underworld, and that the *makaron nesoi*, the fortunate isles or isles of the blessed, were the site where the gods received favoured mortals into a blissful paradise.[16]

In the course of history, then, a Schliemannesque wave began breaking upon the metaphorical shore, with the Maltese island of Gozo proposed as Calypso's island, and the Canaries, Madeira, and Capo Verde cited as possible actual candidates for the ancient mythical site of Elysium. In any case, Nietzsche's blessed isles as well as the volcanic isle located in their vicinity are neither actual (topical) nor rhetorical (tropic). As literary commonplaces they are located between actual geography on the one hand, and rhetorical tropology on the other.

This third poetic dimension, which transcends the dichotomy of actual/topical and rhetorical/tropic, falls nicely into place if one reconsiders Nietzsche's early thoughts on metaphor (mainly in "Über Wahrheit und Lüge im außermoralischen Sinne" / "On Truth and Lie in an Extra-Moral Sense"). Nietzsche's commentaries on the rhetorical/tropic dimension of language remain an area of ambiguity that is central to his work and yet quite unresolved. It is the distinction between the literal and the figurative that Nietzsche does not consider to be clear cut: "Was ist ein Wort? Die Abbildung eines Nervenreizes in Lauten. [...] Wir glauben, etwas von den Dingen selbst zu wissen, wenn wir von Bäumen, Farben, Schnee und Blumen reden, und besitzen doch nichts als Metaphern der Dinge" (What is a word? The illustration of a nerve stimulus in sounds. We think we know something of the things themselves, whenever we speak about trees, colours, snow and flowers, but we really possess nothing but the metaphors of things).[17]

This is the locus where Nietzsche's theory of language intersects with the literary qualities of his writing. His understanding of metaphor is a dominant concept in his critique of the relation of language to reality, while his poetic writing, however innovative and explosive, is nevertheless grounded in his parodic and pastiche-like deployment of primarily Homeric and biblical themes and patterns. Following long poetic and rhetorical traditions, Nietzsche writes antithetically: life-death, body-soul, fire-ice, love-hate, peak-abyss, light-dark, good-evil, to name just a few. What is special in his use of these binaries is that they are proto-Freudian on the one hand (so that they eventually collapse into what Freud calls the primeval word) and explosive on the other (so that they engender a third energetic dimension). In proto-Freudian terms, *On Truth and Lie* wonders about our drive towards truth ("Trieb zur Wahrheit"),[18] presents our eccentric location in the cosmos, and closely links this given eccentricity of ours to our equally given exile in language. Nietzsche examines the roles that illusions and dream images have assumed in language and culture (as a consequence of our recognition that senses cannot grant us direct access to the truth). Instead of attacking these illusions, Nietzsche only takes issue with one: the illusion of truth, suggesting that the only truth there is, is that there is no one Truth. He celebrates a plurality of perspectives (his isles and dawns are in the plural) and reminds us that the presence of languages, in the plural, provides sufficient evidence that the relationship of word and thing is "arbitrary" ("willkürliche Übertragungen"[19] practically anticipates Ferdinand de Saussure). Nietzsche welcomes such arbitrariness as he celebrates the metaphoricity of language. Such metaphoricity is most condensed in *Zarathustra*, whose protagonist not only faces metaphors as words, but also reads the metaphoricity inherent in the landscape surrounding him. It is to this Ligurian-Provençal terrain that Nietzsche has lent geopoetic agency.

One of the first things to strike the reader of *Zarathustra* is the sheer abundance of rhetorical devices, mainly the *figura etymologica*, but also neologistic compounds and skewed idioms. It was Jorge L. Borges, an avid and dedicated reader of Nietzsche, and of *Zarathustra* in particular, who pointed out that etymology is actually helpful beyond its philological force, teaching us that "pontiffs are not builders of bridges and that rubrics are not red." Zarathustra's metaphoricity is less rhetorical than poetic, even though his speeches are generically necessarily rhetorical – a rhetoricity that is enhanced by his legendary ironies punned out of semantic opposites: for instance "Freudenschaft" translated as "passion of pleasure" or "Trauerernst" translated as "tragic reality" (or mournful seriousness), which does not completely capture the span of intended meanings.

For a genuine poet, however, writes Nietzsche in *The Birth of Tragedy*, metaphor is not a rhetorical figure but a vicarious image that he actually beholds in place of a concept. Another way of saying this is that a genuine philosopher is first a genuine poet. The island that either belongs to the blessed archipelago or, like the island of the fire hound, is located close enough to that state of blessedness, is one of the strongest images of this vicarious kind, and by that token transcends rhetorical figuration and stands in for something more profound: a philosophical concept. Poetry, says Nietzsche, precedes thought; and it is the vicarious image of the island that embodies the place of the philosophical concept of the eternal return, so that it can be grasped geopoetically.

"Denn ich liebe dich, o Ewigkeit" (For I love you, oh Eternity!)[21] This declaration of love is repeated, albeit in the mode of hypothesis, many times towards the end of part three, while part four starts with Zarathustra as an old man looking out onto the ocean: "how many seas surrounding me, what dawning human fates. Must I seek the last happiness far away on blessed isles between forgotten seas?" The soothsayer answers that there are no blessed isles anymore, to which Zarathustra exlaims: "No, no, no, three times no! There are still blessed isles, be silent about that, you sighing sadsack!" By twisting and turning his own words, by lending the weight of the eternal return some rhetorical lightness, by adding song, play, and dance, Nietzsche will then be free to call the vicious circle divine: *circulus vitiosus deus* (cf *Beyond Good and Evil*), or: *Teufelskreis*.

"Io, le isole non ho mai capite," says Patrizia, a young and prosperous Roman woman in Michelangelo Antonioni's *L'avventura*, "tutto il mare intorno, poverine" (I have never quite understood islands, the entire sea surrounding them, poor things). She goes on to say that there is no way for her to consider these isolated land masses bracketed by water as *terra*, "land" or "earth" (she and her friends are on a tourist boat in the Mediterranean at the time). While *L'avventura* is a mystery story, its focus is the mysteriously haunting, not to say viciously repetitive, quality of the island as landscape image rather than, as the genre would lead us to believe, a finely tuned detective plot. This slow-paced story is set in a visually composed volcanic archipelago in the Tyrrhenian Sea north of Sicily known as the Aeolian Islands, named for Aeolus, the Greek keeper of the winds, whose benevolence has been an essential element on a variety of mythical occasions. One of these islands had already been chosen ten years earlier as a setting for Roberto Rossellini's *Stromboli: Terra di Dio* (Land of God).

What, one might wonder, has postwar cinema got to do with a work of late-nineteenth-century philosophy? The two works share a curiously similar poetic sense of the island as haunting and vicarious image, as simultaneously geographical site and site of thought, as landscape, seascape, and mindscape, as a site of loneliness and discovery, arrival and departure, adventure and astonishment. How can our grasp of the island transcend that of Antonioni's Patrizia? I read Nietzsche's insular shores in their third dimension between actual/topical islands as geographic accidents and rhetorical/tropic islands as sites of language. Nietzsche's island, then, is a critical component of his doctrine of the "eternal return" as it interprets itself through the island as compact and circular space. Moreover, I suggest a placement of Nietzsche's idea of the insular as a condensation on the one hand, and as a repetition on the other, of those sites, which Nietzsche transformed into his two major expressive tropes: the Alps and the Mediterranean as Europe's most prominent cultural landscapes converging in Liguria.

The influence of Nietzsche's places and displacements on his work cannot be reduced to these sites as pools of metaphor, since "high above the Mediterranean coast or on the shore of Lake Silvaplana," write Krell and Bates, "it is hard to distinguish the vehicle from the tenor of metaphor. In Nietzsche's texts it is impossible."[22] My focus would be less on the tenor's general drift than the vehicle's visual embodiment of that drift. Through *Zarathustra*, conceived in Sils-Maria and Rapallo, and, under an evident Ligurain influence, written between 1883 and 1885 in the Alps and on the Riviera respectively, Nietzsche transformed the German language into his uniquely innovative form of radically felicitous poetic expression. Freud and Benn are under the spell of this Ligurian-Nietzschean expression (Nietzsche, Freud confesses, found words for what remained silent in Freud, while Benn admits that Nietzsche originated all the words, and what Benn and Expressionism fabricated was nothing but exegesis). What do Nietzsche's workplaces have in common with Zarathustra's places of habitation and wandering, which range from the solitary cave as a totally enclosed space, in which he dwells for ten years before greeting the sun, to the blessed isles as totally exposed space, from whose ports he wishes to embark?

Nietzsche calls the "eternal return" the "vision of the loneliest," and his language is imitative of such solitude: it sustains itself on itself, rather than providing a redemptive solution of its tropes into a more communicative literality. Nietzsche's trope of the insular seems to turn around itself exactly as the insular itself does. While the blessed isles do not stand for Zarathustra's lonely wanderings, they place them in a tropological setting of isolation (islands are time-honoured sites for prisons and penal colonies, hospitals, covents, monasteries, and other sorts of institutions). The peaks and shores, caves and islands in *Zarathustra* manifest themselves as condensed spaces where mountain and sea, peak and abyss are hauntingly displaced and at the same time joined together. This paradoxical dimension spoke very much to Freud's concept of dream languages, as well as to Benn's oneirically based Ligurian poetics.

While islands have been emblematic for the adventure genre,

Stone with Serpent, in Weimar (Photograph by the author)

Roughly a century before Nietzsche's composition of *Thus Spoke Zarathustra*, the original Schlangenstein / Stone with Serpent was erected in Weimar's Ilm Park upon Goethe's order. Nietzsche welcomed such forms of encounter between art and nature just as enthusiastically as Goethe had, and saw them prefigured in the paintings of Claude Lorrain. The stone's shape is reminiscent of an ancient altar, and its inscription is dedicated "to the spirit of this place": *genio huius loci*. Intended as the ancient symbol of life and health rather than the Christian symbol of sin and temptation, this serpent has been interpreted as an embodiment of the spirit of place itself, in line with the Persian Zoroaster, who not only inspired Nietzsche's *Zarathustra* but also celebrated the spirit of place for the sake of love of life, landscape, and poetry. Nietzsche, the legendary Alpine-Mediterranean walker, was rendered immobile by a partial paralysis during his final years in Weimar, and never saw this stone. This Stone with Serpent attests to the ironic absence of this spirited place in Nietzsche's life, for Zarathustra's serpent was a good serpent, a vital companion, a Ligurian genius.

Claude Lorrain, *Le Port de Gênes, vu de la mer / The Port of Genoa, Sea View* (oil on canvas). Louvre, Paris, France/ Giraudon/ The Bridgeman Art Library. Used with permission.

French Baroque painter Claude Lorrain (1600–82) sojourned in Rome and Genoa and painted *Le Port de Gênes, vu de la mer / The Port of Genoa, Sea View* in 1627–9. The highly structured land- and seascapes that Claude is known for were painted at a time when landscape was not yet deemed an appropriate painterly genre. Nietzsche, whose sensibilities were more attuned to music than to the visual arts, did, however, experience intense moments of joy in an enthusiastic confrontation with Claude, whose art was as untimely as Nietzsche's meditations in his time. *The Port of Genoa* poetically captures the atmosphere of fishermen at daybreak (we are looking toward the eastern sunrise), as well as the enchanted aspects of the locale. It also validates Nietzsche's assessment of Claude as the painter of the "halcyon" – of supreme calm, quality of light, and beautiful completion, as well as one who is committed to surface: here evident in the detailed wavelets catching the light. Genoa was only one among a number of Ligurian locales Nietzsche stayed in during the 1880s. He was attracted to its seafaring tradition and spoke highly of the city of Columbus's pride and power in which he claims not to have lived in vain: "Ich habe nicht umsonst jahrelang in der Stadt des Columbus gelebt."

Nietzsche's isles are less places of departure and arrival in the usual sense than they are sites of the eternal return as the philosopher's fate, whose *amor fati*, his central mental adventure, is the love of that fate combined with a persistence that obsessively wills the past repetitively forward, for: "nicht zurück kann der Wille wollen" (will cannot will backwards). This eternal return seems to bend the timeline into the very circle that Nietzsche terms vicious, that is to say, characterized by endless repetition. This circle is vicious because its time frame is cyclical, eternal. And eternity, as Woody Allen has it, "is a long time, especially toward the end"; or, to return to Nietzsche, "Alle Wahrheit ist krumm, die Zeit selber ist ein Kreis" (all truth is crooked, time itself is a circle), as the dwarf murmurs to Zarathustra shortly before the latter embarks on his voyage.

Even though Nietzsche's isles at first glance are the ascetic philosopher's nostalgia and utopia, even though they seem canonically blessed rather than inventively haunted, their isolated existence has the potential of the haunted, the vicious, and the circular. Nietzsche called *Zarathustra* his most poetic creation (while *Dawn* and *The Gay Science* triumph in the art of aphorism) and anticipated that its publication would cause him to be regarded as a madman – especially in Germany. Keeping in mind islands as privileged geographical locations for institutions as well as Nietzsche's eventual fall into isolating madness, we witness Antonioni's Patrizia's sympathetic identification with the islands themselves as lonely entities bracketed by a mass of water as having come full circle.

Giovanni Assereto characterizes Liguria as an agglomeration of islands, and intimately intertwines this observation with the verticality of the Ligurian landscape. Matvejević's words on Mediterranean islands and the insular mode of existence as simultaneous exposure and enclosure (and thus isolation par excellence) also confirm Liguria precisely as Nietzsche and others after him saw and envisioned it: as small and remote, liminal and isolated, steep and challenging, self-reflexive and beautiful – in short, as an ideal refuge for self-confrontation, self-therapy, and poetic self-liberation. It is in a related sense that Karl Schlechta puts great emphasis on Nietzsche's "grosser Mittag" (great noon, Mediterranean high noon, or the French *Midi* and Italian *Mezzogiorno*) as the chronotopic time-space that posits "south" and "noon" as synonymous. "Dies ist mein Morgen, mein Tag hebt an: herauf nun, herauf, du grosser Mittag!" (This is my morning, my day is breaking: rise now, rise, thou great noon!). Thus ends *Zarathustra*, while a protagonist as energetic as the morning sun itself yet again leaves his mountain cave.[24]

Harold Bloom has suggested that true (auto)biography comes about, not when (one's) life enters (one's) writing, but rather when (one's) writing becomes (one's) life. The genre of Nietzsche's purported auto-biography (and autobibliography), *Ecce Homo*, has been one question in an extensive literary debate, in light of which one is tempted to classify *Zarathustra* rather than *Ecce Homo* as truly autobiographical (in Bloom's sense as well as that of Charles Wright, who calls "all forms of landscape autobiographical").

With *Zarathustra* in particular, Nietzsche lived his philosophy, hiked, in a geopoetic-nomadic sense, his words and sentences – "Sprüche sollen Gipfel sein"[25] (aphorisms shall be peaks) – as if they were an actual geo-graphic territory. Liguria in particular was the actual earth underneath Nietzsche's wandering feet, to which the writer should, as he repeatedly stresses in *Zarathustra*, book I (written Rapallo), pay heed, while tolerat-ing hard work and contradiction without falling prey to the allure of redemption.

In 1882, six years after his first contact with Liguria, and on location once again, Nietzsche not only compares philosophy with seafaring, but also types into existence, on his Malling Hansen typewriter, what would likely be a divinatory Freudian slip *avant la lettre*: "Leg ich mich aus so leg ich mich hinein so moeg ein Freud mein Interprete sein"[26] (if I interpret myself, I immerse myself; may a Freud be my interpreter). The question whether this "Freud" turned out to be the kind of friend ("Freund") whom Nietzsche had in mind as a reader of his autobiographical geo-poetic oeuvre, is as wide open as the seafaring philosopher's Epicurean seas of existence.

Guilt Trips on Royal Roads:
Freud's Ligurian Affinities

... one could get away with more on the summer Riviera.

F. Scott Fitzgerald

... vom Land kann man nicht reden, ohne ein Dichter zu sein oder andere zu zitieren.

(... one cannot speak of this land without being a poet or quoting poets.)

Sigmund Freud

... Vergessenheit ist keine blosse vis inertiae, sie ist ein aktives, positives Hemmungsvermögen.

(... forgetfulness is no mere vis inertiae, it is an active, positive power of inhibition.)

Friedrich Nietzsche

"C'était septembre, et c'était la Provence"; thus opens Alphonse Daudet's account of Tartarin's last adventures, entitled *Port-Tarascon*.[27] Well, it was September and it was Liguria when Sigmund Freud embarked on a one-night furtive whistle-stop at the Grand Hôtel Savoia in Rapallo, accompanied by his sister-in-law, Minna Bernays, with whom he enjoyed a brief but intense "moment" at the Châlet Nina, the portion of Rapallo's lido that belonged to the Savoia at the time. Nietzsche could not have lodged at the Savoia – for one thing, it only opened in 1899; but more importantly, he was never in a position to afford the kind of luxury enjoyed by the more privileged class of tourist. Nietzsche had come to Rapallo to walk and work – and he had come in winter. Whereas very

On Rapallo's shore (Photograph by the author)

"Also vom Meer ... der Strand ist feiner Schlamm ... ein Stück weiter sind herrliche Klippen ... Bassins ... schräg geneigte Teppichfelsen, auf denen man wie ein Böcklinsches Untier sich wälzt" (Now for the sea ... the beach is fine mud ... a little further on there are wonderful cliffs ... pools ... sloping carpets of rocks, in which one rolls like a Böcklinesque monster) – thus wrote an exuberant Freud in his 1905 letter from Rapallo to Vienna, which in turn he called a place of "nördliche Verbannung" (northern banishment).

much like Freud, albeit far more extensively, various Russian artists, most notably perhaps Wassily Kandinsky and Gabriele Münter, sojourned in Rapallo in 1905, a fit location to accommodate their love as well as their fine artistic output at the time. It was also the place, incidentally, where seventeen years later the Treaty of Rapallo, part of the Genoa Conference, was signed (1922).[28]

For Freud, from childhood on, Italy was a scene of glory and conquest on the one hand and of art and splendour, science and learning on the other. His repeated identification with Carthaginian general Hannibal's storied crossing of the Alps and fifteen-year sojourn in Italy, as well as his repeated reading of Johann Wolfgang von Goethe's *Italienische Reise* and *Römische Elegien* (*Italian Journey* and *Roman Elegies*) are the principal influences in this early formative period. Freud's first journey to what was not yet a part of Italy at the time, but rather belonged to the Austro-Hungarian Empire, was his prolonged sojourn in Friulian Trieste in 1876 (where Hellenist Johann Joachim Winckelmann was murdered). Freud was there on a research grant for several months, dissecting eels at the zoological institute. Subsequently, his friendship and intense correspondence with Wilhelm Fließ (from 1887 to 1902), which comprises numerous letters in which Freud confided his doubts, fears, and guilt-ridden dreams (most famously perhaps the dream of being late to the funeral), were central to the transformation of Freud's image of Italy, and roughly coincided with his growing commitment to self-analysis from 1895 onward; the friendship was also concurrent with his work on *Die Traumdeutung*, in which Freud relied on an extensive number of close readings of his own dreams and other forms of self-analysis.

Such a merging of doctor and patient, of analyst and analysand in self-analysis is not only similar to Benn, particularly with his alter ego Rönne, but was to become an ongoing project that led Freud into ever more recondite and self-reflective regions of his own mind's circularity. A remote, (pen)insular mentality, difficult of access – and certainly not readable within a purely linear concept of time – may in itself be suggestive of the seclusion and isolation of Ligurian terrains that Nietzsche during his most prolific years of self-confrontation had searched for and inhabited roughly two decades before Freud. If Nietzsche's ubiquity in Freud is hardly subtle, the proximity of Nietzsche's Liguria in Freud may appear to be; however, I suggest that it was always secretly familiar (immensely uncanny) to the avid Mediterranean traveller and alleged father of psychoanalysis himself.

"Freud took 24 vacations in Italy (seven to Rome alone) and another three to Italian-speaking regions of the Austro-Hungarian Empire," states Laurence Simmons in *Freud's Italian Journey*, a book that demonstrates how profoundly Italy informed Freud's psychoanalytical elaborations; while, according to Cosimo Schinaia, "in nessun altro paese straniero Freud viaggiò quanto in Italia, dove venne per quindici volte" (in no other foreign country did Freud travel as much as he did in Italy, which he visited fifteen times).[29] Whatever the exact total, it is evident that Freud journeyed to Italy frequently (in his late forties and fifties almost yearly), and certainly more often than to any other place – and he travelled widely: to Greece, Switzerland, Holland, England, and America. Freud tended to tour in the summer, primarily with relatives: at first with his younger brother, Alexander; later with his sister-in-law, Minna Bernays; and eventually with his daughter, Anna.

Freud steered clear of Provence, and compared with his extensive Italian travels, his trips to Liguria were hardly numerous. However, en route from Milan in the summer of 1900, Freud briefly stopped over in Genoa (soon after his completion of *Traumdeutung* in 1899). He seems to have been on his own on this first Ligurian incident, after having travelled in the South Tyrol and on Lakes Garda and Maggiore with Minna. One wonders why Freud did not write home from Genoa on this first occasion, and we can only speculate whether he visited Nietzsche's steep, modest, and remote garret there, in Salita delle Battistine 8.

Before travelling to Milan and Genoa, Freud wrote in a letter to his wife, Martha, about the all-too-northern character ("nordischer Charakter") of the Alpine Lavarone, which he eventually came to appreciate for its purity of air and peaceful mountain greenery; the same letter ends with a far more enthusiastic anticipation of the south: "unser Herz [zeigt …] nach dem Süden […] nach Feigen, Kastanien, Lorbeer, Zypressen, Häuser[n] mit Balkonen, Antiquaren udgl" (our heart points to the south, toward figs, chestnuts, laurel, cypresses, houses with balconies, antiquities and things of that order).[30] Five years later, in September 1905, Freud embarked on his second Ligurian visit, to Genoa and Rapallo, this time in the company of Minna. Apart from these two visits, no further travels to Liguria by Freud have been recorded.

At the turn of the century Freud had not only completed his *Die Traumdeutung*, but had also been to Italy six times (visiting Lake Garda, Venice, Bologna, Florence, Pisa, Orvieto, Milan, and Genoa, among others). However, he had yet to tackle Rome. Freud first set foot in Rome (with his brother Alexander) in September 1901, and he relates this step not only as a sort of ominous way to inaugurate the new century but also as his successful bid to overcome his anticipatory anxiety about the potentially overpowering impact of the eternal city. Freud's writings up to this first Roman visit were mainly concerned with pathology and psychology, whereas his commitment to art and literature as a basis for psychoanalytic inquiry – and to poets as precursors, even partners in crime, as it were, who had engaged in psychoanalysis long before it became an official study – began around the time of his Roman initiation. Among the groundbreaking texts related to this and subsequent journeys to Rome are the analysis of Wilhelm Jensen's *Gradiva* (during his Rome visit in 1907 Freud saw the original bas-relief in the Vatican after having composed his text, realizing that this artwork was Attic rather than Roman), as well as the essays on Leonardo da Vinci (whom he likens to Goethe) and on Michelangelo's *Moses* (inspired by Freud's Rome trips in 1912 and 1913).

While Rome marks a compelling turning point in Freud's career as a writer, my attention is directed towards Freud not primarily as the legendary and meticulously prepared visitor to Rome but rather as a traveller to less obvious destinations such as Rapallo and the Acropolis (of which Frederic Leighton painted an intriguing version including its "Genoese Tower").[31] I contend that Freud's sojourns in Liguria in 1900 and 1905 differ fundamentally from his other Italian journeys. Via Nietzsche, Liguria's seemingly liminal culture silently becomes a central, psychologically saturated terrain like no other for Freud, and his ascent of the Acropolis in 1904 and his stay on the beach of Rapallo in 1905 are incidents most intimately intertwined with his feelings of guilt in general and his unacknowledged literary debt to Nietzsche in particular. Freud repeatedly makes mention of Nietzsche's expressive force, first, specifically, in 1900 (the year of his first brief sojourn in Genoa) in the context of his self-declared periodic muteness and lack of expressive inspiration.

Granted, Freud's journeys to Genoa and Rapallo provide slender Ligurian substance when compared to Nietzsche's extensive Ligurian wanderings on the one hand and Freud's numerous and extensive travels to places such as Venice, Florence, Rome, and Naples on the other. This is partially because of the fact that Liguria played no role whatsoever in Goethe's Italian travels (and only a minor, if any, role in the Grand Tour's itinerary, mainly because of the difficulty of getting there). Even in the early twentieth century Freud complained about the ugly aspect of travelling in the environs of Genoa, because of the immense number of tunnels to be gone through ("arge Tunnelfahrt"). However unpleasant Freud may have perceived some aspects of Ligurian travel to be, it is very clear that he cherished his and Minna's visit to the Villa Pallavicini at Pegli, their eight-night stay in Genoa's Hotel Continental (on a postcard home he characterizes Genoa as "großartig elegant, fast trotzig": thoroughly elegant, almost defiant)[32] – and above all their brief stopover in Rapallo at least as thoroughly as he repressed Nietzsche's presence

there and Ligurian influence on him (Freud's visit in Rapallo is dou-
bly furtive). Freud was in Liguria at least twice, a fact often forgotten,
but mentioned by Cosimo Schinaia on the occasion of the centenary of
Freud's 1905 visit to Rapallo:

> Tuttavia, nonostante queste difficoltà, la presenza di Genova e della Ligu-
> ria nell'opera di Freud è rilevabile e significativa e se ne vuole dare conto
> anche in vista del centenario della sua seconda visita. Si sa con certezza
> di una sua breve visita a Genova da solo, dopo essere stato a Milano nel
> 1900, e di una più lunga a Genova e Rapallo nel 1905. Oltre a ciò, nella
> *Psicopatologia della vita quotidiana* Freud cita le località di Nervi e Pegli, che
> in Germania allora erano famose come stazioni climatiche, dimostrando di
> conoscerle bene.
>
> (In any case, despite difficulties such as these, the presence of Genoa
> and Liguria in Freud's œuvre is detectable and significant, and it is worth
> reminding ourselves of it also in light of the centenary of his second visit.
> We certainly know of one brief visit to Genoa on his own, after having stayed
> in Milan, in 1900, and then of one longer visit to Genoa and Rapallo in
> 1905. Beyond these two instances, Freud in his *Psychopathology of Everyday
> Life* cites the [Ligurian] locations Nervi and Pegli, which in Germany at
> the time were known as famous health resorts; Freud seems to have known
> these places well.)[33]

We all, as it were, "speak Freud." Jacques Derrida in his suggestive
reading of Freud's analysis of Jensen's *Gradiva* provocatively states that
"certain people can wonder if, decades after [Freud's] death, his sons, so
many brothers, can yet speak in their own name. Or if his daughter ever
came to life [*zoe*], was ever anything other than a phantasm or a specter,
a Gradiva *rediviva*, a Gradiva-Zoe-Bertgang passing through at Berggasse 19."[34] It is in any case beyond doubt that we colloquially and cross-
culturally speak of taboos and inhibitions, libidos and anxieties, hyste-
rias, complexes, and compulsions, as if these lexical items of psychoanalytical dimensions had always belonged to our quotidian vernacular.

In other words, "Freud" has become an internationally present and
transdisciplinarily deployable idiom, a kind of modern *lingua franca* in
which one smoothly converses about living and dying, reading and writing, travelling, dreaming, and remembering. But what was the legacy
that Freud relied on? Whose language did he speak? Whose paths did he
pursue? Can we read Freud as the radical innovator alone, or must we

not also acknowledge Freud as a generous gleaner, anxious denier, and guilty forgetter? At the turn of the twentieth century, when Freud, at the outset of his career, embarked on his first Mediterranean journeys, crossing the Alps, reaching Italy, and sending self-centred letters home was a well-established cultural practice of the European elite.

It is astonishing that while Freud's role in challenging taboos is well known, Freud the silent borrower and zealous pilgrim to the Mediterranean's affectively canonized sites has attracted far less attention. To demonstrate that Freud is one of "the usual suspects" rather than an "innocent abroad," I focus on his affinities with three travel writers – two German, one French – to whom he is obviously indebted: Goethe as Freud's celebrated paternal precursor; Nietzsche as his largely unacknowledged quasi-contemporary; and Romain Rolland as his cherished pen-friend, whose identity Freud repeatedly chooses to withhold. While paying tribute to the Goethe-Nietzsche-Rolland triumvirate's substantial influence on Freud, I concentrate on three of his journeys here, and, respectively, on a trio of Mediterranean places as inscribed in three of Freud's texts that owe their origin to these journeys: first, the connection of his 1902 tour of Pompeii and 1907 visit to the Vatican with *Der Wahn und die Träume in W. Jensens Gradiva* (1907); second, the link between his sojourn in Rapallo on the Ligurian Riviera and his letter to Alexander Freud (1905); and finally, his 1904 travels to Athens as retrospectively documented in "Brief an Romain Rolland: Eine Erinnerungsstörung auf der Akropolis" (1936).

Focusing on the early and the very late Freud implies an emphasis on the formative influences preceding his most prolific years between 1910 and 1935, as well as on a mature retrospective, when his unacknowledged debt to Nietzsche becomes important once again. I am concerned with three less obvious and more distant destinations, which share vertical prospects and a proximity to sea and port: Pompeii is situated on a lava spur and was closer to the Mediterranean Sea in antiquity than it is now; Rapallo, where the Ligurian Apennines meet the Ligurian Sea; and Athens with its citadel – the Acropolis – posing on a high, rocky outcrop, close to the Aegean Sea and to Piraeus. My attention is directed not to Freud the legendary post-Goethean tourist on his seven trips to Rome but rather to how his travels and dreams, perceptions, memories, and interpretations of far-off or seemingly peripheral locales – two Italian, one Greek – transcend the commonplace of classical archaeology as Freud's prime trope for mapping his understanding of major mental processes, enabling, instead, a reading of Freud on his own terms.

Freud writes the letter to his brother while in Rapallo in 1905, about two decades after Nietzsche had left the Riviera, three years after his own visit to Pompeii in 1902, one year after his visit to Athens in 1904, but more than a year before his analysis of Wilhelm Jensen's novella *Gradiva*. The Rapallo letter, as the epistolary genre implies, coincides with Freud's sojourn in Rapallo, while only three years pass between his tour of Pompeii and his analysis of Jensen's Pompeiian fantasy (written in Lavarone). All the more striking, then, is the time span between Freud's untypically spontaneous 1904 journey to see the Acropolis, a trip abruptly decided on during a visit to Trieste, and his account of it in 1936 in his last letter to Romain Rolland. In it, Freud analyses his lifelong urge to travel, his so-called memory disturbance, and his relationship to his father, while lamenting the illness that had put a painful end to his journeying more than a decade before the composition of the Acropolis text. This text is marked by the provocative paradox of a remembered memory disturbance, of a memory of memory failure, of a memorial to the dynamics of forgetting — in the service of memory.

That Freud's travels to Italy and Greece provided him with moments of profound insight and intense pleasure has been extensively discussed. Considerably less attention has been paid to the fact that Freud as a theorist of the superego frequently experienced a remarkable sense of guilt as a tourist to the Mediterranean. In this vein, he himself in his letter from Rapallo alludes to a passage in Goethe's 1809 *Die Wahlverwandtschaften* (*Elective Affinities*), when addressing the lenient penalty awaiting leisurely strollers under southern palm trees: "Es wandelt niemand ungestraft unter Palmen." (No stroller under palm trees ever goes unpunished).[35]

Die Wahlverwandtschaften is probably Goethe's psychologically most enigmatic work, and it is telling that Freud repeats Goethe's words from a novel that strives to balance the demands of the senses with those of morality, based on the metaphor of human passion as it is subject to chemical affinity. *Die Wahlverwandtschaften* was a crucial inspiration for Thomas Mann at the time of his composition of *Tod in Venedig* (*Death in Venice*), and it is hardly a coincidence that Freud focuses on this complex story of adultery – in Goethe's novel, the alleged adultery takes place exclusively in the minds of the characters (Eduard and Charlotte, the Captain and Ottilie), while providing its readers (including Freud) with a fine picture of what it means to be in love – of what love is, phenomenologically speaking, that is to say: based on affinity.

In his letter to Rolland, Freud relates how he was overtaken by a sudden feeling of guilt on the Acropolis, bringing up once again a "strafende Instanz" (punishing agency).[36] How does this sense of guilt speak to Freud's initial reluctance and anticipated guilt over visiting Rome? How are his sense of guilt, conscience, and indebtedness to Nietzsche intertwined? Freud, after all, understands traditions and cultures as he understands memories and dreams: as expression in transit and desire in conflict.

Freud allegedly claimed to have read more archaeology than psychology. Although he is likely being provocative in saying so, it is nevertheless clear that he was deeply fascinated by archaeological investigation, and was powerfully drawn to Mediterranean archaeological sites. Graeco-Roman archaeology in the Mediterranean makes for a perfectly Freudian landscape, where nature meets art and present meets past. Accordingly, Freud's *Traumdeutung* is concerned not with the vatic but with the mnemonic potential of dreaming (the time-honoured *oneiros/somnium* rather than *horama/visio*), and in Freud's own dreams it is precisely this oneiric potential that derives from preceding journeys.

In Freud's own self-analysed dreams, Italy figures prominently: as, for example, in an oneiric Rome sequence in which the dream's prime function of "Wunscherfüllung" (wish fulfilment)[37] becomes apparent, and in which Freud expresses his "Sehnsucht, nach Rom zu kommen" (longing to reach Rome). In these dreams, Freud looks upon Rome during a train ride (first dream), sees Rome covered in mist from afar (second dream), and actually arrives in Rome but realizes that its scenery offers anything but what he expected (third dream).[38] The yearning, he suggests, must, for the time being, be satisfied oneirically, since travelling to Rome in his spare time in the summer would be detrimental to his health. It is telling that he revisits this comment in a footnote to the second edition of *Die Traumdeutung* a decade later, confessing his former lack of courage, as well as the fact that he had meanwhile turned into an eager "Rompilger" (Rome pilgrim).[39]

Northern Italy enters the scene in Freud's Adriatic dream about the "Schloß am Meere" (seaside castle),[40] in which condensation and displacement prototypically play dream work's major roles. Intense water memories of three separate Italian journeys in the years immediately preceding *Die Traumdeutung* are here condensed and displaced into a post-Adriatic oneiric mnemotope: a visit to the Friulian castle Miramare in the mid-1890s, a Venetian sojourn in the late 1890s, and an excursion to Aquilèia and Grado in 1898. "Die Örtlichkeiten in diesem Traume sind aus mehreren Reisen an die Adria zusammengetragen" (The locales in this dream are gathered together from various journeys and placed on the Adriatic), writes Freud, explaining the contemporaneous coexistence of various grafted places, compactly and almost inaccessibly condensed into one oneiric moment: a Friulian seaside castle, the Venetian Riva degli Schiavoni, and a canal in Aquilèia.[41]

Freud's general concern with representations of time and space, and more specifically with the mnemonic potential of dreaming, is crucial for an understanding of the mnemotopic landscapes he longs for, dreams of, visits, revisits, and interprets in order to inspire and facilitate his readings of the human mind. Freud's words about dreams and the royal road are well known. It is, however, crucial to read more closely what he actually writes about this royal road or "via regia": "die Traumdeutung aber ist die Via regia zur Kenntnis des Unbewußten im Seelenleben" (the interpretation of dreams, however, is the the via regia that leads to the understanding of the unconscious in the life of the human mind). Importantly, Freud makes this statement about the royal road right after quoting, once again, his book's Virgilian epigraph, taken from the seventh book of the *Aeneid*: "Flectere si nequeo superos, Acheronta movebo" (If I did not move the authorities, I did shake up the underworld), thus defending and illustrating his method of understanding the psyche's subterranean pastures in the mental underworld (in a similar vertical vein, W.H. Auden in his poetic homage to Freud reminds us that Freud "went his way down among the lost people like Dante").[42] Not dreams but the conscious analytical act of reading oneiric-mnemonic structures is what Freud calls a royal road, leading not to the unconscious itself but to an understanding of the subterranean unconscious activities of the mind.

Freud's challenge consists in tracing and placing this royal road in the midst of the maze of roads, paths, and intersections that one encounters when travelling, as Freud does, through the territory of the human mind. What Freud faces in all of his psychoanalytical endeavours are qualities that likewise characterize Liguria – what I have earlier described as a small and compact territory that is steep as well as remote. I am not mounting an argument for a conscious perception of this phenomenological affinity on Freud's part. Rather, I suggest, Nietzsche's spellbinding effect on Freud, grounded as it is in Freud's ephebian complex vis-à-vis Nietzsche's expressive wording, is intimately connected to Nietzsche's Ligurian writings, primarily the sections of *Morgenröthe*, *Die fröhliche Wissenschaft*, and *Also sprach Zarathustra* that formally reflect Liguria's properties. Unlike Freud, Nietzsche was extremely aware of this geopoetic bond and considered it highly and intensely felicitous for his compositions and self-therapies on Ligurian grounds. His royal road was Ligurian, and it was a road into self-liberation – the road not taken by Freud.

Small and steep, compact and remote: Freud's attention to the most minuscule detail in matters oneiric was as unwavering and sincere as his serious and ongoing commitment to small and self-reflective literary forms – for example homophone, pun, joke, symbol, image, and poem. His interest was clearly anchored in the steep, vertical, and, by extension, metaphorical realms of representation and interpretation, in a spatialization of time, which is evident in the attraction that archaeological sites had for him, as well as in his deployment of literary verticality in virtually all his readings (for example, ancient and Dantean versions of the underworld as well as images of the mind as a multi-storey house with corresponding mental layers ranging from the basement to the attic) and his attempt to locate the meaning of words, particularly primeval words ("Urworte") on a vertical axis. A crucial technique that the dream in Freud's view of it deploys when manifestly representing a more latent content or fuller story is "Verdichtung" (condensation); such condensation implies an imagistic compactness similar to that of a poetic image, and is intimately related to the remote, cryptic, and seemingly inaccessible qualities of the dream realm. Mental action is projected onto such places of condensation and as such displaced. And last but not least, such remoteness goes hand in hand with the circular or insular characteristics that inhabit and define Liguria as much as they define Freud's concept of mental time as represented in literary metaphors and geopoetically inclined visualizations. Freud was eager to conquer such mental territory; he, too, understood Genoese psychology of defiant survival, as Dario Martini and Divo Gori claim Nietzsche did (and as Freud himself characterized Genoa: "fast trotzig,' almost defiant).

Before the turn of the century, Freud had developed an interest in archaeology and the work of Heinrich Schliemann (he writes of Schliemann in an 1899 letter to Fließ). But even though he repeatedly likens the human mind not only to the topographies of various types of multi-storey dwelling but also to the geology of Graeco-Roman excavation sites (locating subterranean archaeological layers, situating reliefs, and analysing fragments), only Pompeii, where he enthusiastically travelled with Alexander in 1902, provided him with the perfect way (via!) of retrospectively visualizing the vertical, compact arrangement of the history of a place condensed into a quasi-oneiric landscape image. In the process of reading its mnemotopic features, Freud increasingly turned Pompeii into a perfect manifestation of his vision of the spatialization of time in psychoanalysis.

Excavations in Pompeii had begun in 1748; Goethe visited this "unglückliche [...] mumisierte Stadt" (unfortunate mummified city) in 1787, acknowledging its history thus: "Es ist viel Unheil in der Welt geschehen, aber wenig, das den Nachkommen so viel Freude gemacht hätte. Ich weiß nicht leicht was Interessanteres" (Many calamities have happened in this world, but very few of the sort that would have provided this much joy to posterity. I cannot easily come up with something more interesting).[43] Incidentally, Mark Twain, who saw Pompeii after Goethe but before Freud, with typical irreverence describes Pompeii as an utter disappointment, since before stumbling on its rotten sidewalks (which he claims were at least as dirty and broken before Pompeii's catastrophe as after it), he had imagined that one would go "down into Pompeii with torches, by the way of damp, dark stairways [...]. But you do nothing of the kind. [...] Street Commissioners of Pompeii never attended to their business [...] never mended their pavements [...] Pompeii is no longer a buried city. It is a city of hundreds and hundreds of roofless houses and a tangled maze of streets [...]."[44] Freud no doubt appreciated the insight provided by this array of roofless houses as a fine metaphor for patients whose psyche has been freed of external authority (and is hence able to operate beyond such censorship), and the labyrinth of streets as an exquisite visualization of the vicissitudes of dream interpretation.

In a fresh look at the Pompeiian catastrophe's eerie time warp and the strange connections that its excavations, replications, and interpretations have unveiled, Charles Pellegrino, in *Ghosts of Vesuvius*, unpacks the fossilized Pompeiians' secrets as located between sleep and death, essence and cast, bone and resin – an assessment that Freud's creative imagination would surely have welcomed:

> As if merely asleep within the earth, those Pompeiians who were packed tight inside a bedding plane of fine-grained pyroclastics (which followed the 7:30 a.m. surge cloud) were flash-fossilized for all time. After centuries, their flesh, their hair, and their clothing had disintegrated, leaving behind hollow spaces in the shapes of people. No matter how disquietingly perfect a face may appear after a "hollow" is filled with shape-fitting plaster or resin, each of the casts becomes, in essence, a statue filled with bones. On occasion, an earthquake or other disturbance had collapsed part of a hollow space, permitting an excavator's resin intrusions to replicate only half of a man's face.[45]

Though Goethe was certainly intrigued by the site, he quickly resumed his far more extensive pages on Naples, his exciting passages to and from Sicily, and his dramatic witnessing of Vesuvius's eruptive activities. Freud, by contrast, fell entirely under the spell of Pompeii's exceptional urban mummy, though for the most part he faithfully retraced Goethe's steps in Italy and was intimately familiar with the retrospectively penned *Italienische Reise*.

Goethe's *Italienische Reise* presents the major travelogue in his autobiography *Dichtung und Wahrheit*, in which he defines what he intends by literary writing and truth, thematizing, among other things, the problematic truth-value of verifiable facts and objectively datable events vis-à-vis the complex powers within the intricate network of authorial memory. The relationship between truth and fiction preoccupied Freud as well, and can be reconsidered from an autobiographical vantage point similar to Goethe's, namely as located somewhere between what (f)actually has been the case and what is mnemonically represented and transmitted. The Pompeii that Freud saw in 1902 was, unlike Goethe's, not only largely exhumed but also naturally preserved. During his visit Goethe, by contrast, saw traces of ash in some rooms but correctly predicted the Freudian instance of a past made present as a source of future pleasure.

Freud thoroughly enjoyed Pompeii and was exceedingly intrigued by the scene it presented, for Pompeii is not simply an archaeological site but a re-semiotized cultural landscape, an exhumed city, whose fatal burial under the ashes of Mount Vesuvius, mummification over almost two millennia, and subsequent archaeological excavation provided Freud with a perfect trope that comprises repression as burial, the impossibility of actual forgetting as mummification, and, finally, excavation and reconstruction as psychoanalysis *in nuce*. It is crucial to acknowledge in this context that Freud certainly buries Nietzsche, even mummifies Nietzsche (in that sense Nietzsche is present in Rapallo as a mummy that signals that repression is practically futile), but never actually excavates Nietzsche; this explains, in Freud's own psychoanalytic terms, why his guilt and indebtedness ultimately remain an abiding memory.

Because Freud was more interested in remote origins and primeval scenes and scenarios (which is what the etymology of archaeology suggests) than in the recent past, his tour of the ancient seaport of Pompeii (which had originated as a Greek settlement) gave him an ideal vehicle for envisioning dream work and dream interpretation in their excavated spatial verticality. One should not, however, overlook the intricate intertextual relationship between Freud's experience of Pompeii and his reading of Wilhelm Jensen's *Gradiva: Ein pompeijanisches Phantasiestück* (*Gradiva: A Pompeiian Fantasy*), a novella that Carl Gustav Jung brought to Freud's attention in 1903.

In Freud's view, Jensen's *Gradiva* confirms the Pompeiian paradox of a contemporaneity of ages, which speaks so well to his larger theory of the psychic apparatus.[46] During a subsequent vacation on Lake Garda that same year, Freud began writing his interpretation of the story. In 1907, Freud's first psychoanalytical case study based on a literary piece appeared: *Der Wahn und die Träume in W. Jensens Gradiva* (*Delusion and Dreams in W. Jensen's Gradiva*). Jensen's *Gradiva* was the first literary work that Freud analysed in its entirety, taking poetically invented dreams as seriously as non-fiction ones, although his reading omits a few essential moments of Jensen's post-Goethean fiction – such as the significance of the eruption of Vesuvius, the presence of Ovid, and the role of the lizard as an epiphany. Jensen could not make head or tail of Freud's reading but was obviously flattered by Freud's detailed commentary on this otherwise little-known novella.[47] Freud's omission of the image of the lizard, which Jensen repeatedly emphasized, may not only imply repression of Nietzsche's powerful identification with a lizard basking in the sun but may also be seen as Freud's attempt to evade the Ligurian spell altogether. (Incidentally, as thematized earlier, Italo Calvino in his Möbius-strip geopoetic perspectives compared Liguria's oblong curved boomerang shape to a lizard offering its maximum surface to sea and sun.)

Jensen's story is set in the dazzling noonday light of Pompeii, whose inhumation supposedly happened at the hour of Pan. Poetic neologisms such as "Mittagstraumbild" (high-noon dream-image / phantom) and "Mittagsgeisterstunde" (high-noon witching hour / hour of ghosts and spirits) create the appropriate atmosphere of this post-Nietzschean "great noon." In his Rönne novellas, Benn captures a similar situation as "Mittagssturz des Lichts" (midday downpour of light).[48] In post-Goethean manner, Jensen chooses to creatively populate a Mediterranean place anew. Even though his figure of choice is not Goethe's Nausikaa, Jensen presents his readers with the life of archaeologist Norbert Hanold, who as a very young man loses his sexual desire and instead dedicates himself to his work. During a visit to an Italian museum he is intrigued by a bas-relief that shows a young woman with a distinctive gait, subtle but determined. In a subsequent dream, he is firmly convinced that she perished during the eruption of Mount Vesuvius in the year 79 (the eruption as the earth's ventriloquism), and starts spinning an entire oneiric texture around this appearance, thus finding himself taken back in time to encounter the young woman, who captivates his fancy even more strongly when he imagines her striding across the Pompeiian stepping stones as hot ashes begin to engulf the city – and are about to bury her alive.

In Pompeii, Hanold actually meets not the woman of his fantasy but his childhood friend Zoë Bertgang (the latter part of her name, "Gang,"

means gait), whose style of walking reminds him of the bas-relief figure that he appropriately called *Gradiva*, the striding one. Zoë (a name
that appropriately signifies life), then, literally steps in as Hanold's likely
local therapist (reminiscent, perhaps, of Freud's Minna, who as intellectual equal and travelling companion seemed to be a kind of saviour
for Freud), enabling his gradual recovery from dreams and delusions
as well as his subsequent re-entry into post-analytical life. After reading
Jensen's novella, Freud analysed condensation and displacement ("Verdichtung" and "Verschiebung" as the dream's major working principles)
in Hanold's dream, interpreting the protagonist's foot fetish as a sur-
rogate for the unresolved affection he entertained for his early sweet-
heart. It seems crucial in this context to mention Derrida's reading of
the Jensen-Freud intertext: he aptly points out that

> the "midday ghost" [Gradiva] appears for us in an experience of *reading*,
> but also, for the hero of the novel, in an experience the *language* of which,
> indeed the multiplicity of languages, cannot be abstracted away to leave
> naked pure perception or even a purely perceptive hallucination. Hanold
> also addresses himself to Gradiva in Greek to see if the spectral existence
> (*Scheindasein*) has retained the power to speak (*Sprachvermögen*). Without
> response, he then addresses her in Latin. She smiles and asks him to speak
> in his own proper idiom, German: "If you want to speak to me, you must do
> it in German." A phantom can thus be sensitive to idiom.[49]

As captivated by questions of idiom and gait as Hanold was, Freud
on his subsequent journey to Rome viewed the artwork *Gradiva* in the
Museo Chiaramonti in the Roman Vatican, retrospectively discovering
that it is not Roman but a neo-Attic piece, produced in a workshop in
Athens for purchase by Roman connoisseurs. Post-Goethean collector
Freud (who famously adorned his Vienna office with antiquities – an
ever-reliable daily spectral audience) followed Hanold, treating himself
to a plaster copy of the *Gradiva* statue, which is clearly intended as a
mnemonic visualization of the contemporaneity of ages (or perhaps,
conversely, as an ongoing cultural spectacle that finds in Freud its most
dependable and invigorated spectator).

On his August 1902 journey, Freud traced one major leg of the Grand
Tour's (and Goethe's) principal itinerary. Sigmund and Alexander Freud
crossed the Alps via Bolzano and visited, among other places, Venice,
Rome, Naples, Sorrento, and Pompeii. Goethe, to be sure, was a follower
in his own right. Goethe's father's *Viaggio per l'Italia* had exerted a major

influence on Freud. Freud repeatedly mentions the impact of Karl Philip Moritz and the obsessively philhellenic Johann Joachim Winckelmann, who became acquainted with Greek art in the form of Roman copies, kindling a renewed interest in classical antiquity and the Hellenic world on Italian ground. Freud followed Goethe almost obediently, hence continuing to write the German history of enchantment with Italy, which Goethe had established with Mignon's song as a prime instance in the genre of yearning – and indeed, Freud quotes from Goethe's "Mignon" in his 1902 letter from Sorrento: "Kennst du das Land, wo die Citronen blühen. Wo (*sic*) nicht, will ich [...] beschreiben, was ich gerade [...] sehe" (Do you know [of] the land where lemon trees bloom. If not, I will describe what I am seeing at this moment).[50] Freud happily volunteers his alluring subsequent description of the southern Italian landscape spread out before him as he sits on the patio ("Terrasse") of his Cocumella Hotel room, with citrus playing the lead in the landscape as he orchestrates it for those who remained at home in Vienna.

Freud the Goethe aficionado, like his celebrated precursor, conscientiously prepared for his travels (he thoroughly studied the streets of Pompeii years before he actually set foot on them), and anxiously anticipated what he would see, occasionally experiencing a trancelike state on arrival. Place becomes text and is quite literally read, touched, inhabited, and imbibed on such occasions. In true Nietzschean manner, then, according to Edward Casey, "what, on Freud's view, dreams provide for an understanding of the unconscious mind – a *via regia*, a royal road – the body has provided for place, which by the end of the nineteenth century had come to be as repressed as the libidinal contents of the unconscious mind."[51] Nietzsche was, if not alone, among the few who were willing to reveal an untimely uneasiness with time-honoured moral hypocrisies about physical life and the presence of joy in it.

Like Lord Byron's travels (but very much unlike Benn's fireside trips, armchair journeys, and eventual fellow travelling), Goethe and Freud's Italian sojourns are characterized by a desire to travel for a temporary respite from domestic pressure and professional duty, as well as by a passionate interest in Mediterranean antiquity in general and the cultural landscape of Greece, as replicated in Italy, in particular. The acme of such journeying is a heroic tourist's authorial success as an inalienable consequence of such touring, an almost compulsively reinvented remembrance after a reluctantly completed return from the canonized climes of their cultural dreams.

As I have suggested earlier, the Mediterranean as an actual terrain is simultaneously also a landscape of legend. In this vein, Goethe's epigraph to his *Italienische Reise*, "Auch ich in Arkadien!" reminds us of the phrase "*Et in Arcadia ego*" as a *memento mori* of life's ephemeral nature, while concomitantly contributing a perfect example of the kinds of dreams and delusions cultivated by travelling writers of Freud and Goethe's ilk, whose major objective may have been not clear distinctions between fact and fiction – between actual and literary locales – but rather a geopoetic assessment of the terrain as it evolves between world and word.

The geographical Arcadia is a demanding Mediterranean land but is established as the *topos* of pastoral serenity and Arcadian mythmaking by Virgil. As such, it not only portrays the opposite of the actual Greek terrain's qualities but has been transmitted so consistently that we are likely more familiar with the bucolic *topos* than we are with the real nature of the terrain and its aura – assuming that we are acquainted with its geographic conditions at all. In other words, the real Arcadia is quite unlike the soft dream in which "Arcadia" has long been poetically solidified – in works by Virgil, Jacopo Sannazaro, Philip Sidney, Giovanni Francesco Barbieri, and Nicolas Poussin, to name only a few.[52]

As a consequence of its remote and enclosed character, Arcadia has been perceived as a perfect refuge; but it was hardly a fabled land until Virgil invented literary "Arcadia," providing us with one of the foundational tropes of Western literature. Not entirely unlike Greek Arcadia (but distinct from Atlantis),[53] the Italian Liguria is, on the one hand, part of the Mediterranean and its traditional *genius loci*, while on the other it is also significantly more than the sunny beaches and blue skies that "the Riviera" has come to signify to generations of tourists. Liguria is exceptional in its geographic as well as in its cultural qualities – a crucial fact that Nietzsche recognized (even more than he adored what he perceived as an encounter of Italy with Finland in the Engadine, he welcomed the coexistence of the Alps and the Mediterranaen in Liguria). By contrast, Freud, an otherwise well-read traveller, needs to suppress this distinctly Nietzschean-Ligurian feature. Moreover, Freud increasingly reveals himself as an eager, intense tourist, determined to see as much as possible, regardless of the comfort or preferences of Alexander, his travelling companion.

In this vein, Freud himself related how he cancelled an Italian journey that he and Alexander had envisioned, not to say planned, referring to his fatherly/brotherly rejection as a kind of "Bestrafung" (punishment) of Alexander for his tendency to complain that Freud pressured him into "zu rasche Ortsveränderung" (too many quick changes of location) and "zuviel des Schönen an einem Tage" (too much beauty in one day).[54] Rather than Alexander, then, Freud's companion during his late summer 1905 trip to the Ligurian Rapallo was his sister-in-law, Minna Bernays, to whom he was suspiciously close. On this occasion, Freud writes home to his brother Alexander as follows:

> Dieser Brief – der erste seit der Abreise – ist bereits in Vorahnung der Rückkehr ins gemeine Menschenleben entstanden. Man kommt nämlich zu nichts, die himmlische Sonne und das göttliche Meer – Apollon und Poseidon – sind Feinde aller Leistungen. Ich merke, was uns sonst noch aufrecht erhalten, war das bißchen ernste Pflicht, mit dem Baedeker in der Hand neue Gegenden, Museen, Paläste, Ruinen zu verifizieren; da dies hier und diesmal wegfällt, gehe ich ganz im Wohlleben unter. Also vom Meer. Der Strand ist feiner Schlamm […], ein Stück weiter sind herrliche Klippen, wie wir sie in Capri kennengelernt, Bassins […], schräg geneigte Teppichfelsen, auf denen man wie ein Böcklinsches Untier sich wälzt, ganz einsam und ohne mögliche Zeitschätzung. […] Vom Land kann man nicht reden, ohne ein Dichter zu sein oder andere zu zitieren. Es wächst hier alles, wie zum Beispiel in Sorrent, nur in Palmen ist geradezu Luxus, man darf auf die gnädige Strafe neugierig sein. […] Ende der Woche bin ich zurück, […] bald kommt der letzte Ölbaum, Arancia, Magnolia und so weiter. Herzliche Grüße in Deine nordische Verbannung.

> (This letter – the first since my departure – is already written in anticipation of the return to the life of ordinary mortals. One just doesn't find enough time for anything; the heavenly sun and the divine sea – Apollo and Poseidon – are enemies of all mental activities. I realize that the only thing that has hitherto kept us going has been the remaining sense of obligation to identify – Baedeker in hand – new regions, museums, palaces, ruins; since this obligation no longer exists here, I am simply drowning in a life of ease. For the sea. The beach is fine mud […], a little further down there are wonderful rocks (similar to those we saw in Capri) with pools […], sloping carpets of rocks, in which one rolls and waddles like a monster in one of Böcklin's paintings, completely alone and losing all account of time. […] It is impossible to speak of the land unless one is a poet or one quotes poets. Everything grows here as in Sorrento, except that there is a sheer abundance of palm trees, so that one may well wonder about the merciful retribution. […] I will be back at the end of this week […]. I will soon be passing by the last olive tree, bitter orange, magnolia, etc. Cordial greetings to you in your northern banishment.)[55]

Arnold Böcklin, *Im Spiel der Wellen / At Play in the Waves* (1883). © 2012 bpk, Berlin/Neue Pinakothek; Bayerische Staatsgemäldesammlungen, Munich, Germany/Art Resource, New York. Used with permission.

While *Toteninsel / Isle of the Dead* is probably Arnold Böcklin's best known paint-ing, this 1883 work by the Swiss Symbolist (1827–1901), *At Play in the Waves,* was created around the same time that Nietzsche wrote *Thus Spoke Zarathustra. Im Spiel der Wellen* is compelling in the context of the present study: Benn repeat-edly referred to the expression "Welle und Spiel" (wave and play) as Nietzschean (Nietzsche did use it in his *Dionysos Dithyramben,* where in the poem "Die Sonne sinkt" he writes: "Rings nur Welle und Spiel" (only wave and play around us).

When visiting Rapallo in 1905, Freud probably remembered that Böcklin, too, had sojourned on the Ligurian shore. Even though Böcklin's painting was inspired by a dip in the Gulf of Naples (Ischia), when his travelling compan-ion, marine biologist Anton Dohrn, allegedly dived for a long time and then suddenly surprised a circle of startled female swimmers, Freud likely had in

Upon his many returns from Italy to Vienna, Freud repeatedly – and stereotypically – lamented the imminent loss of the Italian south that his heart so desired. This complaint or disappointment as a *topos* not only already forms part of the Goethean homecoming but also presents us with a traveller who fantastically contrasts Italian joy, sun, and atmospheric clarity to German gloom, doom, fog, and despair.[56]

Freud's allusion to the quasi-oxymoron of the mild punishment or merciful retribution is to Goethe's *Wahlverwandtschaften,* where nobody walks under palm trees without experiencing some sort of retribution for having indulged in such luxurious *otium.* In similar terms, when writing of Sicily, Freud refers to the "unerhörte Schwelgerei, die man sich eigentlich nicht gönnen darf" (the unheard-of indulgence, which really one is not permitted to allow oneself).[57] In the Rapallo letter, Freud uses the attractions of the setting as his excuse for not having written home sooner. This first letter to Austria signals his reluctant preparation for a hesitant return to what he calls a place of "northern banishment," that is, Vienna. He then speaks of the discrepancy not only between the burden of his usual family and professional life in Vienna and his current state of romantic Ligurian bliss (the sun is heavenly, the sea divine, and the troubadours' Provence not far away) but also between the preceding eight journeys with Alexander (for instance to Rome and Athens, where they still had small but serious duties such as reading guidebooks and visiting sites) and his current immersion in joyful, timeless, and probably adulterous well-being. Freud's evocation of a Mediterranean outside of time and history is clichéd, and his ending the letter atmospherically with the Italian words for orange and magnolia is exotic. But there is something more astonishing yet.

Freud smoothly turns to the topic of literary tradition and poetic force, alluding to the *topos* of the ineffable. He reminds Alexander of their excursions to Capri and Sorrento (places well known not only for

---

mind this depiction of the sea populated by mythical creatures while fashioning himself as a frolicking Böcklinesque creature in his letter home to his younger brother in Vienna. A sea in motion without land in sight, an aquatic substructure, and creatures such as joyful centaurs and apprehensive nymphs, laughing tritons and worried mermaids fared well with Freud's favoured realms of poetic-erotic fancy, here reaffirmed in Böcklin's humorously presented nostalgia for myth, which, due to its brooding quality nonetheless enhances downstream drama.

Goethe's famous passages but also for Nietzsche's well-documented visits there), puts great emphasis on the luxurious surfeit of palm trees, and makes a clear but unsourced reference to a merciful retribution as Goethe presents it in *Die Wahlverwandtschaften*. What was Freud's real reason for travelling to a far less fabled land than his former destinations and *delitiae Italiae*? Why does he feel guilty? Why does he repeatedly mention – albeit polemically – retribution? What does he deny and repress, while admitting that one cannot speak of the land (Rapallo, which originates in a vernacular expression for "marsh" and is in that sense ideal for what he likes to do there – roll and wallow) without being a creative writer or quoting one? Why does he silently quote Goethe but not even allude to Nietzsche, whose poetically most forceful work, *Also sprach Zarathustra*, as well as its protagonist, the wanderer Zarathustra himself, were conceived precisely there, and even anticipate some of the major insights about human nature and the power of the unconscious of Freud's *Traumdeutung*? This lacuna is extremely puzzling, especially given Freud's self-analysis and expansive correspondence with Wilhelm Fließ immediately before the Rapallo excursion and his repeated assertions that nobody ever exhibited a more profound and refined self-knowledge than Nietzsche. "Der Wanderer und sein Schatten" (The Wanderer and His Shadow), or perhaps "The Wanderer and His Charts," as Kenneth White has provocatively rewritten Nietzsche's title in 2004, must have been looming large from this Ligurian promontory over Freud's ephebian shoulders. Nietzsche's spectre will have been present in Freud's mental scenario on this seemingly innocent day abroad, on Rapallo's lazy shore.

Even though classical philologist Nietzsche is drawn to the Alps and the Mediterranean as Europe's two major cultural landscapes, envisioning peace of mind in an ideal climate, in order to counteract his various psychosomatic agonies, he significantly deviates (and, sure enough, the otherwise Goethe-inspired Freud follows Nietzsche right into this detour) from the itinerary prescribed by the Grand Tour. Leaving Germany, Nietzsche took up residence in the Alps proper and on the Riviera, where the better part of his most expressive work was created. In his autobiographical *Ecce Homo* Nietzsche recalls (in the previously quoted crucial letter):

> Den [...] Winter lebte ich in jener anmutig stillen Bucht von Rapallo unweit Genua, die sich zwischen Chiavari und dem Vorgebirge Porto fino einschneidet. Meine Gesundheit war nicht die beste. [...] es war dieser Winter und diese Ungunst der Verhältnisse, unter denen mein Zarathustra ent-

stand. – Den Vormittag stieg ich in südlicher Richtung auf der herrlichen Strasse nach Zoagli hin in die Höhe, an Pinien vorbei und weitaus das Meer überschauend; des Nachmittags, sooft es nur die Gesundheit erlaubte, umging ich die ganze Bucht von Santa Margherita bis hinter nach Porto fino. [...] – Auf diesen beiden Wegen fiel mir der ganze erste Zarathustra ein, vor allem Zarathustra selber, als Typus: richtiger, *er überfiel mich.*

(The following winter I stayed in that charming quiet bay of Rapallo, which, not far from Genoa, is cut out between Chiavari and the foothills of Portofino. My health could have been better [...] it was that winter and under these unfavorable circumstances that my *Zarathustra* came into being. Mornings I would walk in a southerly direction on the splendid road to Zoagli, going up past pines with a magnificent view of the sea; in the afternoon, whenever my health permitted it, I walked around the whole bay from Santa Margherita all the way to Portofino. It was on these two walks that the whole of *Zarathustra I* occurred to me, and especially Zarathustra himself as a type: rather, he *overtook me.*)[58]

How can Freud, two decades later, so evidently ignore Nietzsche's rendering of Rapallo as his and his *Zarathustra*'s privileged place? Granted, Freud's experience differed significantly from Nietzsche's. Nietzsche was there in the winter, Freud in the summer; Nietzsche was there alone, Freud with Minna; Nietzsche resided there, Freud furtively vacationed there; Nietzsche suffered from disease, Freud was greatly at ease; Nietzsche hiked the promontory, Freud, in his own words, wallowed on the beach in the manner of a monstrous creature inspired by Böcklin; Nietzsche anticipated no punishment, Freud a lenient penalty or mild retribution. And last but not least, Nietzsche was there first, Freud, at best, second. It is precisely Nietzsche's having preceded him that seems to be responsible for Freud's resentment of time, and that caused him a fair amount of pain and anxiety: the pain of belatedness and the related anxiety of influence that would permeate virtually all his expressive endeavours.

Regarding Italy's canonized magic and Goethe's effect on Freud's writing and thought, one would expect Freud, when experiencing Italy in his own right, to be hindered by such spell-binding visions as those inscribed by Goethe. However, Freud had no difficulty in celebrating Goethe, while establishing himself as a belated but creative Italophile authority.[59] Nevertheless, while he felt at ease with "die Patronanz Goethes" (dated Austrian German for "Goethe's patronage"),[60] Freud was less at ease with Nietzsche, his near contemporary, who was literally too close to home in more than just one sense. It is as difficult to imagine that Freud did not know of Nietzsche's residence in Liguria (and of *Zarathustra*'s contemporaneous conception in Rapallo) as it is to accept that he was not, on much more extensive grounds, profoundly indebted to him. While a variety of critics have elaborated on the Freud-Nietzsche relationship, on Nietzsche as Freud's precursor, and on the nature of Nietzsche's influence on Freud's writing and thought,[61] the geopoetically charged Rapallo incident as Freud's surreptitious visit to the native lands of *Zarathustra* has so far remained unaddressed.[62]

Among Nietzsche and Freud's shared interests are the significance of dreaming; the vicissitudes of the ego; the genealogy of morality and conscience (the superego) in the Judaeo-Christian tradition; the body's mirroring of the pysche; antiquity, mythology, and tragedy (key concepts such as the Oedipus complex and narcissism have their origin in Greek mythology); working through (Freud) and overcoming (Nietzsche); and last but not least the intricate dynamics of remembering and forgetting, a challenging psychomechanics that permeates the work of both Nietzsche and Freud from beginning to end, making Freud's "forgetting" of Nietzsche all the more complex, particularly in light of the fact that Freud's library included the complete works of both Goethe and Nietzsche. Moreover, as documented in detail by Paul-Laurent Assoun, Nietzsche was widely discussed in Viennese circles (particularly from 1902 to 1908 in the "Mittwochgesellschaft"), and particularly by Freud's friends Joseph Paneth (who worked at the zoological institute in Villefranche and had met Nietzsche in Nice) and, later, Lou Andreas-Salomé. Freud evoked Nietzsche in a 1908 meeting of the Viennese Psychoanalytic Society, and he read Nietzsche in Salomé's presence in 1911, the year in which the Congress of Psychoanalysis was held in Weimar, where Nietzsche had spent his last years and ultimately died: "the Freudian court came to sit in the Nietzschean citadel," writes Assoun, "in a place that, symbolically, held the vestiges of the great Goethe." Assoun aptly suggests that Freud set out to discover Nietzsche by being "an admirer – as reticent as sincere – of Nietzsche," but eventually became "a user of Nietzschean pre-metapsychological intuitions."[63]

Grounding his work in the dynamics of reading and influence in Freud's theory of the Attic *Oedipus*, as well as in *Der Familienroman der Neurotiker* (*Family Romance of Neurotics*), Harold Bloom generally qualifies the younger writer's relationship with his precursors as that of a son in rivalry with his respective father figure(s). *The Anxiety of Influence* presents the reader with six Freudian defence strategies, which Bloom classifies as "revisionary ratios," and which are informed by the belated writer's attempt at repressing his precursors' eventually undeniable paternal influence or patronage. Bloom considers Freud and Nietzsche's writings and the impact of literary tradition as opposed to an individual poet's creative will as foundational for his theory of influence (albeit without reading Freud as Nietzsche's son), and it is in this vein that I turn to Freud's Oedipal Acropolis text and the questions it raises about these very guilt and defence mechanisms ("Abwehrmethoden"),[64] which Freud himself, in 1904, held responsible for his mental counteraction of mnemonic meaning in Athens. Bloom's sixth ratio, "apophrades," seems particularly appropriate in the present context. It is a notion taken from Athenian times, when the dead were said to return to the precise places they used to inhabit in life. On this occasion, Bloom takes his highly appropriate epigraph, "[...] Who seem to die live," from Ralph Waldo Emerson, who along with Henry Thoreau was an important Transcendentalist forerunner of geopoetics, a writer and walker with a keen perception of the world surrounding him, and who likewise fascinated Nietzsche.[65]

Reviewing his methodological approach, which took him from self-analysis to the analysis of others (both actual individual patients and fictional characters in literature) to his later work on society, and eventually back to himself, the mature Freud confided in Romain Rolland about a crucial episode of his 1904 journey that kept recurring to his thoughts. On the occasion of Rolland's seventieth birthday, Freud – aged eighty, trapped in domestic monotony because of his poor health (mouth and throat cancer), and thus painfully deprived of the dynamic prospect of the potentially guilty allures of travel – recalled how, on his journey to Athens with Alexander, he climbed up to the Acropolis and first saw the ruins of the Parthenon. In almost Dantean fashion, Freud's open "Brief an Romain Rolland: Eine Erinnerungsstörung auf der Akropolis" ("Letter to Romain Rolland: A Memory Disturbance on the Acropolis") deploys journeying as a trope for life in order to inscribe, poetically and retrospectively, a journey that had taken place thirty-two years prior to this paradox of an expressive Freudian meditation. In this late text, Freud unambiguously presents the desire to travel as a representation of the traveller's unconscious wishes. In it, the idea of wanderlust clearly takes on the main characteristic of the dream, which is wish fulfilment. That a fulfilled travel wish, however, implies the end of a dream as much as the beginning of a reality is precisely the dilemma on whose psychic dimensions Freud compellingly elaborates, eager to confess his late thoughts to

Rolland, the French mystic, novelist, dramatist, essayist, Nobel laureate, Italophile, and, after Freud's death, author of *Voyage intérieur*.

Freud's admiration of Rolland's courage in speaking the truth is unwavering. It is not surprising that on this solemn occasion he reminds us of his high esteem for Rolland's "Wahrheitsliebe" (love of truth) and "Bekennermut" (moral courage).[66] The love of truth paired with the spirit of observation needed to perceive truth is also praised by Goethe in his *Italienische Reise*, referring to the writer's complementary strengths of proto-mimetic "Beobachtungsgeist" (spirit of observation) and poetic "Welterschaffung" (making of a world),[67] that is, the writer's willingness, if need be, to shock, to astonish by radically expressing the new. These qualities are present not only in Goethe and Rolland but also in Nietzsche and, for that matter, in Freud, the adventurous reader of the human unconscious. Freud also shares with Rolland his love of the theatre, of Michelangelo, and of Rome, where Rolland resided for two years, acquainting himself with Italian art (and via art and artefacts, with himself, much like Goethe and his *Gegenstände*) as well as with Malwida von Meysenburg, a friend of Nietzsche's.

Goethe's *Italienische Reise* is based on a poetics of place and mnemonic replacement: "ich mache diese wunderbare Reise nicht, um mich selbst zu betriegen, sondern um mich an den Gegenständen kennen zu lernen" (I embark on this journey not to delude myself, but to get to know myself better in confrontation with the objects),[68] writes Goethe in the present tense, as if he were present once again in his travelogue's act of representation. While rewriting his letters and diaries, Goethe re-experienced himself in Italy. In a fine instance of such retrospection, he continues: "man kann das Gegenwärtige nicht ohne das Vergangene erkennen" (one cannot recognize the present by excluding the past),[69] an insight that perhaps explains why Freud was in awe of him. But while Goethe is consistently open about the beholding subject's role vis-à-vis the objective world, Freud, recalling his Acropolis experience in the 1936 letter to Rolland, by contrast, rigorously continues a kind of self-delusion while curiously oscillating between presence and absence, self and world, and with no obvious will to cognition.

That the Acropolis text says practically nothing about the ruined Parthenon itself (even though on another occasion Freud mentions the overwhelming beauty of its columns) shows Freud in a strikingly unobservant mode and marks his Athens experience as something very different from the one he had in Pompeii. Further, one would have expected Freud to confirm a profound enthusiasm for the Greek school that inhabited the Acropolis from its first conception: "twenty-five centuries ago," recalls Kenneth White,

> three men: a politician, Pericles; an architect: Phidias; and a poet, Sophocles, met on the heights of Athens with the idea of giving a radiant form to the city and making it "the school of Greece." The result was the architectural complex of the Acropolis, and, back of the architecture, a *paideia*, a whole system of poetic and philosophical education making for a live, brilliant culture.[70]

While Freud's text does not breathe a word about the Acropolis as a geopoetic place, a Mediterranean house of poetry, myth, and culture (where Athena and Poseidon offered an olive tree and a spring of salty water), he is very expressive when it comes to other sites, so that his silence about the place itself, in contrast to his eloquence about his mental experience in it, is all the more astonishing. Moreover, Nietzsche's engagement with Attic tragedy and Liguria's theatrically organized humanized landscape (Calvino for instance speaks of Liguria's spectacles and balconies) render Freud's silence even more suspect. A crucial point of cultural interest about the Acropolis is that the Parthenon had been inhabited over the centuries, and unlike Pompeii, only in the nineteenth century became the archaeological site and artificially constructed ruin that Freud visited. Venetian, Byzantine, and Turkish remains had already been removed by that time, and the four remaining buildings had undergone repeated reconstruction.

It is interesting that these reconstructions only reflect the earliest appearance of the site, not its later incarnations. Unlike Pompeii, this ruin resembles a quasi-Romantic creation rather than a Freudian-Pompeiian vision of things past, present, and future. It seems, finally, unlikely that the 1904 sense of guilt that Freud still remembered in 1936 is actually interpreted (truth)fully in this final act of what one would have hoped was a more mature self-analysis; instead Freud's "via regia" seems to be strangely deprived of its full interpretive potential.

In travelling to Athens in 1904, Freud went further than Goethe, further than Nietzsche, and further than Rolland, even if Greece in general and the Acropolis in particular are associated with Goethe's worship of ancient culture and are suggestive of Nietzsche's lifelong Attic interests as well. Wondering whether he had not perchance, gone too far, while trying to uncover why this arrival on the Acropolis felt "too good to be true,"[71] Freud explains the following in hindsight:

Es war mir längst klar geworden, daß ein großes Stück der Lust am Reisen in der Erfüllung dieser frühen Wünsche besteht, also in der Unzufriedenheit mit Haus und Familie wurzelt. Wenn man zuerst das Meer sieht, den Ozean überquert, Städte und Länder als Wirklichkeiten erlebt, die so lange ferne, unerreichbare Wunschdinge waren, so fühlt man sich wie ein Held, der unwahrscheinlich große Taten vollbracht hat. Ich hätte damals auf der Akropolis meinen Bruder fragen können: Weißt Du noch, wie wir in unserer Jugend Tag für Tag denselben Weg gegangen sind, von der … straße ins Gymnasium, am Sonntage dann jedesmal in den Prater oder auf eine der Landpartien, die wir schon so gut kannten, und jetzt sind wir in Athen und stehen auf der Akropolis. Wir haben es wirklich weit gebracht! Und wenn man so Kleines mit Größerem vergleichen darf, hat nicht der erste Napoleon während der Kaiserkrönung […] sich zu einem seiner Brüder gewendet […] und bemerkt: "Was würde Monsieur notre Père dazu sagen, wenn er jetzt dabei sein könnte?

(It had long become clear to me that the better part of one's desire to travel consists in the fulfilment of these early wishes, which is to say in one's not being content with one's home and family. When one first lays eyes on the sea, crosses the ocean, experiences cities and countries as realities that had for the longest time been such distant and seemingly unreachable objects of desire, one then feels as if one were a hero who has accomplished incredibly grand deeds. I could have asked my brother back then on the Acropolis: Do you remember how in our youth we walked the same walk every day, from the … street to high school, on Sundays then every time to the Prater, or on another one of those excursions into the countryside with which we were already so very familiar, and now we are in Athens and stand right on top of the Acropolis. We have, indeed, come a long way! And if one is allowed to compare such small things with much bigger issues, did not the first Napoleon during his coronation as emperor turn to one of his brothers and say: I wonder what Monsieur our father would have to say, if he could be present right now?)[72]

It is significant that Nietzsche, in reflecting on Rapallo and *Zarathustra*, mentions in *Ecce Homo* the authority of Kaiser Friedrich in order to convey his geopoetic sensitivity to place and the emotions and memories so intimately connected with it, while Freud refers to none other than Napoleon in envisaging a historical triumph over the father. This reaffirms the role of the Acropolis as a mental landmark for Freud rather than an actual place of cultural impact.

Reminiscent of his letter from Rapallo, it is here once again Freud's flight from home and his departure to distant, fabled pastures that brings about this rare moment of post-Napoleonic grandeur and heroism, as Freud confesses having experienced it, hypothetically suggesting that he could have, but did not, address Alexander on the Acropolis at the time, either to trigger a shared recollection of their childhood, or else to state that against all paternal odds they had indeed come a long way. Coming such a long way here marks the end of filial piety and implies surpassing the father while conquering the mother.

The Freud of 1936 used either the post-Napoleonic *pluralis maiestatis* (the "royal we") or the first person plural in order to make his younger brother explicitly part of this putative "Überlegenheit der Söhne" (superiority of the sons);[73] in 1904, however, he did not invite his younger brother to share his sense of triumph, simply because this sense of triumph was overpowered by his profound sense of guilt. But why was this act of heroism permeated by a feeling of guilt? Why does Freud call his hope for a revision of what he learnt about antiquity in school, his spontaneous attempt to deny a part of reality (the actual existence of the Parthenon) in order to feel less fortunate and hence less guilty, an "Erinnerungsstörung" (a mnemonic failure or memory disturbance which simultaneously implies both, a failure of memory, and a memory of this memory failure)? One certainly wishes that Freud had written a late text in response to the 1905 Rapallo incident as well. Why does this so-called mnemonic failure have to enter an otherwise successful and satisfying scene of a perfectly accomplished arrival in Greece? In a related and much earlier text, Freud characterizes failure precisely as a consequence of success: "Am Erfolge scheitern."[74] And yet, curiously, towards the end of the same essay, he referred to the "Verbrecher aus Schuldbewusstsein" (criminal out of sense of guilt),[75] one of the rare occasions on which he explicitly uttered Nietzsche's *nomen proprium*:

Ein Freund hat mich darauf aufmerksam gemacht, daß der "Verbrecher aus Schuldgefühl" auch Nietzsche bekannt war. Die Präexistenz des Schuldgefühls und die Verwendung der Tat zur Rationalisierung desselben schimmern uns aus den Reden Zarathustras "Über den bleichen Verbrecher" entgegen. Überlassen wir es zukünftiger Forschung zu entscheiden, wieviele von den Verbrechern zu diesen "bleichen" zu rechnen sind.

(A friend has directed my attention to the fact that the "criminal out of sense of guilt" was also known to Nietzsche. The pre-existence of the sense of guilt and the deployment of the actual deed in order to rationalize this sense of guilt glimmer over toward us from Zarathustra's speeches "On the

pale criminal." Let us leave it to future research to decide how many crimi-
nals should count among these so-called pale ones.)[76]

In the case of Freud's anticipated guilt with regard to his repeated and
allegedly undeserved visit to Rome, for instance, the argument about
pale crimes might hold. But Freud's Acropolis experience was significantly different from his first arrival in Rome – far guiltier and evidently
less resolved. In other words, Freud the Rome-pilgrim became no Ath-
ens-pilgrim; nor did he, as far as we know, ever return to Liguria after
1905, even though his Italian travels continued until 1923. In Athens,
Freud might indeed be seen as the self-judging pale criminal as sympa-
thetically described by Nietzsche in *Zarathustra*, since it is at the end of
his life that Freud seems to take inventory, thoroughly haunted by his
unacknowledged literary debt to Nietzsche.

The Freud brothers' bad mood began in Trieste, on the Adriatic,
and persisted from the moment when Alexander's business acquaintance persuasively encouraged them to embark on their 1904 side trip
to Athens (via Corfu) until the moment when they boarded the ship for
Greece. As a rather meaningful psychic subset, this negative mood puts
an even greater emphasis on the anticipation of guilt and the necessary next step to commit this putative crime, so as to justify, in temporal
reversal, an advanced sense of guilt by a subsequent correspondence, or
rationalizing justification, on the level of action.

The quasi-schizophrenic situation that Freud remembers after having
climbed the Acropolis is intricately intertwined with his sense of "Greece
guilt": the shock of the reality of an Acropolis that as an adolescent
schoolboy he had read about and had since been longing to see – "die
Sehnsucht zu reisen und die Welt zu sehen"; (the longing to travel and
to see the world)[77] – provokes an uneasiness of a different order. Freud
clearly remembers having doubted the actual existence of the Acropolis,
whose putative unreality, one is tempted to conclude, would have liberated him from this astounding sense of displaced guilt. It is remarkable
how, in Freud's text, the person who opens up this delusive possibility is
not identified as being the same as the *alter ego* who perceives it. Rather,
the second person is stunned at the first person's doubt, which calls into
existence a split moment that gives rise to a strong sense of alienation:
"Entweder erscheint uns ein Stück der Realität als fremd oder ein Stück
des eigenen Ich" (either a part of reality appears strange to us, or a part
of our own self/ego does).[78]

Freud's own writing must occasionally have appeared strange and foreign as well as strangely familiar (uncanny) to Freud himself. The anxiety that Nietzsche evokes in Freud the writer – and with Leslie Chamberlain I read both Nietzsche and Freud as intensely talented creative writers – is one that Freud the denier euphemistically talks away by referring to his temporary "inertia" with regard to reading his Ligurian precursor. In a letter to Fließ in 1900, in which, tellingly perhaps, he also mentions his "Conquistadorentemperament" (conqueror's temperament) Freud writes: "Ich habe mir jetzt den Nietzsche beigelegt, in dem ich die Worte für vieles, was in mir stumm bleibt, zu finden hoffe, aber ihn noch nicht aufgeschlagen. Vorläufig zu träge" (I have now acquired a copy of Nietzsche, in which I am hoping to find words for many things that remain mute in me, but I have not yet opened the book. Too inert for the time being).[79] The timing of this seemingly nonchalant last comment regarding Freud's reluctance to open that Nietzsche book is as intriguing as the wording regarding expressive muteness and inert laziness.

Die Traumdeutung, Freud's most extensive psychoanalytic work, first appeared in 1899, but its official publication date was 1900, deliberately marking its decisive, ground-breaking character by tying it to the beginning of a new century. Consequently, the official birth of Freudian psychoanalysis practically coincides with Nietzsche's death in 1900. This year also marks Fließ's first step towards terminating his friendship and correspondence with Freud – as a result of Freud's appropriation of a Fließean concept, another silent borrowing for which Freud later apologized – an apology, however, that Fließ rejected.[80] The second breach – and the one that finally ended the Fließ-Freud interaction – was in 1904, the same year that Freud embarked on his journey to Athens.

The correspondence with Rolland began in 1923 (the year in which Freud's Mediterranean travels ended with a journey to Lavarone, Rome, and Sorrento, among others, in company with Anna Freud), and introduced Freud to the notion of the "oceanic feeling" developed and poetically phrased as such by Rolland as a consequence of his study of eastern mysticism. While Freud's epistolary interactions with Rolland tend to be extraordinarily polite, they are also clearly confessional in tone. In a 1926 letter, Freud speaks of his psychoanalytic practice as neither his fault nor his merit ("nicht meine Schuld und nicht mein Verdienst"), making reference to the fact that psychoanalysis saved some patients while destroying others.[81] In 1929, Freud again touches on Rolland's "oceanic feeling," announcing to him his almost finished *Das Unbehagen in der Kultur* (*The Uneasiness in Culture*, which was also freely, and I would say problematically, translated as *Civilization and Its Discontents*), a very late text of Freud's in which he likens the structure of the unconscious to the palimpsestic structure of Rome, while elaborating extensively on culture and the theme of guilt. Freud explains how he deploys Rolland's term in the book's first pages, but does so only by anonymously acknowledging (if that is not an oxymoron to begin with) its actual author, Rolland: "ich erwähne Ihren Namen nicht, gebe aber immerhin einen Wink, auf Sie zu raten" (I make no mention of your name but at any rate I drop a hint so that one may guess that it is you).[82] It is intriguing to recall in this context that in his psychoanalytical reading of Jensen's novella, Freud focused on the protagonist, Norbert Hanold, and the process of unveiling his past rather than on the author and precursory inventor of this psychoanalytically complex character and plot, Wilhelm Jensen, whose name Freud mentioned only three times, and extremely casually at that.

One wonders why explicitly quoting Rolland's name along with his brilliant geopoetic notion of the "oceanic feeling" was not an option for Freud, who at the same time clearly wanted to acknowledge someone, but not by name, a curious act of which Freud subsequently informs Rolland in a letter. Freud circumvented explicit naming on a number of other occasions as well: for example, in "Vergänglichkeit" ("Transitoriness") of 1915, where he similarly concealed the names of a tacit friend ("schweigsamer Freund") and a young but already renowned poet ("junger, bereits rühmlich bekannter Dichter"), with whom he was taking a walk through a summer landscape, engaging with the poet's thoughts on beauty's transitory character.[83]

While it is known that this walk took place in the Dolomites in the summer before the beginning of the First World War, the names of Freud's companions at the time have yet to be determined. In the case of the Rolland letter, by contrast, Freud added a footnote in 1931, saying that he can now, after the publication of Rolland's *La vie de Ramakrishna* and *La vie de Vivekananda*, reveal his name rather than refer to him only as "[s]einen Freund."[84] Freud mentions the fact that Rolland had written to him about the "oceanic feeling" in a private letter, which Freud seems to consider an unquotable document. While this perspective might weaken the point about Freud's reference to Rolland as an unnamed source, it is nonetheless worth pointing to other passages in Freud where he indicates unnamed influences, such as the aforementioned unidentified "friend" who tried to make Freud more aware of Nietzsche.[85]

Freud's exact motivation for initially not acknowledging Rolland as the originator of this phrase used to express a religious feeling of eternity – a flash of poetic genius, really, and hence extremely attractive to Freud – might be nothing more than an anomaly. But it is striking how much Freud's attention is geared towards the French writer's exact poetic wording. More often than not an imaginative interpreter and a thorough reader, Freud generally shows himself to be quite conscientious in matters of quotation and citation. Literary references abound in his work, as do his praises of an international array of artists and poets of all ages and places.

One of the main reasons why Freud was awarded the Goethe-Preis in 1930 was, in Alfons Paquet's words, Freud's "kühne Deutung der von Dichtern geprägten Zeugnisse" (bold interpretation of testimonies coined by poets).[86] Freud indicates in his acceptance speech what one would perhaps have found more appropriate with regard to his disturbing attitude towards Nietzsche: he calls a writer's relationship to fathers and teachers "ambivalent," in that it is always wavering between "Verehrung" (reverence/adoration) and "feindselige Auflehnung" (resentful/hostile rebellion), reminding us of Bloom's take on literary debts. In Goethe, Freud continues, he admires the "Bekenner" (confessor) as much as the "Verhüller" (cloaker).[87]

As a consequence of the earlier Freud's unacknowledged indebtedness to him, Nietzsche seems to return to a Freud who cannot help but send himself on a second Athenian guilt trip, in 1936, culminating in his admission to Rolland. It is, I submit, Freud's superficial "Greece guilt," covering his denial of his profound debt to Nietzsche, that troubles him again at the very end of his life. Or, to put it another way: Freud partially renders to Rolland and Greece what he owes to Nietzsche and Liguria. Nietzsche not only speaks of guilt and crime in *Zarathustra*, but writes in *Zur Genealogie der Moral* (*On the Genealogy of Morals*): "Das Gefühl der Schuld, der persönlichen Verpflichtung, hat [...] seinen Ursprung [...] in dem Verhältnis zwischen [...] Gläubiger und Schuldner: hier trat zuerst Person gegen Person, hier mass sich zuerst Person an Person" (The sense of guilt, of personal debt, has its origin in the relationship between creditor and debtor: it was here that person was first pitted against person, that person was first measured against person).[88]

At times Freud's confessional post-Acropolis self-analysis may well sound Greek to the reader, since his authorial failure of memory in 1936 emphatically reaffirms the mnemonic failure of 1904 to distinguish truth from fiction and text from pre-text. Having, unlike Goethe and Nietzsche, gone out of his way, all the way to Greece, and having momentarily doubted the reality of the Acropolis as he perceived it, Freud compounded his guilt by denying Nietzsche's presence (even though he first travelled to Genoa in the year that Nietzsche died and the *Traumdeutung* appeared, as well as to Nietzsche's Rapallo in 1905). As with Freud's aforementioned Adriatic dream about the seaside castle, the years and experiences of 1904 and 1936 are here collapsed into one contemporaneous image designed to keep the dream and its potential for wish fulfilment alive, even as Freud continues to repress his authorial affliction regarding Nietzsche, divided to the very end: "Person gegen Person" (person against person).

Even though Freud's communication in Athens with his brother Alexander (who is later dropped in favour of Minna) remains hypothetical, Freud continues to search for words. On the few occasions when he does refer to Nietzsche, he is concerned with the act of expression rather than the act of thinking, with finding words rather than construing theories, with poetic force rather than the demonstration of scientific logic (in a way reminiscent of Jensen's Hanold, the excessive lover who works at maintaining an illusion that unites art with reality). In spite of what he calls inertia, which is clearly a pretext, Freud wants to find, in Nietzsche, "Worte für vieles, was in [Freud] stumm bleibt" (words for many things that remain silent in him). At another point, Freud characterizes Nietzsche's words as "treffend" (felicitous).[89] And during his inert *dolce far niente* on Rapallo's shore (was Rapallo Freud's experience of Provençal *alba* and *gaya scienza,* one wonders?), Freud says that one cannot speak of the place without being a poet or quoting other poets (and while alluding to Goethe's *Elective Affinities* he once again conveniently forgets to mention Nietzsche). Freud is the one who "speaks Nietzsche" without speaking of him, without quoting him, without even anonymously acknowledging him as an influence, as he did in the case of Rolland and others – not even in a moment of self-acknowledged expressive crisis such as this.

Freud the aficionado and creative reader of international literary texts – *Oedipus, Hamlet, The Sandman, Gradiva,* and Sherlock Holmes, to mention only a few – turns to ancient and modern, traditional and new, canonized as well as extremely recent and unknown texts such as Wilhelm Jensen's Pompeiian novella, in which he chooses to engage, following Jung's recommendation and its archaeological setting's power to express his Nietzsche-derived theory. Freud's generally acknowledged debt to poetic tradition renders his anxious flight into putative inertia vis-à-vis Nietzsche in general (for instance on Attic tragedy), and the Ligurian Nietzsche (and his Rapallo residence and conception of *Zarathustra* there) in particular, all the more bizarre.

Freud's Mediterranean-Italian-Ligurian endeavours provide him with mixed blessings and guilty pleasures, including moments of conquest, learning, bliss, and success, as well as of downfall and failure, so that the complex tension between Hannibal and Oedipus, Goethe and Nietzsche, remains unresolved to the very end of Freud's authorial career. The uncanny effect of Harold Bloom's Attic "apophrades" emerges at the exact moment when the precursor no longer seems to have composed the work of the ephebe, but the belated writer seems to be retroactively penning the work of the precursor. Nietzsche and Freud, then, appear strangely familiar to the reader (and probably to one another). In "Spéculer – Sur Freud," Jacques Derrida makes a similar observation about Freud's self-presentation as a posthumous creditor rather than a belated debtor, so as to assure his secondary authorial autonomy.[90]

There is no evidence that Freud ever travelled to the French portion of the Ligurian coast, nor (curiously, given his strong interest in Eros) did he demonstrate any interest in medieval Provence. In contrast to Erika and Klaus Mann, Freud (who lived in Paris at the time when Nietzsche concluded his Ligurian sojourns, in the mid 1880s) never displayed any kind of enthusiasm for the Côte d'Azur. His predilection was clearly for Greek and Roman antiquity; and, as a happy follower of Goethe, Freud indubitably favoured Italy over any other travel destination as the most accessible place in which to view the archaeological remains of ancient times. The Mann siblings considered Nietzsche's Rapallo an utterly boring, uninspiring location, albeit one with a charming past – they mention Lord Byron, Arnold Böcklin, and Friedrich Nietzsche but not Sigmund Freud – yet, unlike the French coast, with a lacklustre present, and as such appropriate for retirement rather than excitement. Freud's Rapallo was quite the opposite: while to him, too, it was the landscape of Böcklin, it was not a landscape of beautiful memory but rather an uncanny territory of repressed acknowledgment which the luxuries of the Hôtel Savoia could not cure; it was also a blissful place of magic vacationing and seductive beaches, rather than the backwater depicted by the Manns about two decades later.

While it has been challenging at least since Nietzsche (and Marcel Proust) to inquire into the intricate dynamics of knowing and unknowing, remembering and forgetting – both voluntary and involuntary, even though such a distinction is to be taken with a grain of salt – a Nietzsche-in-Freud discussion cannot help but address the paradoxical idea of Nietzsche's plea for voluntary forgetting in the service of life, which is practically synonymous (albeit evaluated differently) with Freudian repression, and as such by definition an unsuccessful amnesia, in that one will always need to remember what it is precisely that one so desperately tries to forget, while constantly having to face up to the fact that the unconscious somehow stores everything and forgets nothing.

A voluntary attempt at forgetting such as Freud's with regard to Nietzsche necessarily backfires, for it is, ironically, informed by ongoing acts of solid remembrance. However, despite the intricate network of Freud's ongoing remembering to forget and alleged forgetting to remember (which indubitably complicates the mnemonic issue far beyond the Acropolis), one cannot help but read Freud on his own terms as a defiant, if not triumphant, forgetter. It is not his actual presence in Athens but rather his whistle-stop in Rapallo that is to Freud "too good to be true" – "almost too authentic" (to recall once more Erika and Klaus Mann's assessment of Portofino, just a few miles south of Rapallo), as well as Sharon Kivland's pun *too true to be good* and Susan Sugarman's *paradoxical response to the real* in the context of post-Freudian travel to the Acropolis.

Assessed on his own terms, Freud's complex vis-à-vis Nietzsche may be Oedipal as well as Hannibalean – it is as clearly not Goethean as it is Ligurian. However, the one to whom Freud owes most would likely have been most avid about the Viennese doctor-poet's putative inertia. Although Nietzsche would hardly agree with Freud's word choice, he would, unlike the latter, welcome forgetting as he welcomes the sun – as an active and positive service joyfully rendered on behalf of multiple dawns, noons, isles, and of *alba* and *gaya scienza* as another name for life.

Blind Spots, Alibis, Sceneries:
Benn's Ligurian Complexes

... imagination qui vagabonde.

(... vagabonding imagination.)
Paul Gauguin

... von Palavas bis Portofino die schöne Küste lang.

(... from Palavas to Portofino along the beautiful coast.)
Gottfried Benn

... la psychanalyse ... serait l'autre nom du sans alibi ... l'aveu d'un sans alibi.

(...psychoanalysis ... would be another word for alibi-
lessness ... the confession of an alibi-lessness.)
Jacques Derrida

"Da geschah ihm die Olive" (then the olive befell him) and "der Troubadour kehrt zurück" (the troubadour returns), wrote Gottfried Benn in
1916 and 1943, respectively. These deceptively simple sentences contain
his Ligurian poetics in a nutshell, presenting in condensed fashion what
Benn repeatedly calls "Ligurian complex" (first in 1919), and represent
his most serious challenge as an imaginative geopoetic writer whose
travels, and ideas about travelling, are by no means as straightforward
as those of Dante and Goethe, or Nietzsche and Freud. When Goethe
writes of the Italian citrus, he (or Mignon, his protagonist or persona)

clearly longs for and desires to journey towards the climes of lemons and oranges. When Benn, by contrast, writes of the olive, it is the kind of olive that approaches him, that happens to him, that first befalls and from then on haunts him. And when he writes of the troubadours, these vagrant Provençals and their lyrical geopoetic vocabulary draw nigh without the Modernist poet and medical doctor (verbal laboratist) having to face any sort of dislocation:

> Es ist ein Laboratorium, ein Laboratorium für Worte, in dem sich der Lyriker bewegt. Hier modelliert, fabriziert er Worte, öffnet sie, sprengt, zertrümmert sie, um sie mit Spannungen zu laden, deren Wesen dann durch einige Jahrzehnte geht. Der Troubadour kehrt zurück: trobaire oder trobador = Finden, d.h. Erfinden von Worten (XI. Jahrhundert, zwischen Loire und Pyrenäen), also: Artist. Wer den Reigen kennt, geht ins Labor.
>
> (It is a laboratory, a laboratory for words, in which the poet moves. Here he moulds, manufactures words, opens them up, blasts, shatters them, in order to charge them with tensions, whose nature will then live on through a couple of decades. The troubadour returns: trobaire or trobador = finding, i.e., inventing of words (XIth century, between Loire and Pyrenees), which is to say: artist(e). Who knows the round dance goes to the lab.[91]

Benn's seemingly distanced, provocative, and perhaps pert style comes off almost as an excuse for reverting to the medieval troubadours in order to place his own poetic practices within the tradition of the European lyric, and also geographically in Provence, where he had travelled about two decades before writing this fragment about making poetry.

In one sense, Benn travelled extensively; but, apart from brief professional trips, a few seemingly luxurious escapes to Paris and the French Atlantic and Mediterranean coasts, and two major military displacements – to Brussels in the First World War and to Landsberg/Warthe (now Gorzów Wielkopolski to which Christa Wolf refers, mentioning Benn, in her *Kindheitsmuster*) in the Second World War – he did so primarily in his imaginative writing. Upon first reading Benn's poetry and poetic prose, I was reminded of T.S. Eliot's phrase "suspended in time, between pole and tropic," and also struck by the toponymic density in Benn's texts, feeling as if I were dreaming upon maps and landscapes – an idea, as it turns out, not entirely fanciful in light of the poet's own musings upon books and paintings in Berlin libraries and galleries.[92] The titles of some fifty early poems published in the slim volume *Frühe Lyrik und Dramen* (Early Poetry and Plays)[93] contain few references to time (only birth, youth, hour, night, and death can be categorized as such) but more than twenty explicit references to place and landscape. Most of these places Benn did not know from direct experience; rather, he wrote of locales he never visited or viewed.

It is extremely arduous to find any text by Benn that does not contain some reference to place – that is not built on the radiant visionary power of toponymical adventures. Already in this early collection, Benn's topographical spectrum is both wide-ranging and intense, comprising cornfields, poppy fields, graves, woods, and beaches, as well as the morgue, the hospital, the night café, and the national library – all components of the acutely perceived and well-remembered plains of his northeastern German homeland (to which he refers time and again as "norddeutsche Ebene") as well as the urban cityscape of his residence as a medical doctor in Berlin. The German town Jena turns up as well, once visited by Benn's mother, who was captivated at the time by the landscape of the valley, and wrote a panoramic postcard home, whose mnemonic horizons Benn extends by transforming them into his autobiographical poem "Jena" – a psychological study of his mother's disposition and aesthetic appreciation of place, as well as of the card's modest paper and material quality.[94]

This familiar and affectively charged Jena, however, is in stark contrast to "Alaska" and "East Africa," which, in spite of their actual existence in the world and their representations on maps, are mental entities for Benn with a heightened exotic potential, psychic urges visualized in poetic words, imaginative horizons, and oneiric stimuli, places he dissects without any intention of visiting them. While Benn's travels are dealt with as the famously limited affair he insistently held them to be, the discussions of this putative absence, both critical and autobiographical, as well as of his unequivocal dislike of touring, are not. Ursula Ziebarth relates how Benn's poetic colouring of white and hibiscus-red ("weiß und hibiskusrot") was a powerful motivation for her to travel to Cuba to discover Caribbean hues rather than the dead-snow-white and alive-blood-red of Benn's *poiein*. "Meinen Sie, aus Habana, / weiß und hibiskusrot, / bräche ein ewiges Manna / für Ihre Wüstennot?" asks Benn satirically in stanza two of "Reisen": Do you think from Havana, white and hibiscus-red, an eternal manna would break loose to soothe your desert-urge?[95] In the fourth stanza, he calls travelling a poetically and personally irrelevant experience. In German, the etymologies of travelling, *fahren*, and experiencing, *erfahren*, suggest an intimate connection between what Benn considers, in a rather anti-Goethean and un-

Nietzschean manner, to be two absolutely unrelated forms of existence.

This captures a key point about the ubiquity of places in Benn's imaginative acts of naming: it is not his factual staying or going that matters most, but his belief in the concentration of creative energy in a displaced name as quasi-painterly image, which in turn is reminiscent of Eliot's dislocation of language into meaning, as well as of Freud's condensation and displacement as dream work's major ways of operation.

While Freud brings up Nietzsche only rarely and casually (and never quite names Liguria), Benn celebrates Nietzsche and is spellbound – more than Nietzsche and Freud together – by the toponym "Liguria" itself, which speaks, among other things, to Benn's regressive interest in all sorts of Ur, including his poem "Urgesicht" (which was translated as "Primal Vision" and also supplied the title for E.B. Ashton's edition of Benn's *Selected Writings*),[96] as well as to his frequent celebration of Nietzsche's expressions and abodes. Nietzsche's presence in Benn is neither subtle nor uncanny. While Benn's creative topographical spectrum ranges "from pole to tropic," in Eliot's phrase, his particular obsession is with Nietzsche's Liguria (broadly defined and including Provence, the Côte d'Azur, and especially the segment called the Côte Bleue, close to Marseilles, also known as the Calanques, from the Provençal *calanco*: steep) as a foreign land and language. Benn enthusiastically refers to Nietzsche's "Ausrufe aus Nizza und Portofino" (exclamations from Nice and Portofino) and to Nietzsche's "Welle und Spiel" (wave and play), celebrates what he classifies as Nietzsche's "Provenzalische und Ligurische" (Provençal and Ligurian principles), and calls him his era's "Erdbeben" (earthquake) and "seit Luther das größte deutsche Sprachgenie" (the greatest genius of the German language since Luther). Nietzsche's restlessness and, in particular, his Ligurian wanderings were decisive in stirring up Benn's firm stances against dislocation, on the one hand, and for "Ligurian complexes" conjured up in more permanent abodes, on the other.[97]

The extent of Benn's exposure to the Mediterranean is rather elusive. There is evidence that he visited the Côte d'Azur in the interwar period, but the French Riviera has not been a part of Italy since 1860. Scholars have repeatedly claimed that Benn was not only not a traveller, but that he did not travel to Italy (Paul Requadt and Peter Lingens, among others) – dubious claims when one considers his impressive mastery of self-fashioning. He indulged in variants of the (post-)Romantic *topoi* of loneliness and introspection, while obsessively addressing the necessity of avoiding travel at all costs. Benn actually travelled a fair bit, however, including in Italy – on Lake Garda (Benn admits to Gabriele D'Annunzio's influence on him) and in the Alpine Meran – albeit late in his life and not in Italy's central regions.[98] In all likelihood, he did not see the Italian Mediterranean, but then it is impossible to give evidence for something that (allegedly) did not happen (the same holds true for Freud's absence from Provence).

Benn's fascination with and knowledge about the Mediterranean stem from Homer and the Bible, as well as from Goethe and Nietzsche. For Benn, however, it is the olive rather than the citrus that becomes an emblem of his southerly invention. Even though Benn was acquainted with the rare Ligurian species of olive called the Taggiasca (from the town Taggia on the Riviera di Ponente), known for its intense, aromatic, oil-rich deep violet pulp, he does not visit the olive; the olive visits him. Unlike Goethe's lemons, Benn's olive is not a symbol of longing but an emblem of agency. In 1919, the same year in which Freud elaborated on the uncanny ("Das Unheimliche") as that which is secretly familiar, Benn returned to the phrase "da geschah ihm die Olive" (then the olive befell him) as he had first coined it in the preceding Rönne prose in 1916, in his "Schöpferische Konfession" ("Creative Confession"), a concise poetological entry in which he inaugurated his poetics of "Ligurian complexes." It is important to emphasize that an olive befalling or overtaking the subject is significantly different from an olive tree standing in front of him or even his gaze falling on an olive tree; according to Benn even the article should be dropped, so that the expression "da geschah ihm Olive" (then olive befell him) is the only one with the poetic potential to unfold into a powerful complex that evokes silent, silver olive groves as well as the painstaking olive harvest and the celebration of the first press, while suggesting an analogy between olive and poem (or olive and poetic forms of sheer beauty, hard work, and eventual celebration). At the end of *The Birthday*, Benn explicitly mentions such an "Ernte" (harvest).[99]

Ligurian complexes are formally reflected in Benn's writing as they are in Nietzsche and Freud's, in that his texts are poetic, esoteric, and liberating; they also make their appearance in a wealth of proper and improper nouns that range from "Tyrrhenian islands," "Tyrrhenian Sea," and what Benn terms the Ligurian Sea's "sacrilegious Blue," to "Ponente," "Portofino," "Ligurian complexe(s)," "Ligurian notions," "Ligurian Sea," and the specifically Ligurian "Taggiasca" olive, from Giovanni Domenico Ruffini's native land. Van Gogh's Provence also enters the scene in *Der Garten von Arles*, a novella in the series of prose pieces on which Benn bases his first poetological formulation of the Ligurian complex in 1919, the year, incidentally (or not), not only of Sem Benelli's baptism of the *Golfo dei Poeti* and the Futurist exhibition in Genoa, but also of of Hermann Hesse's *Demian*, Franz Kafka's *In der Strafkolonie*, August Stramm's "Patrouille," T.S. Eliot's "Hamlet" and "Tradition and the Individual Talent," as well as of the murders of Karl Liebknecht and Rosa Luxemburg, the beginning of the Weimar Republic, the founding of the Bauhaus, Claude Monet's *Water Lily Pond*, and Sigmund Freud's "Das Unheimliche."

Most probably Benn never set eyes on Liguria, and he likely saw the Mediterranean only a few times, when accompanying a Berlin art dealer to France in the 1920s. Benn had expressed his major poetic challenge as that of the "Ligurian complex" in 1919, which is to say before he saw the Mediterranean in the south of France, while avoiding Italian-Ligurian terrain entirely. Even if we accept that Benn was allegedly not much of a traveller, but preferred visiting galleries, museums, and libraries to actual exposure and dislocation, we find that when he did travel, his tastes tended to the luxurious — from the magnificence of the French freeways to what the Mann siblings later called the Côte's "Champagnerseligkeit" (champagne bliss).

"The Côte d'Azur," to recall Will Self, "isn't really a place at all – more a state of mind stretched out over hundreds of kilometers of beaches, headlands, outcrops, fish restaurants, walled villas and foul-tempered chiens. This sun-soaked coastline is like the strap of a bikini, suntan-oiled then teased by the imagination."[100] This portrait of the intrinsic character of place, body, and their relationship with psyche very much relies on the latent evocative power that place names hold. Granted, Self's stimulating assessment occurs about eight decades after Benn's four extensive interwar journeys to Paris, the Atlantic, and the French Mediterranean, as well as after his coining of the phrase "Ligurian complex." However, the psychogeographic potential that Self opens up between a place, its name, and one's state of mind and imaginative *teasing* strikes me as curiously responsive to the toponymic density that marks Benn's writing in particular. His spectrum of place names ranges from Alaska to Palau, with a clear emphasis on the Mediterranean-Tyrrhenian-Ligurian-Provençal-Côte d'Azurean complex, and is more often than not marked by this very exotic-erotic desire that Self presents in his provocative twist of the time-honoured *topos* of *genius loci*.

Will Self is a long-distance walker with, like Nietzsche, the capacity to develop an intimate relationship with place. Benn, by contrast, is no aesthete of perambulation. Rather, he stylized himself as a post-Romantic artist who prefers, allegedly, to stay put. The critical discussions of Benn's putative non-journeying, as well as Benn's own pronouncements against touring, are legion. However ambivalent and at times secretive (even repressive) his writings about his travels may be, he nevertheless commented at length in *Frankreich und Wir* (*France and Us*) on his four extensive journeys to France, as follows:

> Ich habe seit dem Krieg vier größere Reisen durch Frankreich gemacht, sowohl nach Paris wie in die Provinz. Zwei von ihnen waren Autofahrten, mehrere Wochen dauernd, zahlreiche tausend Kilometer fuhren wir auf den prachtvollen Routes nationales, glatt wie Billards, geteert, staublos, den besten Autostraßen des Kontinents, und nicht weniger auf den schwierigeren Nebenstraßen. Wir fuhren kreuz und quer durch das Land, vom Mittelmeer zum Atlantik, von Palavas bis Arcachon, von Longwy bis Hendaye und von Jeumont nach Perpignan, wir durchfuhren die Argonnen und Pyrenäen, wir berührten die Provinzen seines keltischen, seines baskischen und seines ligurischen Bluts. Wir wohnten in den großen Hotels, um die die Golfplätze liegen … Hotels, Restaurants, … Strand … Bars … Kaufläden … wir machten geschäftliche, ärztliche, persönliche Bekanntschaften …
>
> (Since the end of the war I have embarked on four extensive journeys through France, to Paris as well as to the provinces. Two of these were road trips which lasted a couple of weeks, and we drove thousands of kilometres on the magnificent *Routes nationales*, as smooth as billiard tables, tarred, dust-free, the best roads on the continent, and we drove no less on the more demanding back roads. We criss-crossed the country from the Mediterranean to the Atlantic Ocean, from Palavas to Arcachon, from Longwy to Hendaye and from Jeumont to Perpignan; we crossed the Argonnes and the Pyrenees, we touched the provinces of France's Celtic, Basque and Ligurian blood. We stayed in the grand hotels surrounded by golf courses … hotels, restaurants, … beach … bars … shops … We picked up with people on business, medical and personal grounds …)[101]

The unenthusiastic reception of Benn's work abroad, particularly in the Anglo-American world (he has been received well in Italy), might be a consequence not only of Benn's flirtation with early Nazism (a consequence which forecloses the compelling discussion of Benn's paradoxical move into inner emigration from 1935 on) but also of the absence of an English edition of Benn's complete body of work – a curious ellipsis, which, in turn, may be the result of the notorious difficulties Benn's intensely condensed poetical and prose texts pose in their unique density of geopoetic toponomy, evocative neologisms, and intriguing nominal constructions.

From 1935 on, when Benn's exclusion from literary life in Berlin began, his tasks as a military doctor included the establishment of files about military injuries and suicides. From 1938 on, Benn's writings were prohibited. Benn continued to write in inner emigration, and his 1941 poem "Monolog" ("Monologue"), which is an unequivocal rejection of Nazi barbarism, was written secretly and published privately twice, before its wider, public distribution in 1950. Initially, Benn introduced his "Monologue" to a pen-friend by camouflaging it as his translation of a fragment of medieval English. However, Benn's English was minimal at best, and his attempt at masking clearly not well conceived.

Even though the monologue is for Benn the mystified form of the poem as such (the poem as monologue, perhaps as prayer, as a language event rather than as situational or even communicative text), the absent audience takes on a heightened dimension in this specific context of Benn's (not so) silent words against Fascist terror, combining, in his double life, external assimilation with the art of soliloquy, while reverting to the verbal brutality of his Expressionist beginnings in *Morgue*. Here, Benn poetically phrases the dilemma between death/suicide versus action/resistance before his eventual celebration of dreams and visions, solitude, and an augmented art of post-Nietzschean Ligurian *poiein* as located above and beyond an impasse such as this.

Benn's invention of Rönne as the persona in uniform and protagonist of his First World War novellas coincides with his composition of night café poems and is the result of a creative mind under a variety of influences, ranging from cocaine and the army to the brothel and F.T. Marinetti. *Der Geburtstag* (*The Birthday*), the last of five Rönne novellas (located between *Die Reise* and *Die Insel*), is an autobiographical piece written in 1916, in which Benn's inscription of his *alter ego* Rönne's troubling midlife challenges the *topos*, as it explosively collides with Futurism's love of youthful force and reckless bravery – a collision that Benn experienced at the peak of his career as an Expressionist writer at that precise moment. In line with Benn's naming of Nietzsche rather than Freud as the inventor of psychoanalysis ("die ganze Psychoanalyse, der ganze Existentialismus, alles dies ist [Nietzsche's] Tat"/ all of psychoanalysis, all of existentialism, all of this has indeed been Nietzsche's doing),[102] Rönne opposes what could have come close to being a Freudian cure (certainly for Rönne and potentially even for Benn), and, opposing action, allows for things to befall him (including the olive).

Benn composed this series of subversive novellas while stationed in Brussels as a military doctor in the First World War. These novellas are written in an outlandish syntax, pervaded, in Nietzschean manner, by the exclamatory mode and an extraordinary punctuation, and rich in evocation through outré compounds and bizarre neologisms (all embedded in a southerly exoticized atmosphere of saffron fields, cinnamon woods, olive groves, islands, oranges and sycamores). It is in this multilayered Expressionist experiment that Benn brings his early poetics to full fruition, inscribing the simultaneity of free-floating nouns at a time when Italian Futurism was in full swing.

In 1919, following his inscription of Rönne, Benn also presents a poetics that returns to his earlier prose and declares the poet's rejection of the word as logical construct in favour of the word as trigger of associations. "Creative Confession" is symptomatic of his ongoing commitment to unsanctioned creativity and unprecedented explosion, which traditional aesthetics and institutionalized art, the bourgeoisie, and eventually Fascism would not so willingly embrace. In it, he lays the foundation for his lifelong Expressionist aesthetics of Ligurian complexes, southerly words, intriguing neologisms, and puzzling compounds, of free associations and a Futurist anti-grammar of the noun: Sea and desert, harbour and olive, pub and tavern, potions and poppies have happened to a Rönne who is drunk on life, who associates freely, and who expresses himself in radical analogies, as Benn recalls in this confessional retrospective on creativity three years later.

As an aesthetic program (or poetology), "Creative Confession" also demonstrates Benn's early experimentation with genre. He writes cryptic prose to poetically approach an explanation of his creative stance by way of a retrospective confession, which is interspersed with quotations from two of his autobiographically informed First World War novellas collected as *Gehirne* (*Brains*) – *Der Geburtstag* and *Querschnitt* (*Cross-section*).[103] Benn unveils an early pessimism with regard to reality, while installing his artistic existentialism by confirming his continuous interest in the mnemonic dynamics of the creative mind.

Gottfried Benn: "Schöpferische Konfession"
Ich finde nämlich in mir selber keine Kunst, sondern nur in der gleichen biologisch gebundenen Gegenständlichkeit wie Schlaf oder Ekel die Auseinandersetzung mit dem einzigen Problem, vor dem ich stehe, es ist das Problem des *südlichen Worts*. Wie ich es einmal versucht habe darzustellen in der Novelle "Der Geburtstag" (Gehirne); da schrieb ich: "da geschah ihm die Olive," nicht: da stand vor ihm die Olive, nicht: da fiel sein Blick

auf eine Olive, sondern: da geschah sie ihm, wobei allerdings der Artikel noch besser unterbliebe. Also, da geschah ihm "Olive" und hinströmt die in Frage stehende Struktur über der Früchte Silber, ihre leisen Wälder, ihre Ernte und ihr Kelterfest.

Oder an einer anderen Stelle derselben Novelle: "groß glühte heran der Hafenkomplex," nicht: da schritt er an den Hafen, nicht: da dachte er an einen Hafen, sondern: groß glühte er als Motiv heran, mit den Kuttern, mit den Strandbordellen, der Meere Uferlos, der Wüste Glanz.

Oder in einer anderen Novelle schreibe ich weichliche Freudengrüße über "Anemonenwald." Allen Leichtsinn, alle Wehmut, alle Hoffnungslosigkeit des Geistes enthülle ich oder trachte ich zu enthüllen als Schichten dieses Querschnittes von Begriff. Da sollte einer sein, der ging durch diese kleinen Blumen, im Wald, durch die verwehenden Gebilde, er dachte, das ist noch nicht so weit, wir brauchen uns noch nicht so zu beunruhigen, es ist ja bis zum Abschluß noch sehr weit, dies ist nur "zwischen den Stämmen feines, kleines Kraut; anderes würde kommen bis in das Unendliche hinein, Anemonenwälder und über sie hinaus Narzissenwiesen, aller Kelche Rauch und Qualm, im Ölbaum blühte der Wind und über Marmorstufen stieg, verschlungen, in eine Weite die Erfüllung." – Dann aber nach Jahren, eben des Lebens Jahren, sah er, "dies war der Anemonenwald gewesen, um ihn gebreitet, am Saum den Hauch."

Mich sensationiert eben das Wort ohne jede Rücksicht auf seinen beschreibenden Charakter rein als assoziatives Motiv und dann empfinde ich ganz gegenständlich seine Eigenschaft des logischen Begriffs als den Querschnitt durch kondensierte Katastrophen. Und da ich nie Personen sehe, sondern immer nur das Ich, und nie Geschehnisse, sondern immer nur das Dasein (Da-sein), da ich keine Kunst kenne und keinen Glauben, keine Wissenschaft und keine Mythe, sondern immer nur die *Bewußtheit*, ewig sinnlos, ewig qualbestürmt, – so ist es im Grunde diese, gegen die ich mich wehre, mit der südlichen Zermalmung, und sie, die ich abzuleiten trachte in ligurische Komplexe bis zur Überhöhung oder bis zum Verlöschen im Außersich des Rausches oder des Vergehens.

(For what I find within myself is not art. Much rather, and in forms similar to the biologically bound concreteness of sleep or disgust, I am internally confronted with the examination of the single creative problem that I am facing – the problem of the *southerly word*. What I mean is what I once tried to portray in the novella "The Birthday" (Brains), where I wrote: "Then the olive befell him." Not: Then the olive stood before him; and not: Then his gaze fell upon an olive, but rather: then it befell him. And as a matter of fact, even the article should be dropped; thus "olive" befell him, and the structure here in question pours out over the olives' silver sheen, the silent olive groves, their harvest, and the celebration of the first press.

Or as I put it in another passage of the same novella: "Grand and ardent drew nigh the harbour-complex." Not: He then strode down to the harbour; and not: He then thought of a harbour, but rather: Grand and ardent it drew nigh as a motif, with its cutters and beach brothels, the sea's boundlessness, the desert's gleam.

What I am saying is reminiscent also of another novella, in which I have written of soft exclamations of joy about "anemone-woods." I am here unveiling (or attempting to unveil) every carelessness, every wistfulness, every hopelessness of the mind as strata visible in the cross-section of a term. There should be somebody to tread softly through these small flower patches in the woods, over their scattering formations, he pondered, it is not quite finished yet, no need for us to worry, it is still a very long way to the end. This is merely "delicate small herbage between the tree trunks, other kinds would come and reach into infinity, anemone-woods, and above and beyond them narcissus-meadows, all the chalices' fume and agonies, in the olive tree the wind bloomed, and over marble stairs fulfilment rose, entwined, into a distance." – Then, however, years later, years of his life later, he understood: "These had been the anemone-woods, spread all around him, breeze at their edges."

It is without any consideration of its descriptive character and purely as an associative motif that the word simply fills me with sensations. And then I sense absolutely concretely its quality of the logical term as the cross-section through condensed catastrophes. And since I never see others, but always only the I, and never see events, but always only existence (Da-sein), since I know of no art and no faith, no science and no myth, but always only of *awareness*, eternally senseless, eternally excruciating, it is in a sense this very awareness against which I defend myself by means of a southerly devastation. It is this awareness which I am striving to divert into Ligurian complexes, to the point of exorbitance, or of dissolution in a frenzy of ecstasy or transience.)[104]

Benn's Modernist commitment to a trans-mimetic and anti-Romantic construction goes hand in hand with the destruction of Realist and Naturalist traditions. His *Ligurian complexes* run parallel to T.S. Eliot's *objetive correlatives* and Ezra Pound's *images*, in that objects (words, images) poetically condense, enclose, and augment subjectivity and validate awareness by diverting it into Modernist aesthetic significance.

Besides the Berlin art dealer who in the 1920s took Benn with him to Paris and around France, including famous locales on the Mediterranean coast such as Marseilles and Hyères,[105] the globetrotter Ursula Ziebarth, a committed collector and fascinating (travel) writer, is likely the only person to persuade Benn to travel in later life. She tells the story of their journey to Lake Constance in the mid-1950s, where they followed in Goethe's putative footsteps. They also closely examined prison gates and monastery windows in Constance, as well as the former abode and deathbed in Meersburg of the nineteenth-century poet Anette von Droste-Hülshoff. Benn was strongly attracted to Droste's myopia (incidentally, Goethe was also myopic), a condition he understood as intimately related to her physiological impressionism (which Benn related to Nietzsche's increasing loss of sight as well). In Benn's mind, myopia is a form of concentration that necessarily cuts out any sort of distraction.

Intrigued by the monastic aspects of Droste's life in the castle at Meersburg (which overlooks Lake Constance as Freud's Miramare overlooks the Adriatic, and Nietzsche's Èze the Mediterranean Sea), as well as by her myopia, Benn entered into an intra-poetic dialogue with her. "Er hatte etwas gemeinsam mit der Toten, von der ihn ein Jahrhundert trennte," writes Ziebarth; "tief, tief trunkene Flut hatte sie gesagt und er hatte geantwortet mit trunkene Flut, trance- und traumgefleckt" (He had something in common with the dead poet, from whom he was separated by a century: deeply drunken tide, she had written, and he had answered: drunken tide, trance- and dream-chequered).[106] Benn and Ziebarth also travelled to the Abbey Library in the Swiss Saint Gall, convincingly combining the obvious physical movement of travel with Benn's profound interest in monastic stasis, learning, vision, and concentration.

By inspired study and careful research, Benn does some justice to the names he poeticizes, which are the source rather than the consequence of his extensive literary topographies. His ongoing geopoetically informed reflections on the existential conditions of writing become evident in his plea for monastic robes, and disclose his admiration for self-disciplined concentration as well as material modesty (to which Kenneth White points as well).[107] The attention paid to a variety of ascetic and hermetic scenes can be understood as one way of analysing his own life of working and writing in small rooms, and is reminiscent of Nietzsche: poets are, according to Benn, "Einzimmerbewohner" (one-room-inhabitants),[108] and he traces a straight line from monastic ascetic solitude to art: "Einsamkeit, Askese, Mönchstum – Kunst" (solitude, asceticism, monasticism — art).[109] All of Benn's rooms had very limited views, but were consistently inhabited by a mind embarking on journeys that others had or might have experienced before him: Goethe and Nietzsche first and foremost, but also van Gogh, Gauguin, and Joseph Conrad, among others.

Nietzsche's restlessness and his Ligurian wanderings were decisive factors in stirring up or at least confirming Benn's stance against such disruptive dislocations, and stand in intimate connection with the Ligurian complexes conjured up in Benn's permanent residences. Both Ziebarth and Peter Lingens refer to the unparalleled importance of Jens Peter Jacobsen's *Niels Lyhne* in this context as Benn's lifelong novelistic companion (incidentally, Italophile Rainer Maria Rilke was an avid reader of *Niels Lyhne* as well). The protagonist is a poet who writes little and travels much – a habit that hinders his much-desired escape from his own condition, and also hampers his creativity and imaginative output. Niels's conversation with the visual artist Erik Refstrup, who had invited him to visit (a favour that found immediate accommodation in Niels's schedule), inquires into the whereabouts of the muse. The failed poet's reply is naturally that writerly genius is intimately bound up with the new impressions that travel offers. While this was certainly true for another author whom Benn greatly admired, Joseph Conrad, who set sail from Marseilles (and later settled in England to write his stories of the sea in English, which was not his native tongue — this linguistically exilic mode of composition fascinated Benn), Erik's eventual assessment of Niels's situation in chapter eleven of Jacobsen's novel states the opposite: talented people who insistently search for new travel impressions ended up losing poetic inspiration altogether: "They travelled, Niels, looking for new impressions. That was their obsession. The South, the Orient, it was all in vain, it all glanced off them like off a mirror."[110] Not even a mimetic outcome is achieved after such escapist travel, according to Jacobsen's novel, not to mention a more Modernist variant of creative expression.

The Benn paradox one needs to highlight, however, is that it is precisely this novel, with its embedded revelations about the anti-art of travel, that the mature Benn habitually took with him when he did travel: "er pflegte das Bändchen mitzunehmen auf Reisen" (he used to bring this little volume along on trips),[111] according to Ziebarth. It seems as if Benn carried with him a written confirmation of his own wavering belief, almost as an act of self-defence or at the least a preventive reminder. Related to this contradiction, which seems to hold Benn back while at the same time letting him move on and away, is the more delicate question of how exactly Benn's inner emigration relates to his purported avoidance of any form of displacement – an antipathy that was partly responsible for the blind spots in his poetic Ligurian alibi and that cannot be excused only by Benn's preference for "staying put," even though it is closely related to it.

This becomes particularly evident when one looks at how the poet does not end his "inner emigration" at the end of the Second World War, but rather intensifies it into the very metaphysics of absolute expression, to which his *Statische Gedichte* and *Fragmente* bear witness. Benn's "Schutzdach Platane" (plane tree, protective roof), a phrase from "Mediterran," a poem written in 1927 after his journeys to France, seems to have announced in an untimely manner what the Mediterranean myth and the Ligurian complex were increasingly to imply later on.[112]

Critics tend to agree that what Benn takes from Nietzsche is the desire to affirm existence through the potential of artistic creation – an assertion prefigured in Nietzsche's Ligurian writings ranging from *Dawn* and *The Gay Science* (including the *Songs of Prince Vogelfrei*) to *Zarathustra*. That this aesthetic potential, however, is not just broadly southern (nor exclusively southerly) – even though Benn's poetry might run that risk in that it ranges from Peru to Palau to the Mediterranean and the Caribbean – but strictly Provençal and Ligurian is a point that seems to have escaped Benn scholars despite the fact that Benn put great emphasis on Nietzsche's "Provenzalische und Ligurische" (Provençal and Ligurian principles)[113] as an explosion of poetic forces that transcends thematic approaches on the one hand and literary longing on the other.

Two Italian critics are worth noting as exceptions to this oversight: Marco Meli, in an examination of Provence and Benn, and Lia Secci in a brief assessment of Benn and Liguria. Meli traces the static limitation and solitude of Benn's *alter ego* Werff Rönne in Brussels during the First World War, showing how Benn's mental landscapes become increasingly southern French; Secci, by contrast, whose short, unpaginated contribution unfortunately abounds with errors in German, draws no distinction between Benn's singular and plural use of (the) Ligurian complex(es), but nevertheless provides the only piece, that directly addresses the inspirational energies of the actual Ligurian landscape (Tigullio, ports, olives, agaves) and its neighbour Provence. Speaking of the "sublimazione estetica del paesaggio mediterraneo" (aesthetic sublimation of the Mediterranean landscape), Secci chronologically explores Benn between 1910 and the 1920s, including his practical deployment of the Ligurian complex in the late poem "Mittelmeerisch."[114]

It is with reference to Provence / the Côte d'Azur / Liguria that Benn's toponymic art is not based on invention exclusively – in part because Provence and Liguria are neither Kokomo nor Orplid but actual cultural landscapes; in part because Benn adopts them from two contemporary artists, a philosopher-poet and a painter, both of whom experienced and cherished these lands *in situ* and repeatedly praised their qualities of colour, light, and air. Vincent van Gogh is, next to Nietzsche, Benn's most evident intertext. Of van Gogh Benn writes in the novella *Der Garten von Arles* (The Garden at Arles): "Und Sonnenblumen [...] immer wieder Sonnenblumen. Er wußte es, stand er auf, er wußte es, der in der Provence malte unter jenem Himmel über Oliven und Wein. Er malte, er war besessen von Unerinnerlichkeit" (And sunflowers, time and again sunflowers. He knew it when he got up, he knew it, he who painted in Provence under those skies above olives and vines. He painted, he was obsessed with unrememberability).[115]

While Benn himself repeatedly and explicitly named Goethe and Nietzsche as his most influential precursors, he fictionally inscribed van Gogh as a character in his Rönne novella *Der Garten von Arles*, where he referred to the painter not by name but as "der Idiot von Arles" (the idiot from Arles),[116] an obvious reference to van Gogh's fall into madness in Provence. Benn shared with Nietzsche and van Gogh the northern upbringing and the cultivation of solitude in Protestant homes,[117] and thus felt some affinity with both Nietzsche and van Gogh's eventual escapes into madness. This becomes clear when, in a typical combination of nostalgia and cynicism, Benn speaks of his own brain as injured ("lädiertes Gehirn").

Benn's principal engagement is with poetic form, which I regard as a place where Nietzsche's philosophy of language and geopoetic Expressionism and van Gogh's proto-poetic painterly representation (van Gogh also wrote poetry) are able to meet on the grounds of approximating solidity of verbal form in an act of borrowing light and colour as well as Van Gogh's intuitive line as the crucial elements of painterly composition.

In spite of his professed antipathy to travel, Benn did visit Provence and the Côte d'Azur, and knew their troubadour tradition as well as he knew their qualities of light and colour.[118] It is crucial to discern that, while Benn repeatedly refers in French (his mother's native tongue and thus close to Benn's heart) to the *Mediterrannée* as his poetic dreamland, he conceives of Liguria (which, as far as we know, he did not see) as a marine horizon rather than a steep land, emphasizing its horizontal sea rather than the vertical lines of its sculpted topography. It is, however, more than a "südliche Horizontale, die den Blick schweifen läßt gegen die nördliche Vertikale in ihrer Starrheit" (a southern horizon that allows the glance to ramble in the face of a rigid northern verticality),[119] as the second stnza of Benn's "Reise" (1916) in its vertically unhemmed horizon makes clear:

Das Auge tief am Horizont,
Der keine Vertikale kennt.
Schon schwindet der Verknüpfungsdrang.
Schon löst sich das Bezugssystem.
Unter unter dunklem Haut-Gesang
Erhebt sich Blut-Methusalem.

(The eye deep at the horizon, unaware of any verticality. The urge towards connections vanishes instantly, the system of coordinates dissolves, and under dark skin-song arises blood-Methusaleh.)[120]

While his seas do provide what Lacroix calls *un horizon aux désirs*, Benn's presentation of such an engulfing horizontality curiously includes Methuselah as a "rising" Ur-ancestor, who is one on an entire spectrum of associative Ur-presences in Benn. These range from runes and lures to lemurs (*Lemuren* means both prosimians and spirits of the dead – a coincidence that is typical of Benn's sense of humour), to tellurian and Ligurian. Ur-words contain their opposites (Freud, Jakobson), and are located on the vertical, metaphorical axis of selection rather than the horizontal, metonymical axis of combination. Further "horizon" and "aphorism" share the same etymology, from the Greek *horizein* ("to bound"); it would surely be difficult to call Nietzsche's aphoristic composition horizontal or flat (a meaning that "horizontal" acquired late in its history), as in Goethe's distribution of prosaic plains versus poetic verticality. Incidentally, *Gebundene Rede* means "poetry" (and Benn's "Reise" clearly forms a bounded speech, part of this category). The beginning of this poem invents a marine dream scene, while its ending thematizes grammatical hierarchy and logical conjunction *ex negativo*, as spatial coordinates dissolved. Nietzsche's Liguria is vertical and insular but offers an outlook upon the open sea and its horizons. And while Benn's Ligurian poetics are in one sense horizontally oriented and conceive of the vertical dimension as a cerebral burden of logic and rational authority that has to be overcome by whatever means possible, "Reise" ends with an excursion into biblical naming, and it is Noah's ancestor Methusaleh, along with Peru and the various dreams of the South Sea, that Benn borrows from Paul Gauguin's book *Avant et après,* written in 1903 in Atuana on the Marquesas.[121]

Benn was clearly familiar with this work of Gauguin's, and quoted from it (albeit without indicating the exact source) in relation to van Gogh: "A Arles, les quais, les ponts et les bateaux, tout le midi devenait pour lui [van Gogh] la Hollande" (In Arles the piers, the bridges and the boats, the entire south became Holland to him), writes Gauguin, who had decided to abruptly end his brief friendship with van Gogh and subsequently openly ridiculed his former friend. Benn recapitulates:

> Gauguin schreibt an einer Stelle über van Gogh: "In Arles wurde alles – Quais, Brücken und Schiffe, der ganze Süden – Holland für ihn." In diesem Sinne wird für den Lyriker alles, was geschieht, Holland, nämlich: Wort, Wortwurzel, Wortfolge, Verbindung von Worten; Silben werden psychoanalysiert, Diphtonge umgeschult, Konsonanten transplantiert; für ihn ist das Wort real und magisch, ein moderner Totem.
>
> (Gauguin writes somewhere about van Gogh: "In Arles, the quays, the bridges, the boats, the entire south became Holland to him." In this sense everything that happens becomes Holland to the poet, namely: word, verbal root, verbal sequence, connection of words; syllables are psychoanalysed, diphthongs retrained, consonants transplanted; for the poet the word is at once real and magical: a modern totem.)[122]

This passage immediately follows Benn's statements about the troubadours and their art of *trobar* as located between "Finden" (finding) and "Erfinden" (invention), and unravels much about the poetic word in Benn's conception – not only as proper name, but as an entity with a life of its own. It is also reminiscent of Benn's coining of the "Ligurian complex" and shows a clear connection between poetic language, literary *topoi,* and geopoetic writing in Benn's sense as well. Further, it is yet another occasion on which Benn deploys concepts that thoroughly intrigued Freud – here it is the totem; earlier it was the complex; at other times, hypercathexis (an additional charge of instinctual energy), repetition compulsion, and neuroses (which he hilariously rhymes with the mimosas at Cannes: *Neurosen – Mimosen*), as well as the dream as a form of poetry, with which Benn is even more obsessed than Freud.

Benn clearly sees van Gogh's perception and artistic deployment of Provence's clarity of light, purity of form, and brilliance of colour (yellow and blue in particular), which the Dutch painter had perceived in

those Arlesian gardens and Provençal lands that Benn decides to poeti-
cize in his own realms of textual imagination. Here, the poet studies the
painter, whose work ranges from sunflower still lifes to olive trees, and
on to expressive renderings of a burnt landscape scoured by the Mistral,
imprinting not only its glory but also the violent heat and harsh winds
of the climate in quasi-archaeological patterns, which turn the inside
out and are strongly evocative of Liguria's erosive imagery and difficult
beauty as well.

"Haben wir noch die Kraft," asks Benn with a ring of doubt, "die Bilder
tieferer Welten zu entwerfen?" (do we still have the strength to invent
images of deeper worlds?). Benn's work of the 1930s explicitly reacts
to Nietzsche's Ligurian-Mediterranean, turning it into his "Mythe Mittelmeer,"[123] which stands in stark contrast to his "keine Mythe" of 1919.
Nietzsche lived a significant part of the 1880s on the Italian and French
Rivieras, almost exactly at the same time as van Gogh's Arlesian sojourns
in Provence. Nietzsche comments less on Goethe's modes of fascination
than on his own physical ease in experiencing Genoa and San Remo
on the Riviera di Ponente, and Rapallo and Portofino on the Riviera di
Levante, and eventually Nice on the French Riviera (Côte d'Azur).

Benn, by contrast, cannot rely on an Italian journey of his own (his
whistle stops in Merano and on Lake Garda happen late in his life). As a
military doctor he writes his *alter ego* Rönne's Provençal Arles into existence and realizes that the olive befalls him – Rönne, for whom the body
is hardly Nietzschean-Ligurian air, health, and walking, serving the mind
and freeing the imagination, but rather stench, decay, and mutilation
as the consequences of war and disease, endangering the mind on the
threshold that is Rönne's/Benn's.

Benn is well read rather than well travelled, and decides for Ligurian
modes and troubadour principles that render agency to place, botany,
and landscape, as the perfect mental climes for his aesthetic, refusing to
represent what he could have seen had he been willing (as he was not)
to venture beyond the French border (in contrast to Freud, who did not
venture to cross the Italian border). Benn does not visit the Italian Liguria but celebrates it as Nietzsche's terrain of choice and counterweight
to Christian morality (to which Benn refers as Nazarene as opposed
to the Provençal), while Freud visits Liguria but represses the fact that
Nietzsche had been there before him (Freud circumvents Provence as
Benn circumvents Liguria).[124]

Benn makes an enormous effort to acquire a profound reading knowledge of his densely poeticized Ligurian regions:

Ich versuchte von Berlin aus mit Hilfe von Bildern und Steinen in den Museen und den Büchern aus den Leih- und Staatsbibliotheken hinüberzuäugen in die beschenkteren Reiche aus Marmor, Öl und Orangen und jene Eroberungen zu betreiben, die dem lädierten Gehirne allein gegeben sind.

(In Berlin I tried with paintings and statues in the museums and books borrowed from the lending and national libraries to peek over to the more favourably endowed realms of marble, olives, and oranges, to complete those conquests that are the only ones left to the injured mind.) [125]

Curiously, Benn's poetics is not a pure expression of desire in intuited, evocative imagery, but rather relies on travel experience as transmitted primarily by Goethe und Nietzsche:

Eigentlich kann alles, was meine Generation diskutierte, innerlich sich auseinanderdachte, man kann sagen: erlitt, man kann auch sagen: breittrat – alles das hatte sich bereits bei Nietzsche ausgesprochen und erschöpft, definitive Formulierung gefunden, alles weitere war Exegese. [...] Er ist, wie sich immer deutlicher zeigt, der weitreichende Gigant der nachgoetheschen Epoche. [...] Alles, was Inhalt, Substanz, Gedanke war, vielmehr schien, riß er mit seinem Krakenhirn, seiner Polypennatur an sich, spülte etwas Meerwasser, tiefblaues, mittelländisches darüber, fuhr ihm unter die Haut, zerriß es und siehe, es war nur Haut, zeigte seine Bruch- und Wundflächen und trieb weiter, wurde weiter getrieben zu neuen Meeren, rings nur Welle und Spiel.

(Virtually everything that my generation discussed, thought about, and thought apart, one could perhaps say: suffered through, one could also say: talked into bits and pieces – all of that had already been expressed and exhausted, had already found definite formulation in Nietzsche; what followed was nothing but exegesis. He is, as has become increasingly evident, the far-reaching giant of the post-Goethean era. All that was or rather seemed to be content, substance, thought, he pulled towards himself with his octopus-brain and polyp-character, splashed some dark-blue Mediterranean seawater over it, went underneath its skin and tore it apart, and it was indeed nothing but skin, and showed its fractured and wounded surfaces, and then drifted on, was taken away to other seas, surrounded only by wave and play.) [126]

While Benn unequivocally reads himself and his Expressionist generation as thorough poetic interpreters of Nietzsche's Ligurian work, clearly unlike Nietzsche, whose "Reich erstreckt sich von Portofino bis Zoagli" (realm extends from Portofino to Zoagli) and whose "Spaziergänge führen täglich an die genannten Grenzen [s]eines Reichs" (walks lead him daily to these borders of his realm),[127] Benn's practice is a matter of exclusively mental construction of a "süße Ekstase, die die Ferne bringt" (sweet ecstasy which distance provides / which provides distance), mainly from Brussels, Berlin, and Landsberg, the three places in which he primarily lives his professional life in various stages of deliberate isolation.[128]

What is the point, one might wonder, in discussing art that is modernistically expressive rather than traditionally mimetic, in drawing such fine distinctions between the personal experience of an actual place's reality as a condition for a local and localizable phanopoeia on the one hand, and, on the other, the poetic invention enriched by knowledge of place imagery as read and toponymically taken in and desired, as Benn did after Nietzsche and van Gogh? While Benn never saw Liguria, it was in Liguria that Nietzsche suffered immensely from deteriorating vision. As far as we know, Homer was blind, and yet his epic topography was precise, enabling Heinrich Schliemann to make his archaeological discoveries based on the epic's mapping of the Trojan territory.

Since Homer, however, the representation of land and sea has come with complications. "The paradox of Ithacan topography is that the island is described in remarkably accurate detail as part of a largely fictional story line."[129] Where is the borderline between fiction and truth, imagination and reality to be drawn (after Freud)? The sharp generic distinction between poetry and prose, or between letter or diary and travelogue, might need to be deliberately relaxed in order to do justice to Benn and Nietzsche's verbal energies, which cross generic and stylistic borders in every direction. Their prose is highly poetic and abounds with condensed and displaced images of Mediterranean land- and seascapes. But they are landscapes made of words, thoroughly inspired by the power of Nietzsche's poetic expression, coined on Ligurian terrain under halcyon skies. Benn transforms these into his own metaphors, which are beautifully difficult to access, and at the same time offer liberating horizons.[130]

Why are van Gogh's Provence and Nietzsche's Liguria, as specific instances of Benn's Mediterranean, not taken at face value in scholarship? Granted, a poetic complex called Ligurian by someone who never really geopoeticizes this land in the way local knowledge would prescribe it and a Dutch visual artist given to madness, self-mutilation, and eventual suicide under Provençal skies might not lead to an immediately satisfying answer as to why Benn turns Provence, Côte d'Azur, and Liguria into names for his poetics, with a particular emphasis on Nietzsche's specifically charged "Ausrufe aus Nizza und Portofino" (exclamations in Nice and Portofino) as Ligurian principles of geopoetic expression.[131]

The Riviera's azure sea and halcyon sky, its harbours and olive groves, rose gardens, and peach and almond blossoms (which are also van Gogh's) are poetologically labelled Ligurian and are literally inscribed first and foremost by the southerly word *Blau*, whose sound comprises the entire colour palette of vowels from the open "a" to the closed "u," thus opening up an intensely undulating synaesthetic experience:

> Blau, welch Glück, welch reines Erlebnis [...] dies einzige Kolorit [...] dies ewige und schöne Wort! Nicht umsonst sage ich Blau. Es ist das Südwort schlechthin, der Exponent des ligurischen Komplexes [...] das Hauptmittel zur Zusammenhangsdurchstoßung [...] Phäaken, Megalithen, lernäische Gebiete – allerdings Namen, allerdings zum Teil von mir sogar gebildet, aber wenn sie sich nahen, werden sie mehr. Astarte, Geta, Heraklid – allerdings Notizen aus meinen Büchern, aber wenn ihre Stunde naht [...] die Stunde des Gedichts. Worte, Worte – Substantive! Sie brauchen nur die Schwingen zu öffnen und Jahrtausende entfallen ihrem Flug. Nehmen Sie Anemonenwald, Narzissenwiesen, Ölbaum, Marmorstufen, Olive oder Theogonieen. Botanisches und Geographisches, alle die [...] verlorenen Welten, hier ihre Blüte, hier ihr Traum.
>
> (Blue, what bliss, what sheer experience! This only hue, this eternal and beautiful word! Not in vain do I say blue. It is the southerly word per se, the exponent of the Ligurian complex, the main means for the breaking up of context, Phaeaces, monoliths, Lernaean pastures, yes indeed: names, yes indeed, partly invented by myself, but when they draw nigh, they are far more than that. Astarta, Geta, Heraclitus, yes indeed, notes from my notebooks, but when their hour comes, it is the hour of the poem. Words, words, nouns. They only need to open their wings and millennia come out of their flight. Consider for example anemone woods, narcissus meadows, olive tree, marble steps, olive and theogonies. The botanical and the geographical, all the lost worlds, here their blossom, here their dream.)[132]

This Blau is Benn's major act of poetic condensation, a colour straight out of van Gogh's night-blue part of the palette, rather than a place of the mind alone, and a colour taken from Nietzche's evocations of halcyon skies, high noons and midnights.

Benn inaugurated his poetology of the Ligurian complex, one year before *Der Garten von Arles* (1920), echoing *Der Geburtstag* (1916), where he had already said that the olive befell or overtook Rönne ("da geschah ihm die Olive"), and that, especially in the version which lacks the article, "die in Frage stehende Struktur über der Früchte Silber" (the structure in question about the olives' silver sheen), is poetically enabled for the first time. Similarly, the harbour-complex approached him, glowed towards him: "groß glühte heran der Hafenkomplex" (as opposed to the protagonist's walk to the port, which according to Benn is poetically invalid).

Benn wants to divert consciousness into Ligurian complexes, an endeavour reminiscent of Ezra Pound's *image* as a representation of an "intellectual and emotional complex in an instant of time" as well as of Eliot's *objective correlative* (Benn was familiar with both poets).[133] That the German for "Ligurian complex" – "ligurischer Komplex" – capitalizes the noun but not, as in English, the toponymical adjective somewhat takes away, however, from Benn's otherwise nominal poetology, in which word means noun and is placed upon the page as a picture is placed upon a wall. He stages landscape in ways reminiscent of Nietzsche's crimson sail placed on the surface of the Ligurian Sea, and his poem "Ein Wort" of 1941 is emblematic of this, in that it posits the compound noun ("Flammenwurf," "Sternenstrich") in the company of monosyllabic nouns ("Wort," "Satz") as a momentary spark, and parallelizes it with the sun's radiating power as an epiphany or an "ad-venture" (taken at face value as a marvel that occurs rather than a risk that one takes) in an otherwise dark cosmos.

> Ein Wort, ein Satz – : aus Chiffren steigen
> erkanntes Leben, jäher Sinn,
> die Sonne steht, die Sphären schweigen
> und alles ballt sich zu ihm hin.

> Ein Wort – : ein Glanz, ein Flug, ein Feuer,
> ein Flammenwurf, ein Sternenstrich – ,
> und wieder Dunkel, ungeheuer,
> im leeren Raum um Welt und Ich.

> A word a phrase – : from cyphers rise
> Life recognized, a sudden sense,
> The sun stands still, mute are the skies,
> And all compacts it, stark and dense.

A word – : a gleam, a flight, a spark,
A thrust of flames, a stellar trace – ,
And then again – immense – the dark
Round world and I in empty space.)[134]

Other than the visual function of unusual Nietzschean punctuation, which is suggestive of Imagist poetry, the title and anaphora of a word make one think of this word as the southerly word "blue," while the neologisms "Flammenwurf" and "Sternenstrich" (the latter is not unlike van Gogh's *Starry Night*) hint at heightened forms of expression and sculptural grandeur. In this poem, the collapse of the mimetic mirror and the expressive lamp (to recall M.H. Abrams's terms) into something akin to a window, perhaps, of mimesis and poiesis into an in-between land begins to take clear shape.

That Benn's geopoetic writing is situated at the crossroads of geography and psychoanalysis, that his "spheres" and "ciphers" are rather more psychoanalytic and geographical than cosmic, is evident not only in the "complex" that he absorbed on the one hand from an international modernist discourse of which Ezra Pound's definition of the "image" as a "complex" was very much a part (Pound had even referred to the Provençal Arles as a "living complex"), and on the other from the psychoanalytic work and climate in post–First World War Berlin (with Karl Abraham and Richard Huelsenbeck at the centre). Benn's choice of the term "hypercatharsis" also confirms such an assessment.

In his 1925 "Ostafrika" (East Africa), which has been read primarily on its glaringly exoticist terms, Benn silent affirms Freud's 1913 *Totem und Tabu*, lending it a geographic twist: "keine Gedanken, keiner / trösten den Denker wie / Überbesetzung seiner / mittels Geographie" (No thoughts, none ever / comfort the thinker like / its hypercathexis / via geography). Even though the term "Überbesetzung" sounds less scientific than the English translation (Freud relished the vernacular), Benn in no uncertain terms uses the noun in Freudian fashion: "Überbesetzung seiner" (that is, of the thought). Freud had defined hypercathexis as narcissistic "Überbesetzung" of one's own thoughts, classifying it, together with melancholy (for which Benn also had a weakness), as a prime manifestation of compulsive repetition. Benn's accumulations and condensations of toponymic vocabulary speak to this process of repetition compulsion, of which "East Africa" is but one example. All of his acts of geopoetic naming, ranging "from pole to tropic," to recall T.S. Eliot, Benn subsumed early on, in 1919, under the concept of Ligurian complexes.

Benn's focus remained on the Mediterranean, whose beauty he at least partially ascribed to Sparta's heroic spirit, to Liguria's defiance, and to the overall influence of a Greece which Benn renders as primal, as Nietzsche had in *The Birth of Tragedy*.

"Mittelmeerisch" (1943) is a poem in which rhyme itself is called Mediterranean. It is a poetic monologue that advises us not to challenge eternity, since the metaphysical will not manifest itself permanently – reminiscent of the difficult beauty and fragmentary paradise of Pound's *Pisan Cantos*. Benn recommends a southerly construct to counteract the Germanic myth, a *credo quia absurdum,* a jump into the paradox of place between reality and infinity as an artist's primary mandate. This poem's ruins and roses refer less to actual objects than to their verbal potential for beauty and decay. "Mittelmeerisch" evokes isles and archipelagos and opposes the nordic myth's cold and foggy realms of "Niflheim," the whisper of its charming trumpets ("Lurengeflüster") and runes as its oldest written characters ("Runen") to a series of southern artefacts or Mediterranean still lifes: "im Orangengeruch Trümmer" (ruins immersed in a scent of orange), "Kiesel in der Asche der Rosen" (minerals in the ash of roses), thus fulfilling its own intrapoetic imperative: "Schaffe den Dingen Dauer – , strömt es vom Mittelmeer" (create things which last, is the message that streams from the Mediterranean). Out of an unmoved state of being, the poem condenses a wealth of materials and impressions into the contemporaneity of juxtaposition. It is in this sense that Benn's poetry stands for sculpted words, for new combinations as an expression of the desire to last, to not end, and to perpetuate southerly words and promontory-type sentences (to recall Ernst Bertram).

Benn's late writing maximally approximates the pictorial and presents a series of still lifes that melancholically mark the end of what they create. Van Gogh's still lifes are of suns and sunflowers, marking high noon's hour of Pan, where things seem to stand still, while betraying their ultimate secret. Benn's view, however, is a window view opening up to what Freud called the inner land abroad: "Vor meinem Fenster liegt ein Tal" (in front of my window lies a valley), he writes in the title poem of *Statische Gedichte* (1944), which is reminiscent of the early Rönne's "Sessel" (armchair) in Brussels, in which he is seated right by the window, leaning back and conjuring up Ephesus as well as ruins and cypresses, lagoons and olives, while deploying the Ligurian complex as an at least momentarily efficacious self-therapy even if losing consciousness rather than gaining it is desired.

In the light of Benn's various prose comments on desks facing windows, the metaphor of the window is particularly apropos to replace those of the mirror and the lamp (to use M.H. Abram's terms): the window and its relationship with seeing the outside from the inside as well as framing that which is external is an opportune place on the threshold, where a momentary collapse takes the place of self and world, extending into the intermediate realm of the poetic word image as anticipated in the transferential realm or "Zwischenreich" (the title of a Benn poem as well as of Freud's concept of transference) of Benn's self-declared Nietzschean-Ligurian complexes.

The window is the place where the vision begins, where landscape is remembered as reflective and at the same time projective of consciousness. And Benn's statement that "Schreibtisch oder Fensterplatz entwickeln mehr Substanz als Landschaft, sie schaffen ihr Audruck, überdauern ihre Nebensächlichkeiten, ihren unklaren Saisoncharakter" (Desk or window seat develop more substance than landscape; they create expression and survive landscape's banal characteristics as well as its unclear seasonal character) probably overwrites his own contradiction when he says that in "Hannover war Landschaft um mich herum, die habe ich immer als notwendige Voraussetzung für Lyrikproduktion empfunden" (In Hannover I was surrounded by landscape, which I always considered to be a necessary condition for any kind of lyrical writing).[135] Further, "Fensterplatz" is an unusual word for a place in one's house and usually refers to a window seat on trains or planes, so that the room, the desk, and the window become even more significant elements in Benn's various visualizations of the act of creative inscription:

> Ein alter Schreibtisch steht bei mir im Mittelpunkt. Ich verfüge nur über ein Zimmer für meine ärztliche Praxis und meine Schriftstellerei. [...] Hier kritzele ich mit einer schwierigen Handschrift, die ich selber nicht lesen kann, bis es so weit ist, daß ich an die Schreibmaschine gehe, die auf dem Mikroskopiertisch steht. [...] Das Zimmer is parterre und liegt nach dem Hof. Es blickt auf eine Kaninchenbucht [...] auf Wäscheleinen [...] auf Hortensien [...]. Sein Abschluß wird gebildet von der gegenüberliegenden Häuserfront, die grau, abgemörtelt und zerfallen ist. Es ist ein Zimmer, und es ist ein Schreibtisch, von dem sich schon mancher gebildete Mensch mit Erstaunen abwandte. Hier entwickeln sich seit 1945 gewisse Dinge. Sie sind allerdings geistig vorbereitet durch einen dritten Tisch vom Abend vorher: in meinem Stammlokal (zwei Stunden). Bierlokal, wo ich an einem bestimmten Platz lese, sinne, Radio höre, [...] Briefe [...] studiere. Also

drei Tische. Der entscheidende ist der mit der Schreibmaschine. [...] Alles
etwas beengte Tische.

(In my case, an old desk sits right in the centre. I have at my disposal only
one room for the doctor's office and my writing practice. Here I scribble
with a difficult handwriting that not even I myself am able to decipher; I
scribble until the point is reached when I can move over to the typewriter,
which sits on the other table together with the microscope. The room is
located on the first floor and faces the backyard. It looks out onto a rabbit-
shed, laundry lines and hortensias. And it ends with the opposite wall of
houses, grey, the mortar falling off. It is the kind of room and the kind of
desk from which many an educated person has turned away in astonishment. It is here that since 1945 certain things have been taking shape. They
are mentally prepared, however, by means of a third table, on the previous
evening: in my favourite pub (two hours), beer hall, where I sit on a specific chair and read, ponder, listen to the radio, leafing through my letters.
Three tables then. The decisive one is the one with the typewriter. All three
tables are rather cramped.)[136]

This emphasis on an exact placement and its relationship with spatial
composition shows Benn's profound belief in the significance of a physical arrangement, and is also reflected in his production of poetic still
lifes – a painterly genre, in the sense not of the emblematic or allegorical
implication that the still life had in the fifteenth and sixteenth centuries
but rather of the later commitment to exotic details and flowers, as well
as the self-reflectivity and quasi-poetic self-referentiality of composition
of a *nature morte*, which deals with immanent issues of the genre's own
implied stasis in a specific light as well as a carefully chosen placement.
That the table that houses the typewriter as well as the microscope is the
most crucial one of the three speaks to Benn's repeated emphasis on the
printed letter as visual presence, as well as to his dedication to myopic
minuteness and microscopic precision.

Spatial arrangements such as these are likewise connected to the crucial role that the visit to the museum or gallery plays in Benn. Museums
communicate a telling sense of places and displacements, and are sites of
replacement as well. I would argue, with Philip Fisher's view on painting
in mind,[137] that paintings are windows for Benn, and that the museum as
a venue for an organization of art which allows for pedagogical as well as
sensory-aesthetic experience is the kind of museum that Benn frequent-
ed in Berlin – not the crowded popular space that we might think of, but
rather a kind of secularized cathedral, where the poet in quiet solitude

is able to live his elitist exoticism almost mystically, stealing glimpses into promised lands elsewhere, thus learning from the autopoetic system that the museum might be.

It is intriguing that, coined in the seventeenth century in French, the *trompe-l'œil* (which means "to trick the eye") was perfected in Liguria (some polemically claim that it suited the canny Ligurians) and is particularly common on the eastern Italian Riviera (which is steepest, most compact, and where space is scarce) where facades and interiors are endowed with false painterly windows and shutters, curtains and flowers, as well as architectural details seen in perspective, such as arches, architraves, balustrades, and porticos, rendered so ingeniously that, as the name of the genre suggests, they do deceive the eye, seemingly opening up new outlooks, creating niches, enlarging rooms, and granting further vistas, without actually having to provide them. The *trompe-l'œil* makes space in that it creates an illusive vision where the familiar and that which promises to transcend it incessantly jostle for the beholder's attention – it is, in that sense, a combination of painting and window that supplies more illusions than just the one of three-dimensionality. It also visually reaffirms Benn's "Hypothese von Realität" (hypothesis of reality) and his celebration of *als ob* (as if), particularly in the Rönne sequence.[138]

Fisher's insights into the characteristics of the museum could not be more appropriate for a reading of Benn's museal muses and painterly windows of opportunity as a relief from what is otherwise a self-imposed captivity in small and multipurpose rooms. Ordinarily, a window occurs on a wall in much the same way, location, and proportion as a painting would: for that reason a work of art takes effect as an alternative to a window. Both painting and window interrupt the wall, breaking it open to offer respite from the restraining insistence on the here and now that is the imprisoning aspect of the four walls of every room. A mirror is, in spatial terms, a counter-object to either window or painting, since from its position on the wall it can only reinforce the room itself by pedantically reduplicating a part of it, making it occur twice as a form of pseudo-relief from itself. The mirror, in this sense, is diametrically opposed to the *trompe-l'œil*, which pretends to extend the small room into alcoves and balconies, gardens and terraces, and as such is a fine admixture of painting and window that allows Benn to take leave of temporal and spatial limitations and to take a step back from reality in favour of illusion.

In contrast to the mirror's double insistence on the room, windows and paintings take effect as an escape from it. They subsidize a realm of freedom from the here and now of the room, a realm of spatial freedom

Portofino Castle (Photograph by the author)

The window – be it shut, open, or ajar – is for Benn the place where the vision begins. "Schreibtisch oder Fensterplatz entwickeln mehr Substanz als Landschaft, sie schaffen ihr Ausdruck, überdauern … ihren unklaren Saison-charakter" (desk or window seat develop more substance than landscape; they create expression and survive landscape's … seasonal character), he proclaims, while at the same time stressing that he always regarded landscape as a neces-sary condition for poetic composition. Portofino's landscape, partially visible through the open window, with a hint of the Ligurian Sea reflected in the windowpane, is a combination that perfectly captures Benn's idea of mnemonic landscape expression as both reflective and projective of the poet's creative sensibilities, while the cypresses as trees of mourning may be read as this land-scape's emphatic and perhaps defiant exclamation of life and liberation "in spite of" ("trotzdem"), as Nietzsche said.

Vincent van Gogh, *Les Oliviers/Olive Trees* (1889). Museum of Modern Art, New York. Used with permission.

Dutch post-Impressionist painter Vincent van Gogh (1853–1890) composed his 1889 *Les Oliviers* (*The Olive Trees*) in the asylum at Saint-Rémy-de-Provence. Benn was thoroughly enchanted with Vincent's art, and likely saw a selection of it in an exhibition in Berlin in 1914. Benn refers to van Gogh as "der Idiot von Arles" (the idiot from Arles), who, according to Benn, painted two suns in one picture and to whom Benn's autobiographical protagonist Rönne feels uncannily close. Benn was strongly attracted to Vincent's swirling Provençal compositions, bold colours, torn-up surfaces, rough beauty, and turbulent intensity: "He knew it," Benn writes, "he who painted in Provence under those skies above olives and vines." While Benn's reference to "zwei Sonnen" (two parallel to our option within time to step free of ongoing experience by dwelling for a moment within ourselves and our inner sense of memory and imagination (Nietzsche's high noon is a perfect moment for that).

Benn's inner sense of memory and imagination extends as far as Liguria, which ranges from the olive – as botanic and geographic marker of the border between the Alps and Mediterranean – to the palm tree that in turn marks the threshold of the European continent. Benn must have seen both olive and palm tree when accompanying the Berlin art dealer on road trips through France, including the Riviera. He might have thought of Liguria as the ultimate Ur, and instead of making yet another compound of it (as in Goethe and Freud's *Urwort,* Goethe's *Urpflanze,* or Freud's *Urszene*), Benn turned instead to the primary (and perhaps primal) complex that he termed "Ligurian."

The Ligurian Sea was once called *mare ligusticum,* which allows for a potential relationship with *ligustrum,* a southern plant in the olive family, which Benn repeatedly mentions and to which he seems given as much as to the various contradictions that are inherent in his dreamscapes: "aus dem Efeu des Grabes, aus dem Meer von Nizza, aus dem Eis des Engadin mischen sich die Farben u die Widersprüche des Traums" (The colours and the contradictions of the dream are fused out of the grave's ivy, out of Nice's sea, and out of the Engadine's ice) [139] he writes in three untitled and undated lines that not only pay imaginative homage to Nietzsche's main abodes but also remember and anticipate Benn's own sacrilegious blue of the Ligurian-Tyrrhenian Sea: "Tyrrhenisches Meer. Ein frevelhaftes Blau." [140]

---

suns) is obscure (even though Vincent painted various works with a variety of coexisting planets), the two possible candidates Benn might have had in mind are the 1890 *Wheat Field with Crows* and the 1889 *The Olive Trees,* even though in both paintings the white areas above look like two uneven clouds rather than two suns. Benn was not only profoundly taken by Vincent's undulating marine features of inland motifs but was also intensely drawn to the olive, which could be called his Ligurian poetics in a nutshell: "da geschah ihm Olive" (then olive befell him) is a phrase of Benn's that analyses how the word "olive" unveils the entire Ligurian complex of "der Früchte Silber, ihre leisen Wälder, ihre Ernte und ihr Kelterfest" (the olives' silver sheen, the silent olive groves, their harvest and the celebration of the first press). Kenneth White wrote a fictive dialogue with van Gogh (in *Van Gogh*), which makes fine connections between museums, galleries, and geopoetics, with an emphasis on aura, poetic energy, and the power of place that accords well with Benn's re-invention of van Gogh's art.

Postface: Liguria Rediviva

… my islands shift and change, now here, now there, dazzling, white, granite.

H.D.

… les paysages … il faudrait y porter attention parfois plus qu'aux états d'âme.

(… landscapes … sometimes one ought to attend to them more
than to mental states.)

Pierre Mertens

… seeing the landscape, sketching a mindscape,
gathering together the elements of a world.

Kenneth White

Emphasizing the need for a precise territory in order to break the spell of the traditional canonization of Italy's alleged magic, this book's comparative gesture consists in spelling out Liguria's geopoetic dimensions. *The Azure Spell of Liguria* traces a (post)-Nietzschean return to this site and focuses its inquiry on the expressiveness of Friedrich Nietzsche (1844–1900), Sigmund Freud (1856–1934), and Gottfried Benn (1886–1956), as well as on the crucial role that Liguria (broadly defined and including Provence) as a geographically and poetically saturated territory has played as an intersection (via Nietzsche) for these three writers. The Alps and the Mediterranean coexist within the boundaries of this small and compact, steep and liminal, remote and proto-insular world, an amphitheatrical locale framed by natural borders of rock and sea, with the Martime Alps and the Ligurian Apennines sweeping down to the marine stage of the terrain's northwestern Mediterranean shoreline – the Côte d'Azur, the Riviera.

It is with good reason that in "Dall'opaco" ("From the Opaque," or, perhaps more accurately, "From Opaqueness") Italo Calvino has described the Ligurian world as "un teatro il cui proscenio s'apre [...] sulla stricia di mare alta contro il cielo attraversato dai venti e dalle nuvole" (a theater whose stage opens on the void, on the high strip of sea against the sky crossed by winds and clouds).[1] Calvino's marvellously complex piece on geographic, geological, and geometric perspectivism does not simply describe the geopoetic paradigm that he is after but avidly tries to capture it. Calvino studies the points of the compass, plumbing the depths of the Ligurian terrain's form and shape, while disentangling the elusive nature of sun and shade, south and north, east and west, and at the same time reflecting on the practice of writing as the kind of commemoration that points to the future rather than to the past, and as such is an homage to Nietzsche rather than Freud.

"It is not expected of critics as it is of poets that they should help us make sense of our lives; they are bound only to attempt the lesser feat of making sense of the ways we try to make sense of our lives." Thus begins Frank Kermode's *The Sense of an Ending*. The first chapter is titled "The End," and Nietzsche's presence is made clear throughout the book, including when Kermode addresses the "gaiety of language" in times of solitude, hostility, and even confinement.[2] That the word "postface" may well indicate a similar contradiction in terms – what is recto, what is verso, what comes before and what comes after? – is very much in line with Calvino's hermetic acts of orientation, disorientation, and reorientation, and preventively saves these final pages of *The Azure Spell of Liguria* from becoming a mere epilogic conclusion. Instead, these last pages are intended to encourage a sympathy (an affinity without pity) for Nietzsche's struggle, if not refusal, to find endings, to which his repeatedly updated prefaces to all major works as well as the better part of his numerous epigraphs and hybrid endings bear witness. The ubiquitous Janus-faced quality of Nietzsche's writing reflects Liguria's Janus-faced terrain and has, indeed, made it challenging to pin him down, to come to terms with him: "wir können mit Nietzsches Denken nicht fertig werden," according to Rüdiger Safranski, "weil er selbst nicht damit fertig geworden ist" (we cannot come to terms with Nietzsche's thought since he himself did not come to terms with it).[3]

In the fourth book of *The Gay Science*, "Sanctus Januarius" (initially the final book before Nietzsche added the fifth book and an appendix of songs for the volume's second edition five years later), Nietzsche reso-lutely celebrates the first month of the year 1882 as "schönster Januarius" (fairest month of January) in an epigraph composed in Genoa in the moment of realization that his own blood, not only that of San Gennaro, has become enlivened once again: "Nietzsche *redivivus*," one is tempted to say.[4] This postface is composed in such a Nietzschean spirit, favouring the impending outlook of the future side of Janus's face, even though (or perhaps precisely because) it is situated so close to the back cover of the book. Rather than summing up, drawing a balance, or offering conclusive remarks, then, these pages shall project questions and per-spectives that are significantly deserving of future research, thought, and consideration but that the present study touches only in passing. While the Latin *redivivus* has been used to refer to a later artist or writer who relies on the work of an earlier one, it is crucial to recall what it literally means: to enliven, to return to life; as such, it has a strong affinity with Nietzsche's insular concept of time, spelled out in Liguria, as well as with his Ligurian liberation into expression that others have been exploring after him. In all likelihood Nietzsche would joyfully grant each and every one of them their own dawn: "Es giebt so viele Morgenröthen, die noch nicht geleuchtet haben" (there are so many dawns that have yet to shine) – thus Nietzsche's epigraph to *Dawn*, as borrowed from the Rig Veda, an ancient Indian sacred collection of vedic Sanskrit hymns (from *veda*: knowledge).[5]

Regarding future prospects, then: One theme to tackle further would certainly be the *topos* of midlife (or "Mittag des Lebens": midday/noon of life, as Nietzsche has it) as a time-honoured form of almost theatrical *peripeteia* (in that Nietzsche addresses it as "Du heiterer schauerlicher Mit-tagsabgrund"/ You serene uncanny midday-abyss) that the writers and characters examined in the present study have envisioned at moments of either distress or ennui: Dante the exiled poet (forbidden to remain in or return to Florence) and Dante the pilgrim set out to wander through Romance and other territory, wondering about the implications of the "mezzo del cammin di nostra vita" (half of our life's way).[6] Goethe was not allowed to depart, so that his nocturnal stealing away for Italy nec-essarily takes place incognito, six days after his thirty-seventh birthday: "Früh drei Uhr stahl ich mich aus Karlsbad, weil man mich sonst nicht fortgelassen hätte [...] hier war nicht länger zu säumen" (I slipped out of Carlsbad at three in the morning; otherwise, I would not have been allowed to leave [...] I could not wait longer).[7]

Nietzsche resigned from his professorship at Basel just before turning thirty-five, and embarked on his nomadic journey that was to become the occasion of *Dawn, The Gay Science,* and *Thus Spoke Zarathustra*. Nietzsche's *alter ego* Zarathustra leaves his home at age thirty to travel to the mountains: "Als Zarathustra dreissig Jahr alt war, verliess er seine Heimat [...] und gieng in das Gebirge."[8] Freud escapes domestic and professional fatigue on his trips to Italy primarily in midlife, while Benn tries to come to terms with his midlife crisis and wartime experience through an autobiographically inspired Werff Rönne's various forms of mental travel, movie going, and other sorts of exotic-erotic escapism. Rönne's thirtieth birthday occurs in 1916, as does Benn's own, and provides sufficient reason for an Expressionist novella of that year (titled with a definite article *Der Geburtstag* [*The Birthday*], as if it were the only one). One year later, Benn notes: "Du, es ist Mittag! *Ganz* jung ist vorbei" (Hey, it is midday! All that young is over). What – beyond their common geopoetic denominator of writing and wandering – might these instances of midlife crises have in common? How has this literary *topos* evolved, from Dante's twelfth and thirteenth centuries, to Benn's (post)war writing and the present?

Another topic that invites expansion is Benn and Italy. In stark contrast to Nietzsche and Freud's sojourns in Italy and Italy's influence on them, as well as the various publications that trace, analyse, and comment on them,[9] Benn's actual Italian journeying was minimal (apart from visits to Meran and Lake Garda, that is), so that this subject may well be more esoteric, and perhaps controversial. What is certainly intriguing, however, is that Benn draws attention to Italy in seemingly random, certainly fragmentary, but very concrete ways and detailed observations. He speaks, for example, of Italian war memorials, of the actress Eleonora Duse, of the fruit market on Piazza Grande in Trieste, of upscale restaurants on the Riviera, of the Ligurian Taggiasca olive, of Nietzsche's Turin, and, of course, of Gabriele D'Annunzio and Filippo Tommaso Marinetti. Even before coining the "Ligurian complex" Benn emphasized that "Italien war da" (Italy was present).

Benn and Italy, then. This intriguing subject may be approached in a way similar to Virginia Woolf's elaborations on women and fiction (not many women had written much fiction at the time when Woolf embarked on her fine analysis). Incidentally, Woolf also plays a role in Kermode's elaborations on ending. When Woolf was invited to lecture on this theme, she began her speech by scrutinizing the various possible implications and ramifications of the seemingly straightforward topic assigned to her.

Women and fiction: what does that mean? Women writing fiction? Women in fiction? Women reading fiction? "When you asked me to speak about women and fiction," Woolf writes, "I sat down on the banks of a river and began to wonder what the words meant." They might mean female novelists, she ponders; or "women and what they are like; or it might mean women and the fiction that is written about them; or it might mean that somehow all three are inextricably mixed together." While she finds this latter option "most interesting," she is intensely aware of the fact that it is precisely this kind of complex meaning that makes difficult the sort of conclusion a lecturer would be expected to offer. As a creative writer, however, Woolf takes the liberty of opening up horizons rather than drawing conclusions, imbuing all her subsequent deliberations on women and fiction with astute perception as well as a fine sense of humour.[10]

Benn and Italy: what does that mean? Benn in Italy? Italy in Benn? Benn and what he is like when somehow in touch with Italy? Or, perchance, "all three inextricably mixed together"? And to what end? Beyond the various critical controversies with regard to whether Benn was ever in Italy (and if so where, and if not, why not), as well as beyond his explicitly phrased "Ligurian complex," Marinetti and Italian (including Ligurian) Futurism would have to enter the scene far more prominently than I allowed for within the framework of the present study. Further, a discussion that I touched upon in the preface likewise invites elaboration: namely that Benn has been more extensively read in Italy than in other countries and more often translated into Italian than into other languages (this contrast is particularly stark between Italy and Anglo-America). An analysis of this reception promises to shed new light on the dynamics of international Modernism in general and German Expressionism and Italian Futurism in the context of Fascist Modernism in particular.[11]

An intriguing set of works that merit further investigation with regard to the Nietzsche-Freud complex are a variety of fictionalized encounters between Nietzsche and Freud in novel, play, and film – as, for example, in Luis Martin Santos's 1986 *Encuentro en Sils-Maria* (in which Joseph Paneth plays a significant role as a mediator of the encounter between Nietzsche and Freud), Irvin Yalom's 1993 novel *When Nietzsche Wept*, Henri-Charles Tauxe's 2000 surreal tragicomedy *Le tunnel du fou: pièce en un acte*, and the 2007 feature film *When Nietzsche Wept*, directed by Pinchas Perry and heavily reliant on Yalom's bestseller. All of these works imaginatively stage an encounter between Nietzsche and Freud – be it with Freud as the doctor who accompanies Nietzsche on the 1889 train from Turin to Basel (as in Tauxe), or, as in Yalom, with Freud's friend Josef Breuer and Nietzsche striking some kind of mutually therapeutic deal. Here, Breuer not only tells Nietzsche that his books are excellent but also reads Nietzsche to Freud and submits to him that Nietzsche has everything to offer. This is interestingly precisely the moment when Freud admits to having read Nietzsche's "book," albeit without specifying which one, at Lou Andreas-Salomé's instigation (a situation which, in spite of Nietzsche's immense scepticism towards such transference, surely puts any sort of troubadour scheming to shame).

Important issues to be raised in this fictional context would concern the transferential realm between the roles of doctor and patient (partially reminiscent of my present analysis of Benn's Rönne in this respect), the narrative dynamic of the talking cure, and the propriety of turning actual historical figures into literary characters while at the same time reinventing them on their own terms. The 1990 eleven-minute film *Rönnes Reise*, directed by Karin Reiss and starring Ulrich Mühe, the lead actor in Florian Henckel von Donnersmarck's *Das Leben der anderen* (*The Lives of Others*), might also enter such a discussion of fictionalized biography and featured history. *Rönnes Reise*, however, was not commercially released.

Hillert Ibbeken and David Gilmour have recently pointed to another Italy. While geologist Ibbeken relates intriguing stories about Liguria and Calabria as off-centre Italian locales, Gilmour unveils Italy's nationhood as fragile, persuasively arguing that its federation was Garibaldi's artificially imposed (con)fusion in 1861 – a mistake that followed the 1860 Treaty of Turin, which officially ceded Nice and Savoy to France. Situating Italy between France and Greece, while unravelling its geographic, cultural, and ethnic variety from the Alps to Sicily, as well as its centrifugal impetus as an immediate consequence of such a spectrum, Gilmour points to the nation's insular character: its more than four thousand miles of coast make it vulnerable to invasion and prone to infection.

Although Kenneth White coined the term "geopoetic" only in the later decades of the twentieth century, geopoetics is a time-honoured pre-national approach (the troubadours practised it) and at the same time a post-, inter-, and probably "transnational" affair (to use the term that has recently gained such currency). The focus of geopoetics is hardly the nation, nor is it the national language, nor is it the region in the sense of restrictive or reactionary localisms; rather, it is the territory, its aura, and its creative (multi)lingualism. Geopoetics strives for the kind of vibrant dialogue between mind, world, and word that is suggestive of Virginia Woolf's appreciation of Samuel Taylor Coleridge's idea of the accomplished writer's necessarily androgynous mind. Seated by the window in her study, Woolf sees a woman and a man getting into a taxi cab: "the sight was ordinary enough," she comments; "what was strange was the rhythmical order with which my imagination had invested it; [...] The sight of two people coming down the street and meeting at the corner seems to ease the mind of some strain [...] Perhaps to think [...] of one sex as distinct from the other [...] interferes with the unity of the mind."

Granted, Coleridge did not speak of androgyny as a way to ease women's passage into the scene of writing and authorship; rather, "he meant, perhaps, that the androgynous mind is resonant and porous; [...] that it is naturally creative, incandescent, and undivided."[12] In this sense of being vibrant, permeable, imaginative, radiant, and complete, the geopoetic mind becomes quasi-synonymous with this androgynous mind, in that it likewise refuses to deepen the gap between word and world, focusing instead, for creativity's sake, on a potential fusion of such travelling entities. With Coleridge, Woolf (herself a traveller to Italy and Provence in 1908 and 1912) claims that every great writer has an androgynous mind. And, with Kenneth White, I submit that every great writer has a geopoetic mind – a mind intensely susceptible to its territorial, auratic, and verbal surroundings and their respective synergies.

In "Lapis Lazuli," William Butler Yeats defies tragedy, on Nietzsche's terms, by way of gaiety, positing art as the only justification for life. Even though Lear and Hamlet are explicitly mentioned, the poem's final word is "gay," and it is this word that "transfigur[es] all the dread." In the fashion of the troubadours' *gaya scienza*, Yeats celebrates joy against the odds as the technical skill required for poetic composition on the one hand and survival on the other. In 1935, poet Harry Clifton gave Yeats a present: a carving from the Ch'ien Lung period showing the ascent of a mountain suggestive of that in Dante's *Purgatory* (the carving is on display in Ireland's National Library). When composing "Lapis Lazuli" in 1938, Yeats ekphrastically inscribed this carving, in which are seen three "Chinamen," "a musical instrument," and a "long-legged bird" (probably a crane), as "symbol of longevity." Woolf calls a man and woman getting into a cab an ordinary scene and points to the literary importance of an ideally androgynous mind's investment in it. Similarly, Yeats transforms an ordinary enough collectible into a post-tragic scene of geopoetic splendour.

Even if longevity and gaiety are his poem's major themes, Yeats's ending presents us with a curious scene, carved, as it were, right into the lazurite rock that triggered the poem's title and now tears open its surface. If this stone's saturated blue shows "discoloration" or "accidental crack or dent," such flaws are perceived as "a water-course or an avalanche" or a slope. Yeats thus transforms the geological material of a stone that reached him from far away into a poetic landscape near at hand. This geopoetic act of carving joyfully keeps its precious secrets in ways reminiscent of the troubadours' *trobar clus* and *gaya scienza* – and of Nietzsche: "der Stein ist mehr Stein als früher" (the stone is more stone than it used to be), and "im Steine schläft mir ein Bild" (an image lies dormant in the stone and waits for me).[13]

In the prologue to the Mesopotamian epic *Gilgamesh*, possibly the oldest written story on earth, the azure stone enters the scene as well, when the King of Uruk's (present-day Iraq) story is initially presented as hermetically encased in copper and engraved in lapis lazuli: "find the cornerstone and under it the copper box that is marked with his name. Unlock it. Open the lid. Take out the tablet of lapis lazuli. Read how Gilgamesh suffered all and accomplished all."[14] Even if the *Gilgamesh* fragments were actually engraved on twelve tablets rather than one, and not in lapis lazuli but (in cuneiform) in clay, it is in the word "azure" (Persian *lāzhward*) that stone and text are here geopoetically fused into a precious visual-verbal unity. One may be tempted to spell out yet another toponymically derived state of being on this occasion: after (or before?) Kenneth White's "nordicity," "atlanticity," and "littorality," Predrag Matvejević's "mediterraneity," and the current study's "ligurianity," one should probably add "lazurity" and wonder whether Stéphen Liégeard was aware of the fact that "l'Azur" was a name (geological rather than geographic, but geopoetic nevertheless) before he baptized his favourite shore.[15] Would he have "recognized strangeness," in White's sense, as a part of his making of a wor(l)d?[16]

Broadly defined, Liguria reaches from Joseph Conrad's Marseilles in the west to Nietzsche's Genoa in the centre and on to Shelley's Lerici in the east. Its aura, however, may well extend farther: to Orhan Pamuk's Ligurian remains uncannily kept in the post-aqueous archive of the Bosphorus, and all the way to Mesopotamia and Badakhstan. In the fifth book of *The Gay Science*, which he added in 1887 as a sort of "second coming" (Yeats again) or second ending, Nietzsche posits his "open sea" in quotation marks. Such a sea is hardly meant as a political invitation to conquer, nor does "our sea" equal *mare nostrum*, as the Romans called "their" Mediterranean. Inspired as it might be by seafaring Columbus and the idea of an ongoing navigation towards joyful wisdom (or gay science), Nietzsche's open sea is a metaphor for a fearless facing of future horizons, for the experience of another dawn that has yet to shine:

wir [...] fühlen uns [...] wie von einer neuen Morgenröthe angestrahlt;

Gaetano Previati, *Tramonto in Liguria/Sunset in Liguria* (1912). Private collection, used with permission.

Gaetano Previati (1852–1920) was associated with the Scapigliatura in Milan (the Italian equivalent of the French "Bohème" in both the visual and the verbal arts), as well as with neo-Impressionist Divisionism (which practised a separation of colours into optically interactive dots or patches). In 1907, he was involved in the composition of the Dream Room at the Venice Biennale, which was an overdue acknowledgment of Italian Symbolism. Previati sojourned for long periods in Liguria, primarily in Lavagna (southeast of Rapallo, on the Riviera di Levante), where he died in 1920.

Portraying a Ligurian sunset, *Tramonto in Liguria* remembers late Romanticism's oneiric and visionary sensibilities, while at the same time skipping sentimentality and engaging instead, in primary colour and great detail, with

unser Herz strömt dabei über von Dankbarkeit, Erstaunen, Ahnung, Erwar-
tung, – endlich erscheint uns der Horizont wieder frei [...] endlich dürfen
unsere Schiffe wieder auslaufen, auf jede Gefahr hin auslaufen, jedes Wagnis des Erkennenden ist wieder erlaubt, das Meer, unser Meer liegt wieder
offen da, vielleicht gab es noch niemals ein so "offnes Meer." –

(we [...] feel [...] as if a new dawn shone on us; our heart overflows with
gratitude, amazement, premonitions, expectation. At long last the horizon
appears free to us again [...] at long last our ships may venture out again,
venture out to face any danger; all the daring of the lover of knowledge is
permitted again; the sea, our sea, lies open again; perhaps there has never
yet been such an "open sea." –)[17]

Nietzsche wrote this inconclusive revival after completing four books
of *The Gay Science*, as well as *Zarathustra* and *Beyond Good and Evil*. And yet
even in his curious punctuation he signals the problematic of an end-

---

the solar and marine aspects of Liguria. Previati's painting shows emblematic
citrus fruit trees on the left, while placing, in a fashion reminiscent of Claude
Lorrain's *Port of Genoa*, the sea to the beholder's right, which is to say that the
image is oriented towards the southeast, capturing the golden reflection of the
sun setting in the west/Ponente (particularly on the horizon and the citrus),
while at the same time facing the eastern Levante, and implicitly awaiting
sunrise.

The German "Dämmerung" is a part not only of Richard Wagner's 1867
operatic apocalypse *Götterdämmerung* (*Twilight of the Gods*) and Nietzsche's
1888–9 pun on Wagner: *Götzendämmerung oder wie man mit dem Hammer phi-
losophiert* (*Twilight of the Idols, or How to Philosophize with the Hammer*); it also
captures both moments of twilight, dusk and dawn, and speaks to this liminal
phenomenon as it combines local perception with creative anticipation (in line
with Nietzsche's equation of midday/noon and midnight: "Mitternacht ist auch
Mittag"). Some languages have metaphorically deployed the twilight image to
evoke an incipient understanding, *alba* or dawn: "es dämmert mir" (it dawns on
me).

Liguria, finally, is conceived not only as an enclosed recess and a refuge but
also as an outlook and a vantage point from which to revisit a geopoetically
intense and compact wor(l)d, which by facing place in Edward Casey's sense
reaffirms Nietzsche's Epicurean sea of existence, while confirming Kenneth
White's geopoetic wor(l)d, which begins where one is.

ing. First he inserts the conventional period that promises such closure. But then he follows it with a dash, thus undermining the validity of a conclusive period, while tearing open once again the geopoetic territory at hand, as if yet another dawn was drawing nigh – and this second edition of *The Gay Science* ends not with this passage but with an appendix of songs in the manner of the troubadours as poets of dawn, wind, dance – and of Provence.

Geopoetics, taken at face value, is world making. It tacitly reverts to Goethe's idea of "Weltliteratur" (world literature) as the kind of writing that according to Kenneth White "opens space" and "looks beyond the borders," preparing "sensitive grounds, subtle territory," and ongoing encounters of the "earth-thing" with the "mind-thing." Such a geopoetics "works out a new mindscape. Its basis is a new sense of land in an enlarged mind. World, open world begins where one is. Every territory, while maintaining its presence and compactness, is open, if one knows how to read it."[18]

And indeed, Liguria has maintained and affirmed its steep presence, its poetic compactness, its challenging enclosures and contradictions — and its openness to the sea. Benn quickly and enthusiastically absorbed Nietzsche's pathbreaking and liberating expressions in and of this territory; and even Freud's resistance to his forerunner soon turned out to be futile – he, too, essentially succumbed to Nietzsche's staging of poetic expression in a variety of geopoetically conceived Alpine-Mediterranean-Ligurian-Provençal amphitheatres. Freud and Benn followed their pioneer's lead; they, too, were overtaken by Zarathustra; Liguria's difficult beauty befell them, too, projecting them into a geopoetic future under its complex azure spell.

Notes

Preface

1 Translated by Martina Kolb. Unless otherwise stated, all translations into English are my own.

2 According to the *Oxford English Dictionary*, "to befall" is dated and ascribes the agency to the one who or the thing that befalls somebody or something, more often than not some sort of accident, disease, or disaster (as in the German *befallen* which is used, for instance, when plants suffer from lice), although there are also examples of a powerful good that may befall people. I have translated Benn's *geschehen* as "befall" because unlike "happen to," "befall" is directly followed by a dative case and expresses the recipient more directly than a prepositional phrase (an alternative could be "the olive overtook him"). Further, Benn's usage itself is dated and has a biblical ring to it. The olive that befalls the subject here, however, results in an overtaken poetic recipient's poetic bliss rather than in any sort of doom or disaster.

3 Cf Deleuze and Guattari, *Mille plateaux*, which connects Marx, Nietzsche, and Freud's versions of philosophical materialism with contemporary science; and Bonta and Protevi, *Deleuze and Geophilosophy*.

4 Matvejević's open and creative concept is not only opposed to an ethnically and locally defined *mediterraneity* as an exclusively regional characteristic but gains even more momentum in contrast to extremely exclusive nationalistic doctrines such as Fascism's *italianità*.

5 Quoted from memory and translated. Klaus Theweleit delivered his speech on Benn during a round-table discussion at the Deutsches Literaturarchiv Marbach in Germany in 2006, at the symposium "Gottfried Benns Doppelleben oder wie man sich selbst zusammensetzt," which was held on the occasion of the fiftieth anniversary of Benn's death. Klaus Theweleit is the

author of the 1972 study of Fascist consciousness titled *Männerphantasien* (*Male Fantasies*, 1987), as well as of *Buch der Könige* (*Book of Kings*) – in which Benn, partially fashioned as Orpheus, figures prominently, along with a variety of other controversial Modernists, among them Ezra Pound – and a recent biography of Jimi Hendrix. In the only television interview conducted with him, Gottfried Benn, on 3 May 1956 (only about two months before his death), in every reply to Thilo Koch's questions, put heavy emphasis on what he had already stressed throughout his career as a poet: the poet's solitude on the one hand, and his life within his native language on the other.

6　Ashton, ed., *Primal Vision: Selected Writings of Gottfried Benn.* The English translators in this volume are E.B. Ashton, Babette Deutsch, Richard Exner, Francis Golffing, Michael Hamburger, Eugene Jolas, Ernst Kaiser, Christopher Middleton, Therese Pol, Vernon Watkins, and Eithne Wilkins. And see Sander, ed., *Gottfried Benn: Prose, Essays, Poems.* Translations in this volume partially overlap with those in the earlier *Primal Vision*, and the English translators in this volume are Joel Agee, E.B. Ashton, Robert M. Browning, Alexandra Chciuk-Celt, Joseph B. Dallet, Babette Deutsch, Richard Exner, Franz Feige, Patricia Gleason, Michael Hamburger, Ernst Kaiser, E.L. Kanes, Max Knight, Christopher Middleton, J.M. Ritchie, Karl F. Ross, Gertrude C. Schwebell, Richard Sieburth, Vernon Watkins, Kerry Weinberg, and Eithne Wilkins. There is also Ritchie, *Gottfried Benn: The Unreconstructed Expressionist,* which includes a smaller series of English translations of Benn's poetry and prose by Annabel Brown, R.J. Kavanagh, and J.M. Ritchie. Nietzsche translator Walter Kaufmann also translated some of Benn's early poetry (the *Morgue* cycle of 1912) in Kaufmann, ed. and trans., *Twenty German Poets: A Bilingual Collection,* 266–73.

7　Despite Ernst Bertram's questionable conduct during the Third Reich, it is his thorough understanding of Nietzsche's composition (particularly in the "Portofino" chapter of *Nietzsche: Versuch einer Mythologie*) that illustrates extremely well what the present study intends with its geopoetic approach to shared form of word and world, of word and syntax imitating place and geography, and of Liguria's impact on Nietzsche's major writings as well as on those of post-Nietzscheans Freud and Benn.

8　Laplanche and Pontalis, *Vocabulaire,* 72.

9　While the Latin suffix -(*i*)*tas* directly translates into the English -*ty* and the German -*tät* (and Romance variants such as -*tat*, -*té*, -*tà*, -*dad*, etc.), it is sometimes rendered as -*hood*, -*ship*, -*ness* or -*dom* in English and -*heit* or -*keit* in German (as for instance in *fraternitas* – *fraternity*/ *brotherhood* – *Brüderlichkeit*).

10　Kenneth White, *On the Atlantic Edge,* 67.

11 Ibid., 3, 5, 44.
12 Ibid., 45.

Part I

1 Benn, "Ich finde," in *Szenen und Schriften in der Fassung der Erstdrucke*, 154. This is Benn's first mention of "Ligurian complexes" (in 1919). Various later texts, in which he repeatedly takes up this paradigmatic name as the paragon of his aesthetic principles and poetic challenges, are discussed in "Blind Spots, Alibis, Sceneries" below.

2 Cf Hay, *Young Romantics*; Andronik, *Wildly Romantic – The English Romantic Poets*; Guiccioli, *Lord Byron's Life in Italy*; Howarth, *The Greek Adventure*; Cameron, ed., *Romantic Rebels*; and Hunt, *Lord Byron and Some of His Contemporaries*.

3 Pamuk, *Kara Kitap*, 21–4; and Pamuk, *The Black Book*, trans. Freely, 16–20. Even though I welcome the English translation's explicit mention of the Ligurians in this context of the Celts and the Genoese, it is curious that Pamuk's Turkish original says "Likyalı[lar]," which means "Lycians," while "Ligurians" would have been "Ligurlar." But the issue remains compelling. While one context of Pamuk's chapter is that of Genoese conquest, another is that of "Ionic columns," with Ionia geographically close to Lycia (between these two Anatolian territories lies Caria). The earlier English translation of Pamuk's novel, by Güneli Gün (*The Black Book*, 1995) likewise chooses "Ligurian" (15) for "Likyalı," rather than referring to Anatolia. Such a connection, however, would stress a geopoetic bond between Lycia and Liguria – for instance, the coincidence of high mountains (Taurus and Maritime Alps) and the Mediterranean Sea, the encounter of nature and culture in rock architecture (for instance the Lycian rock tombs or the Ligurian dry walls). Cf Clarke, *Notes on the Ligurians, Aquitanians, and Belgians*, 3: "With regard to the name of Ligyes, or Ligures, it is natural to think of others of the same form, as Lukìa (Lycia), Lukaonia, Ki-Likîa (Celècia), Lakonia, Lukania, in Southern Italy, the Le-Leges, and the present Lesghians."

4 *Complete Poems of Hart Crane*, ed. Simon, 33.

5 Uzuner, *Istanbul Blues*.

6 Matvejević, "Mediterranean Images and Oblivion," in Jodice, ed., *Mediterranean: Essays by George Hersey and Predrag Matvejević*, 106.

7 Blume, *Côte d'Azur*, 9.

8 Girard, *Gênes, ses environs et les deux Rivières*, 1.

9 Room, *Placenames of the World*, 99.

10 Waters, *The French and Italian Rivieras*, vi and 1.

11 Silver, *Making Paradise*, 166 and 178.

12 Self and Steadman, *Psychogeography,* 112; and Stein and Niederland, eds, *Maps from the Mind,* 133.

13 Matvejević, "Mediterranean Images and Oblivion," in Jodice, *Mediterranean,* 107.

14 Cf Pemble, "Destinations," in *The Mediterranean Passion,* 39 ff.

15 Mary Blume draws attention to a similar dynamic with regard to exchangeable place names: "At the same time that California was inventing its own dream, both Cannes and Nice had new quarters named La Californie: paradise, El Dorado." (Blume, *Côte d'Azur,* 67).

16 Liégeard, *La Côte d'Azur,* 30.

17 Ibid., 3.

18 Mann and Mann, *Das Buch von der Riviera*; and Ross, *From Liguria with Love.* Cf Grandjonc, ed., *Emigrés français en Allemagne, Emigrés allemands en France: 1685–1945,* especially 122–3, 139–40, and 155–6, with contributions by Rita Thalmann, Gilbert Badia and Hélène Roussel, and Barbara Vormeier on the years 1933 to 1939, when France received more than 50,000 refugees from Nazi Germany (among them a fair number of artists and writers such as Heinrich Mann, Alfred Döblin, Walter Benjamin, Lion Feuchtwanger, Max Ernst, and Hans Hartung), as well as on 1939 to 1945, when various exiles ended up serving in the French army. Cf also Herzer, ed., *The Italian Refuge,* 141–58 and 218–27, for Klaus Voigt's "Jewish Refugees and Immigrants in Italy, 1933–1945" and John Bierman's contribution on "How Italy Protected the Jews in the Occupied South of France, 1942–1943." Voigt writes that, in spite of expulsion orders that were carried out, "Genoa stands out as a city whose officials lived up to a well-deserved reputation of liberality. The port's big shipping companies were also opposed to expulsion, but for a selfish reason: to avoid loss of their best clients during a time when the traffic in tourism and passenger transport had already fallen into a steep decline" (147). Voigt also points to lawyer Lelio Vittoria Valobra, under whose direction the Delegation for Assistance to Emigrés was organized in Genoa. Valobra eventually fled to Switzerland (155).

19 Richardson, *Things Seen on the Riviera,* 115.

20 Ibid., 153.

21 Liégeard, *La Côte d'Azur,* 4.

22 de Marinis and Spadea, eds, *I Liguri,* 533.

23 Liégeard, *La Côte d'Azur,* 2.

24 Ibid., 2.

25 Dante Alighieri, *De vulgari eloquentia.* Cf *The Divine Comedy of Dante Alighieri: Inferno,* 304–5.

26 Cf Monteverde, *I Liguri.*

27 Miltoun and McManus, *Rambles on the Riviera.*

28 For example, Matvejević's *The Mediterranean*, and Braudel's *Les mémoires de la Méditerranée.* Braudel's study focuses on the prehistoric and ancient past of the Mediterranean and was written during the author's German captivity from 1942 to 1945.

29 *Dichtung und Wahrheit* is the title of Johann Wolfgang von Goethe's autobiography, and has been translated alternatively as *Truth and Fiction* or *Truth and Poetry.* True, the collective noun *Dichtung* in the narrow sense means lyrical poetry. However, Goethe's provocative binary primarily builds on the broader sense of the term, in that literary qualities of poetry and other creative genres are considered in Platonic opposition (*mythos* versus *logos*) to what Goethe philosophically calls (but crucially debates as) truth (Wahrheit).

30 *The Divine Comedy of Dante Alighieri: Purgatorio,* 22–3.

31 Girani and Galletti, *Una terra fatta a scalini,* 5.

32 Dwyer Hickey, *Last Train from Liguria,* 65.

33 One might argue for a visual resemblance between Galata and Genoa. When I showed Claude Lorrain's *Seaport of Genoa* to a Turkish friend, she thought, at first glance, that it was an image of Constantinople (the impression being grounded in the sea, the slope, and the spontaneous confusion of the Galata Tower built by the Genoese with the Lighthouse or Lanterna in Genoa's seaport, both constructed in the Middle Ages).

34 For the cross-cultural aspect as well as the sea-bound spirit of place, cf Galley and Ladjimi Sebai, eds, *L'homme méditerranéen et la mer,* where Claude-Hélène Lacroix deliberates on the Mediterranean Sea not as a geographic divide but as an invitation to the imagination: "La Méditerrannée, qu'est-ce que c'est? Une mer entre les terres (d'Italie, de Gaule et d'Afrique). Comme telle, elle est *espace* de différenciation. [...] elle donne un horizon aux désirs [...]. La mer deviant donc espace de révélation – espace entre les terres [...]. La mer ici est l'espace qui permet et garantit l'originalité créative" (What is the Mediterranean? A sea between the lands [of Italy, of Gaul, and of Africa]. As such, it is a space of differentiation. It provides a horizon for one's desires. The sea becomes a space for revelation. A space between the lands. The sea is here the space that allows for and grants creative originality) (671–4). This assessment, which starts with a question of definition, is certainly reminiscent of Matvejević's creative doubt about the actual existence of the Mediterranean beyond our imagination, of Kenneth White's elaborations on the border between sea and land, and of Will Self's "Côte of Desire."

35 Quoted from memory. Toril Moi delivered her lecture at Yale University's Whitney Humanities Center (during the 1999 symposium "Changing the Map: The World of Comparative Literature").

36 White, *On the Atlantic Edge,* 75 and 65. "Couthy" ("couthie") is Scottish vernacular and means "kindly."

37 Benn, *Essays und Reden in der Fassung der Erstdrucke,* 306.

38 As a refrain, "Provence knew" appears repeatedly in Pound's early poem
"The Flame." Cf Baechler and Litz, eds, *Personae: The Shorter Poems of Ezra
Pound,* 48; and Eliot, "Introduction" to Pound's *Selected Poems,* xii–xiii.

39 Cf "Occitan Poetry," in Preminger and Brogan, eds, *The New Princeton Encyclopedia of Poetry and Poetics,* 851, where it is rightly pointed out that "Provençal
has the disadvantage that it seems to refer specifically to Provence [...] which
is only one part of the larger area where the language is spoken. Languedoc
refers to another part of the territory [...] Occitan is free from both such
misleading connotations." Since I am primarily concerned with place, however, I prefer "Provençal" for the language of the territory referred to, even
if it is not exclusive of it. The Provençal of those days was the literary *koine* of
troubadour poetry and is not synonymous with the Provençal/Occitane variants of today's Provence. For the geographic domain of Provençal's dialectic
fragmentation as ethnic cultural language, cf Bec, *La langue occitane.* And for
enlightening insights into the Romance territory and its poetic heritage, cf
Menocal, *Shards of Love.* As well as tracing the Arabic influence on European
poetry (notably on that of the Provençals), Menocal astutely excavates and
originally presents more than just one literary "scandal" in her chapter of the
same title (suggesting that "trobar" is Arabic rather than Latin derived and
refers to the root of "to sing" rather than "to find").

40 *Purgatorio,* 223.

41 Cf *The Encyclopædia Britannica* (Chicago: Encyclopædia Britannica, 2002)
and Touring Club Italiano, ed., *Attraverso l'Italia del 900,* 106–7.

42 Cf Kanceff, ed., *Viaggiatori stranieri in Liguria;* and Ragazzi, ed., *Kandinsky,
Vrubel', Jawlensky e gli artisti russi a Genova e nelle Riviere,* 87ff.

43 Quoted in Powers, *Italy in Mind,* 70–7.

44 James, *Collected Travel Writings,* 394–6.

45 Pound, *The Cantos,* 493.

46 Calvino, *La strada di San Giovanni,* 107. My translation, but cf Parker 144–5,
who translates more freely.

47 Ibid., 110. My translation; but cf Parker, 150.

48 Knowlson, ed., *The Theatrical Notebooks of Samuel Beckett: Waiting for Godot,* 55.

49 Bertram, "Portofino," in *Nietzsche: Versuch einer Mythologie,* 285; and Bertram,
"Portofino," in *Nietzsche: Attempt at a Mythology,* trans. Norton, 234. Form
means "Satzform" (syntax) here.

50 Matvejević, *The Mediterranean,* 10.

51 Calvino, *La strada di San Giovanni,* 97–8; cf Parker, 130, who translates more

freely. Calvino also compares Liguria's oblong curvy shape to a lizard offering its maximum surface to sea and sun.

52 Jakobson, "Linguistics and Poetics," 62–94; and Jakobson, "Two Aspects of Language and Two Types of Aphasic Disturbances," 95–113.

53 Goethe, *Italienische Reise*, 314; Goethe, *Italian Journey*, 302.

54 Cf Emil Levy, *Petit dictionnaire provençal-français*, 80, 221, and 328: "cluire" as "enfermer, renfermer, *clus* couvert, avec profondeur" (i.e., enclosed, profound), "lais" or "lai" as "sorte de poésie, chant des oiseaux" (i.e., light, easy), and "ric" as "puissant, distingué, remarquable" (i.e., rich, powerful, distinguished, remarkable). In *The New Princeton Encyclopedia of Poetry and Poetics*, "trobar clus" is characterized as "allusive, oblique, and recherché in vocabulary and rhymes," which is to say refined in the material and formal aspects of composition.

55 Pound, *The Cantos*, 464–6 and 531. Illustrator Aubrey Vincent Beardsley was associated with the Symbolists and acquainted with William Butler Yeats. Cf *The Cantos*, 177–80, for Pound's translation of Guido Cavalcanti's "Donna me prega" ("A lady asks me").

56 de Marinis and Spadea, eds, *I Liguri*, 35.

57 *The Divine Comedy of Dante Alighieri: Paradiso*, 132–3, and *Purgatorio*, 86–7, 94–5, and 112–13: "Ivi così una cornice lega / dintorno il poggio, come la primaia; / se non che l'arco suo più tosto piega" (There, just as in the case of the first terrace, a second terrace runs around the slope, except that it describes a sharper arc); 116–17: "quella banda / de la cornice onde cader si puote, / perché da nulla sponda s'inghirlanda" (along the outside, nearer the terrace-edge, no parapet was there to keep a man from falling off); 158–9; and 236–7: "Quivi la ripa fiamma in fuor balestra, / e la cornice spira fiato in suso / che la reflette e via da lei sequestra; / ond' ir ne convenia dal lato schiuso / ad uno ad uno; e io temëa 'l foco / quinci, e quindi temeva cader giuso" (There, from the wall, the mountain hurls its flames; but, from the terrace side, there whirls a wind that pushes back the fire and limits it; thus, on the open side, proceeding one by one, we went; I feared the fire on the left and, on the right, the precipice).

58 White, *On the Atlantic Edge*, 59: "Region is a word that rings no bell with me, awakens no deep resonance. It's a purely administrative term. Whereas a strong sense of living in a place requires a lot more than administration. As to regionalism as a cultural policy it leaves a lot to be desired. […] I prefer to speak of territory. What distinguishes a territory from a region is that it has an aura."

59 Freud, "Über den Gegensinn der Urworte." An example for such an *original, primeval,* or *Ur-word* (not on Freud's list, but crucial for the steepness in

question) is the Latin *altus*, meaning high and deep, encompassing height and depth as located on one and the same vertical axis (reminiscent, in turn, of Hart Crane's "high in the azure steeps").

60 Cf Wilkins and Bergin, eds, *A Concordance to the Divine Comedy of Dante Alighieri*, which has no entries for either Liguria or the Mediterranean. Including Dante's non-poetic texts, Paget Toynbee's *A Dictionary of Proper Names and Notable Matters in the Works of Dante*, however, has entries for both terms, as does Giovanni Andrea Scartazzini's, *Enciclopedia dantesca.*

61 For these kinds of landscape, cf especially cantos II, V–VIII, XI–XIII, XVIII, XX, and XXXIV of the *Inferno*. Dante alludes to the Mediterranean ("in mezzo mar"; "in midsea") in *Inferno* 128–9, exhibits the epic Mediterranean quest through Ulysses ("mare aperto"; "open sea") in *Inferno* 242–3, and explicitly makes mention of "Cipri e Maiolica" (Cyprus and Majorca) in *Inferno* 260–1.

62 *Paradiso*, 78–9, 250–1, and 342–3. For a further reference to the Mediterranean, cf *Paradiso*, 68–9: "Bari," "Gaeta," and "Catona."

63 *Purgatorio*, 4–5.

64 Ibid., 30–1.

65 Cf Siculus, *Biblioteca storica*.

66 Kenner, *The Pound Era*, 171. Similarly, Benn calls rhyme itself Mediterranean ("Mittelmeerisch ein Reim").

67 Miltoun and McManus, *Rambles on the Riviera*, 365 and 359. The Brocken (Blocksberg) has made its appearance in works ranging from Goethe's *Faust* and Heinrich Heine to Thomas Pynchon's *Gravity's Rainbow*, Coven's *Black Sabbath*, and the Liars' "They Were Wrong, So We Drowned," among many others.

68 *Italienische Reise*, 29.

69 Cf Kanceff, *Viaggiatori stranieri in Liguria*, who quotes various medieval sources that refer to Genoa as Zenoa and to the Genoese as Zenoexi. *Dante Alighieri on the web:* www.greatdante.net. "De vulgari eloquentia," ch. XIII, p. 19. And Dante Alighieri, *De vulgari eloquentia*, trans. Sally Purcell. Manchester : Carcante New ZPress, 1981, p. 30.

70 *Inferno*, 306–9.

71 "Epistole" and "Egloghe," in *Opere*, 330–4 and 356–9.

72 de Marinis and Spadea, eds, *I Liguri*, 17–18; Cicero, *Orations*, 17. Virgil, *Georgics*, 26.

73 Heinrichs, *Fenster zur Welt*.

74 Banville, *Shroud*, 32 and 17.

75 Goethe, "Noten und Abhandlungen zu besserem Verständnis des West-östlichen Divans," 26.

76 Nietzsche, *Also sprach Zarathustra*, for example, 244 and 245.

77 Nietzsche, *Werke in drei Bänden*, vol. III, 1238 and 1331–2; Nietzsche, *On the Genealogy of Morals, Ecce Homo*, 297–8. In his letters, Nietzsche points out: "*Ecce Homo* [...] gibt einiges Psychologische u. selbst Biographische über mich und meine Literatur: man wird mich mit einem Male *zu sehen bekommen* [...] Dieser *homo* bin ich nämlich selbst, eingerechnet des *ecce*." (*Ecce Homo* discloses a fair bit of psychology and even biography about me and my writing: I will become visible all at once. For I am this *homo*, including the *ecce*); *Werke in drei Bänden*, vol. III, 1238 and 1331–2.

78 *Zarathustra*, 135.

79 Frye, *Anatomy of Criticism*, 204. And White, *On the Atlantic Edge*, 25. White appropriately makes mention of Ralph Waldo Emerson in this context, another fine connection regarding Nietzsche's fascination with the American Transcendentalist, his take on nature, scholarship, and the circular, as well as his emphasis on walking on one's own feet.

80 White, *On the Atlantic Edge*, 24–5.

81 *Zarathustra*, 90. Nietzsche also calls Zarathustra's speeches and teachings "Feigen" (figs). The German "feige" can also signify cowardly. It is remarkable how Nietzsche plays with both semantic dimensions of this homophone in *Zarathustra*.

82 Benn, *Gedichte in der Fassung der Erstdrucke*, 307, 336, and 55.

83 Freud, *Briefe, 1873–1939*, 264.

84 Nietzsche, *Werke in drei Bänden*, vol. III, 1289–90.

85 Nietzsche, *Briefwechsel*, 13 and 60.

86 Both, the *academy* and the *lyceum* were located outside the city walls of Athens. The Platonic academy was named after Akademos, whereas the Aristotelian lyceum received its name from Apollo Lyceus. In the first line of Plato's dialogue "Lysis," Socrates walks along the road which connects the academy with the lyceum. Cf Plato, *Complete Works*, 688.

87 Nietzsche, *Briefwechsel*, 20, 482, and 47–9. Cf *Italia Benedettina II: Liguria monastica*, and *Italia Benedettina V: Storia monastica ligure e pavese*.

88 White, *On the Atlantic Edge*, 51.

89 Nietzsche, *Werke in drei Bänden*, vol. III, 1338; and Nietzsche, *Briefwechsel*, 333, 321, 475, 466–7, and 479.

90 Columbus, *The Four Voyages*, 27–8.

91 Benn, *Prosa und Autobiographie in der Fassung der Erstdrucke*, 81.

92 Harries, "The Philosopher at Sea," 21, 29, and 40.

93 Benn, *Essays und Reden*, 495–6.

94 Nietzsche, *Briefwechsel*, 479.

95 *Zarathustra*, 167, 190, and 216.

96 Cf Ovid, *Metamorphoses*, 240.

97 Matvejević, *The Mediterranean*, 7, 10, and 206. This translation has "rudder" but it should be "tiller."

98 Stein, "Landscape," in *Gertrude Stein's America*, 45. There exists an interesting prose variation of this piece by Stein: "After all every one is as their land is, as the climate is, as the mountains and rivers or their oceans are as the wind and rain and snow and ice and heat and moisture is, they just are and that makes them have their way to be subtle, and even if the lines of demarcation are only made with a ruler after all what is inside those right angles is different from those on the outside of those right angles, any American knows that"; in Stein, *Wars I Have Seen*, 165.

99 Casey, *The Fate of Place*, ix.

100 Hartman, "Romantic Poetry and the Genius Loci," in *Beyond Formalism*, 327.

101 Goethe, *Italienische Reise*, 45; *Italian Journey*, 57. This translation renders "an den Gegenständen" as "in the objects" which fails to stress the sort of confrontation or vis-à-vis that Goethe clearly emphasizes.

102 Nietzsche, *Werke in drei Bänden*, vol. III, 1289–90 and 1322.

103 Cf Petrarca, *Africa;* and Boccaccio, *Decamerone.*

104 Cf Tögel, *Berggasse – Pompeji und zurück*, 39–40.

105 Highet, *Poets in a Landscape*, 70. In a similar vein, Kenneth White refers to John Milton and the idea that "nobody is a poet in his own country" (*On the Atlantic Edge*, 56).

106 Cf Le Corbusier, "Other Icons: The Museums," 15–23.

107 Silver, *Making Paradise*, 25.

108 White, *On the Atlantic Edge*, 28.

109 Cf Ragazzi, ed., *Kandinsky, Vrubel', Jawlensky*, for example, 16, 29–30, 164–5, 214–20, 266, 284, for painterly examples of Ligurian motifs, including Alexej von Jawlensky's western Liguria (Bordighera) as well as Nikolaj Nikolaevič's and Kandinsky's and Gabriele Münter's sojourns in and portrayal of eastern Liguria (Rapallo, Santa Margherita, La Spezia) in the later nineteenth and the early twentieth centuries. It is also worth mentioning in this context that in the aftermath of the failed 1905 revolution, for a substantial group of Russian writers and artists, the Ligurian Riviera became a place of refuge and inspiration.

110 Cf Hibbert, "The Ways to Italy," in *The Grand Tour*, 91ff. Tobias Smollett, James Boswell, and Matthew Todd are exceptions to the rule.

111 Mann and Mann, *Das Buch von der Riviera*, 7.

112 Ibid., 142–4.

113 Ibid., 150.

114 Ibid., 152–3.

115 Ibid., 153, 158–9, and 160.
116 Erika and Klaus Mann travelled together not only to the Riviera but also to
the United States and to North Africa. Klaus Mann's *Der Vulkan* (*The Volcano*) is a famous novel about German exiles during the Second World War.
Klaus Mann died in Cannes of an overdose of sleeping pills and is buried
in the Cimetière Grand Jas. Erika Mann, an intellectual refugee from the
Third Reich (the entire Mann family, in fact, went into exile), was one of
the few women journalists after the war who covered the Nuremberg Trials
and gained access to the defendants. Benn's firm stance against emigration
was apparent already in his 1933 radio speech addressed to German exiles,
in particular those on the Riviera.
117 Mann and Mann, *Das Buch von der Riviera*, 182 and 184.
118 Silver, *Making Paradise*, 23; and Mann and Mann, *Das Buch von der Riviera*,
13.
119 Cf Goethe, *Wilhelm Meister's Apprenticeship*, 83. John Frederick Nims translates the refrain more liberally (and colloquially) as "Oh that's the way [...]
off today." In Browning and Hamburger, eds, *German Poetry from 1750–
1900*, 55–7. Jerome Rothenberg's translation, which is based on Samuel
Taylor Coleridge's, by contrast, renders the refrain of "Mignon's Song" in
a more archaic way as: "Thither with thee [...] would I wend [...] thither
let us steer." In Rothenberg and Robinson, eds, *Poems for the Millennium:
Volume III*, 81–2.
120 Mörike, *Du bist Orplid, mein Land*, 63; and "Weyla's Song" translated by
Charles Wharton Stork, in *The German Classics*, 372.
121 Benn, *Gedichte in der Fassung der Erstdrucke*, 464–5.
122 Calvino, "Dall'opaco," in *La strada di San Giovanni*, 107; "From the
Opaque," in *The Road to San Giovanni*, 145.
123 Cf Ortheil, "Schön in der Schwebe," in *Merian: Ligurien*, 27–8. Ortheil's
title is ambiguous in that it means "beautiful in suspension" as well as
"thoroughly suspended."
124 Matvejević, *The Mediterranean*, 7–12.
125 Ibid., 12.
126 de Man, "Conclusions: Walter Benjamin's The Task of the Translator," in
The Resistance to Theory, 86. Although for at least two decades de Man's
reputation has suffered severely as a result of the posthumously discovered articles he wrote for the Belgian collaborationist newspaper *Le Soir*,
his readings of Nietzsche and Rilke, as well as his fine analysis of imitative
form in literary writing cannot be discarded on these grounds. Further,
this recurrence to Hölderlin is compelling in the connection one might
establish between mise-en-abîme on the one hand and "harte Fügung"
(*harmonia austera* or tough composition) on the other.

127 One wonders whether Gottfried Benn was familiar with John Hersey's 1944 novel *A Bell for Adano*, which relates the story of an Italian-American officer in Sicily during the Second World War, who gains the respect of the inhabitants of the coastal town of Adano by assisting them in finding a replacement for the bell in the town's campanile that the Fascists had melted down.

128 Silver, *Making Paradise*, 101 and 116; and Mann and Mann, *Das Buch von der Riviera*, 16.

129 The Beach Boys, "Kokomo." The song, written by John Phillips, Scott McKenzie, and Terry Melcher, was recorded by the Beach Boys in 1988, released as a single, and became a number one hit in the Unites States, Japan, and Australia. "Kokomo" was first released in an album in 1989, *Still Cruisin'*.

130 http://britishexpats.com/forum/showthread.php?t=296744 (retrieved 13 July 2010, 10:52 a.m.). I took the liberty of correcting a variety of ortho-graphic errors.

131 Freud, "Das Unbehagen in der Kultur," *Studienausgabe* IX.

132 Self and Steadman, *Psychogeography*, 105–6.

133 Fraser, *The Songs of Peire Vidal*, 100–1. Peire Vidal, so the story goes, fled the court of Raimon Barral, Viscount of Marseilles, after having stolen a kiss from the Viscount's wife, Alazais de Rocamartina (a place near Aix-en-Pro-vence), and dressed up in wolf skins to woo Loba de Panautier of Carcas-sonne, but was savaged by her dogs and went on to marry the daughter of the Emperor of Byzantium in Cyprus. There are a couple of variants of this Provençal song of Vidal's, whose auxiliary title is "Ab l'alen tir vas me l'aire" (the poem's first line). It explicitly names the toponyms Provence, Rhône, Vence, and Durence, and stresses that it is indeed Provence that has provided the singer with the "gai saber," with memory ("sovenensa"), knowledge ("sciensa") and understanding ("conneisensa").

134 Cordes, *Troubadours aujourd'hui*, 105.

135 Apollinaire, "Les fenêtres," in *Fenêtres*, 80; and *Selected Writings of Guillaume Apollinaire*, 140–3.

136 Cf Phillipotts, *Stories from Herodotus in Attic Greek*; and Reynolds and Minter, *The First Marathon*.

137 Goethe, *Italienische Reise*, 25 and 17. Since I consider Auden and Mayer's rendering of "Beobachtungsgeist" as "powers of observation" and particu-larly of "Welterschaffung" as "cosmological theories" (*Italian Journey*, 38 and 30) to be problematic, I have provided my own English translations in parentheses on this occasion: "spirit of observation" and "creation of a world."

138 *Italienische Reise*, 53; *Italian Journey*, 64.

139 Assereto, *Storia d'Italia,* 171; and Gabrielli, *Storia d'Italia,* 781.
140 Casey, *The Fate of Place,* 286.
141 Benn, *Prosa und Autobiographie in der Fassung der Erstdrucke,* 274.
142 Brooke, "Lerici," in Rolleston, *Talks with Lady Shelley,* 7–9.
143 James, "The Birthplace," in *Complete Tales of Henry James,* 403–65.
144 James, *Collected Travel Writings / Italian Hours,* 398–400. Incidentally, Henry James also set a portion of his novel *The Ambassssadors* on the Riviera. It is remarkable how James in another act of understatement seemingly opposes Shelley's poetry with his own prose. James's prose certainly qualifies as one example of what Ezra Pound demanded of poetry: that it "must be as well written as prose." Cf Kolb, "Poetry Must Be as Well Written as Prose."
145 As opposed to the English expression "to be silent", the German verb "schweigen," despite its taciturn semantic dimension, is syntactically speaking an active verb.
146 It is crucial to recognize in this "Fläche" not only Bertram's plain of silence, but also Goethe's opposition of prosaic "Fläche" and poetically expressive steepness – an implication that the translation of "Fläche" as "surface" does not capture ("surface" translates into German as "Oberfläche").
147 Mann and Mann, *Das Buch von der Riviera,* 166–7.
148 Norbert von Hellingrath in Frey and Lorenz, *Kritik des freien Verses,* 103–4; and von Hellingrath, "Kunstcharakter der Pindarübersetzung," in *Hölderlin-Vermächtnis,* 20; and Carson, *Eros, The Bittersweet,* 35.
149 Calvino, *La strada di San Giovanni,* 101.
150 Liégeard, *La Côte d'Azur,* 403. Gerardo Dottori's *Il Golfo della Spezia* is located in a private collection in Perugia and is shown on the cover of the present book.
151 Nietzsche, *Die Fröhliche Wissenschaft,* 525.

Part II

1 Giuseppe Mazzini, quoting Johann Wolfgang von Goethe to Friedrich Nietzsche during their chance encounter.
2 Schlechta III, 1217, and *Ecce Homo,* 1127, *Zarathustra,* 363.
3 CF Buddensieg, 27–64: "Genua – Hafen, Gärten, Paläste" (Genoa – harbour, gardens, palaces).
4 Martini and Gori, *La Liguria e la sua anima,* 259.
5 *Jenseits von Gut und Böse,* 201.
6 Buddensieg, 2.
7 *Ecce Homo,* 336–7.

8 Kaufmann and Hollingdale, 297–8. This translation renders Nietzsche's "fiel mir ein" as "occurred to me," which is weaker than "befell" or "overtook"; however, the translators append footnotes to the German original that show nicely the shared etymology of "einfallen" and "überfallen," with which Nietzsche clearly played in this passage.

9 *Zarathustra*, 37.

10 *Die fröhliche Wissenschaft*, 45 and 411.

11 Goethe, *Italienische Reise*, 298–9.

12 Kaufmann, *Gay Science* 354–5, and Schlechta, *Nietzsche's großer Mittag*, 32 and 47.

13 *Zarathustra*, 142.

14 Ibid., 131–2.

15 Ibid., 83.

16 CF Wilhelm J.J. Heinse, *Ardinghello und die glückseligen Inseln: Eine italiänische Geschichte aus dem sechzehnten Jahrhundert* (1787).

17 *Über Wahrheit und Lüge*, 312.

18 Ibid., 311.

19 Ibid., 312

20 "Definition of a Germanophile," in *Selected Non-Fictions*, 203–4.

21 *Zarathustra*, 254–7.

22 Krell and Bates, *Nietzsche's Work Sites*, 6.

23 *Zarathustra*, 41.

24 *Zarathustra*, 363; and Nietzsche, *Thus Spoke Zarathustra*, trans. Kaufmann, 327.

25 *Zarathustra*, 41.

26 Quoted in the brochure of Kolleg Friedrich Nietzsche/Klassik Stiftung Weimear 2012.

27 Daudet, *Port-Tarascon*, 1.

28 Cf Ragazzi, ed., *Kandinsky, Vrubel', Jawlensky*, in particular 26–30 (including Münter's 1905 painting *Baia di Rapallo*), and 215–20 (including Kandinsky's various Rapallo paintings of 1905–6).

29 Simmons, *Freud's Italian Journey*, 15; and Schinaia, "Freud e Genova," 475; and Tögel, ed., *Sigmund Freud*, 5–7 and 391–8. Tögel documents a total of seventeen Italian journeys on Freud's part within the temporal framework of his book.

30 Tögel, *Sigmund Freud*, 127–8.

31 Cf Jirat-Wasiutyński and Dymond, eds, *Modern Art and the Idea of the Mediterranean*, Figure 7.5: Frederic Leighton, *The Acropolis in Athens with the Genoese Tower* (1867).

32 Tögel, *Sigmund Freud*, 204–5.

33 Schinaia, "Freud e Genova," 476. In this context, Freud also wrote on the

homophonic potential of Nervi as the Ligurian town, on the one hand, and, on the other, as the Italian noun for nerves – *nervi*.

34 Derrida, *Archive Fever*, 95.

35 Goethe, *Die Wahlverwandtschaften*, 181. Freud had already alluded to this Goethe passage on a postcard to Minna in September 1902. See Tögel, *Sigmund Freud*, 157 and 206.

36 Freud, *Studienausgabe* IV, 288.

37 *Die Traumdeutung*, 141 ff.

38 Kivland, *Freud on Holiday Volume I: Freud Dreams of Rome* (York: Information as Material, 2006) unpaginated, pages 3–4.

39 *Die Traumdeutung*, 205 ff.

40 Ibid., 447ff.

41 Ibid., 448.

42 Ibid., 577. And Auden, "In Memory of Sigmund Freud," in *Selected Poems*, 93.

43 Goethe, *Italienische Reise*, 198–9, and 204.

44 From Mark Twain, *Innocents Abroad*, quoted in Powers, ed., *Italy in Mind*, 309–11.

45 Pellegrino, *Ghosts of Vesuvius*, 185.

46 Cf Downing's *After Images*.

47 For Freud's correspondence with Jensen about *Gradiva*, see Jeffrey Sammons, "Wilhelm Raabe's and Wilhelm Jensen's Scandinavian Fictions: A Contrast in Nationalisms" in Parente and Schade, eds, *Studies in German and Scandinavian Literature after 1500*, 116–28.

48 Freud, *Der Wahn und die Träume in Jensens Gradiva: Mit der Erzählung von Wilhelm Jensen*, 162 and 170.

49 Derrida, *Archive Fever*, 86.

50 Tögel, *Sigmund Freud*, 159.

51 Casey, *The Fate of Place*, 243–4.

52 The Latin phrase *Et in Arcadia ego* is elliptical; it does not spell out the copula verb *esse*, which is acceptable in Latin but has led to ambiguity in translation and hence to various interpretations, oscillating between something like "Even in Arcadia I am present" on the one hand, and "I, too, was in Arcadia" on the other. The former is close to the Latin syntax, while the latter accords well with Nicolas Poussin's second Arcadia painting, which no longer portrays the skull that was placed on the sarcophagus in the painting's first version. The phrase was first visually represented in Giovanni Francesco Barberini's baroque painting *Et in Arcadia ego*, where it is inscribed in a stone with a skull sitting on top of it. Here it likely intends the first meaning of the phrase as a *memento mori*, that is to say death reminding the two young men in the painting that, even in Arcadia, nobody is spared from dying. In Poussin's painting

The Shepherds of Arcadia the wall is replaced by a sarcophagus, conjuring up the idea that rather than death, the dead soul announces its existence in the realm of the dead. The second version of Poussin's painting tellingly omits the skull from the sarcophagus and has the shepherds converse instead with a beautiful woman. It is interesting to recall the ancient discussions surrounding Plato's rejection of mimetic art in this context, which considered inscriptions in the first person as particularly problematic in that the artist is not the reader. Such inscriptions could only circumvent their fate of necessarily being lies if they applied to every reader who would possibly pronounce this first-person phrase. This lowest common denominator that would apply to all humans (and to all readers who pronounce the first-person phrase) is death. It is, then, death that will come to the mind of the reader as the only commonality, and it is this very awareness of death's uncanny presence that saves this inscription from being a lie. Goethe employs the *Auch ich in Arkadien* phrase as a motto for his *Italian Journey* but later on deconstructs the ambiguity by saying *Auch ich in der Champagne*. Goethe's irony tries to cope with the misery that he witnessed as imposed by the French Revolution, rather than making mention of a poetic phrase or metaphorical presence of death alone. It is, however, really via Friedrich Schiller's beginning lines of the "Resignation" poem that the phrase more prominently entered German literature: "Auch ich war in Arkadien geboren, / auch mir hat die Natur [...]" (Even I was in Arcadia born, / Even to me did nature [...]), which suggests something like an *arcadianity* of places such as the southern German Marbach (in Virgil's sense of Arcadia as the land in which poets are born). Cf Brandt, *Arkadien in Kunst*. And for a parodic treatment of the theme, Stoppard, *Arcadia: A Play*, which elaborates on the complex relationship of the past (including the literary past) with the present, and in which not only translations from the Latin and the study of hermits and the Romantic imagination play a significant role, but in which Lord Byron is given the uncanny presence of an unseen house guest.

53 Although the legendary island Atlantis, said to have existed in the Atlantic Ocean and after a failed invasion by Athens to have sunk beneath the sea, is archaeologically associated with Thera (Santorini), the surviving portion of a larger isle destroyed by a volcanic eruption, Atlantis has more in common with Pamuk's imagined scenario underneath the Bosphorus (and perhaps with Freud's *invasion* of Athens as well) than with an actually existing terrain such as Arcadia or Liguria, whose civilization is not lost.

54 *Die Traumdeutung*, 418.

55 Freud, *Briefe, 1873–1939*, 263–4.

56 A north-south opposition played out in the Germanic versus Romance context dates back at least to Gaius Cornelius Tacitus's *De origine et situ Ger-*

manorum (generally rendered as the *Germania*), while a friendlier encounter portraying a potential compatibility of German and Italian climes is envisioned in Friedrich Overbeck's allegorical painting *Italia and Germania*, where the two places are embodied by two women, one with dark hair and a southern laurel wreath, the other with blond hair and a northern flower wreath, and a background showing a coastal landscape on the one hand, and a gothic town on the other. The two women tenderly hold hands, and Overbeck's painting is indeed an allegory of friendship which was spurred by his loss of Frankfurt painter-friend Franz Pforr, who died young in Albano Laziale near Rome. Overbeck's painting is representative of the early nineteenth-century German Nazarene movement, which set out to revive spirituality in Christian art.

57 Tögel, *Berggasse – Pompeji und zurück*, 85.

58 *Ecce Homo*, 336–7. *Ecce Homo*, trans. Kaufmann, 397–8. When Nietzsche walks from Rapallo to Santa Margherita and Portofino, he walks directly south on the western ridge of the peninsula. In 1886, Friedrich Wilhelm von Preußen, the future Kaiser Wilhelm II, was a guest at the Castello Carnavon at Portofino Mare.

59 I understand Freud's authorial repression and anxiety as post-Nietzschean rather than post-Goethean, and cannot discern Freud's difficulty in facing Italy after Goethe, as Richard Block does (emphasizing Goethe's more than Italy's spell), with which what Block classifies as haunted and castrated epigones (Nietzsche and Freud among them) can only have a phantasmic encounter. While interested in literary (and psychoanalytically defined) influence, the present study is, unlike Block's, geopoetically oriented and hence attuned to literary writing and its intimate relationship not with an elusive Italy at large but with a precise Liguria.

60 *Studienausgabe* X, 294.

61 Among these critics are Paul-Laurent Assoun, Harold Bloom, Renate Müller-Buck, Daniel Chapelle, Jacques Derrida, Reinhard Gasser, Peter Gay, Catherine Géry, Günter Gödde, Ernest Jones, Ronald Lehrer, Andrea Loselle, Marika Lucchetti, Michel Onfray, Sophie Salin, Michael V. Ure, Eric Vartzbed, Aldo Venturelli, and Richard Waugaman.

62 I have previously ventured into Freud's Rapallo excursion in "Guilt Trips on Royal Roads: Freud's Mediterranean Affinities," *Quaderni di Studi Indo-Mediterranei* II (2009): 329–46. The present discussion marks an expansion of my thoughts expressed in it, and I thank the journal editors for granting me permission to reprint portions of this article in the present study.

63 Assoun, *Freud et Nietzsche*, xviii, xxix, 11–12.

64 *Studienausgabe* IV, 291.

65 Bloom, *The Anxiety of Influence*, 137 ff.

66 *Studienausgabe* IV, 285.

67 Goethe, *Italienische Reise*, 17 and 25.

68 Ibid., 45.

69 Ibid., 165.

70 White, *On the Atlantic Edge*, 9–10.

71 *Studienausgabe* IV, 287.

72 Ibid., 292.

73 Ibid.

74 *Studienausgabe* X, 236 ff.

75 Ibid., 252–3.

76 Ibid., 253.

77 *Studienausgabe* IV, 288.

78 Ibid., 290.

79 Freud, *Briefe an Wilhelm Fließ, 1887–1904*, 437–8.

80 It is worth reminding ourselves in this context of beginning and ending professional friendships and collaborations that some of Freud's insightful and successful colleagues were not sufficiently content with following in Freud's footsteps but developed instead a spectrum of ideas that Freud found did not accord with his own claims. Among these are Carl Gustav Jung and Alfred Adler, who repeatedly diverged from what they considered Freud's too-exclusive emphasis on sexuality, and refused to accept Freud as the only totalizing theorist. From the beginning, there has always been a fair bit of resistance to Freud, not only from outside, but from within psychoanalytic circles as well.

81 *Briefe, 1873–1939*, 385.

82 Ibid., 406.

83 Freud, *Studienausgabe* X, 225.

84 *Studienausgabe* IX, 197.

85 *Studienausgabe* X, 253. Likely Joseph Paneth.

86 Ibid., 289.

87 Ibid., 296.

88 *Genealogie der Moral*, 305–6.

89 *Briefe an Wilhelm Fließ*, 438, and *Die Traumdeutung*, 524.

90 Derrida, *La carte postale*, 313ff.

91 Benn, *Szenen und Schriften*, 223. The word "Artist" in German refers to what would be an "artiste" in English, in other words, a professional entertainer such as a singer, dancer, acrobat, or circus artist(e), rather than a poet or painter, which would translate as "Künstler."

92 Eliot, *Four Quartets*, 49.

93 Benn, *Frühe Lyrik und Dramen*.

94 *Gedichte in der Fassung der Erstdrucke*, 187. Cf Bohusch, ed., *Interpretationen*

moderner Lyrik, 89–92, on Benn's poem "Reisen," and Ranicki, ed., *1000 Deutsche Gedichte und ihre Interpretationen*, 236–43, for Benn on the uselessness of touring. Further, one may well suspect Nietzsche's influence on Benn in the context of Benn's "Jena"; Nietzsche begins his youth poem "Nach Pforta" similarly by pointing to a "friendly valley" ("im freundlichen Thale"), which Benn seems to have taken up by "im lieblichen Tale" (in the lovely valley). See Dreßler, Schmidt, and Wagner, *Spurensuche*, 103.

95 Or in Ritchie's translation in *Gottfried Benn: The Unreconstructed Expressionist*, 118, which unfortunately captures "Wüstennot" only as need and hardship, but not as longing and desire, which the German "Not" equally implies: "Or do you think Havana / White and hibiscus-red / Would offer eternal manna / In your waste land for bread?"

96 Edgar Dacqué's thoughts on origin and the lost paradise made a strong impression on the later Benn; Dacqué's *Das Verlorene Paradies* deploys a legion of Ur-compounds and presents the "Urmensch" on a geological basis, while reading psyche in archaeological terms ("Schichtungen oder Zeitalter der Seele," 69ff) reminiscent of both Freud and Carl Gustav Jung.

97 For Benn's numerous references to the Mediterranean, the Tyrrhenian Sea, the Riviera, and Liguria, cf *Gedichte in der Fassung der Erstdrucke*, 55, "Tyrrhenisches Meer. Ein frevelhaftes Blau" (Tyrrhenian Sea. A sacrilegious blue); 70, "tyrrhenische Inseln" (Tyrrhenian islands); 145, "Tyrrhenische See" (Tyrrhenian Sea); 159, "Ponente" (that is: Western Riviera); 175, "tyrrhenische Meer" (Tyrrhenian Sea); 195, "Mediterran" (Mediterranean); 240, "Méditerrané [sic] (Mediterranean Sea); 307, "Mittelmeerisch" and "Mittelmeer" (Mediterranean); 336, "ligurische" (Ligurian); 394, "Méditerrané" [sic] (Mediterranean Sea); and 419, "Portofino." Cf *Essays und Reden in der Fassung der Erstdrucke*, 44, "nach ligurischem Komplexe" (relying on the Ligurian complex); 81, "der helle Staub der Méditerrannée" (the light dust of the Mediterranean); 306, "das Ligurische" (the Ligurian); 510, "ligurische Begriffe" (Ligurian concepts); 520, "ligurische Komplexe" (Ligurian complexes); and 532, "ligurischen Meeres" (of the Ligurian Sea). Cf *Prosa und Autobiographie in der Fassung der Erstdrucke*, 42, "Mittelmeer" (Mediterranean Sea); 49, "Ponente" (that is: Western Riviera); 50, "Ligurischem Meer" (Ligurian Sea); 201, "Mittelmeer" (Mediterranean Sea); 212, "Mittelmeerländer" (Mediterranean countries); 265, "Tyrrhenermeer" (Sea of the Tyrrhenians); 274, "ligurischen Komplexes" (of the Ligurian complex); 300, "das ligurische Meer" (the Ligurian Sea); 326–7 and 376–7, "ligurische Komplexe" (Ligurian complexes); and 476, "Méditerranée" (Mediterranean). Cf *Szenen und Schriften in der Fassung der Erstdrucke*, 154, "ligurische Komplexe" (Ligurian complexes); and 227, "mittelmeerisches Prinzip" (Mediterranean principle).

98 Hof, *Benn*, 233. Gardone, from where Benn wrote a postcard, houses the "Vittoriale degli italiani," a shrine that d'Annunzio turned into his monumental residence.

99 Benn, "Ich finde," in *Szenen und Schriften in der Fassung der Erstdrucke*, 154. This piece is alternatively titled "Schöpferische Konfession." And Benn, *Prosa und Autobiographie*, 51. In "Gottfried Benn's Return to the Future: Four Translations and Commentaries," *Italian Poetry Review* V (2010): 125–44, I have ventured into English translations of Benn's poetry and prose. The present chapter marks an expansion of my ideas about Benn's Expressionism and Marinetti's Futurism expressed in this article (as well as a revision of a portion of my translations of Benn into English). I thank the journal editors for granting me permission to reprint sections of my previous work.

100 Self and Steadman, *Psychogeography*, 112.

101 *Essays und Reden*, 77.

102 Ibid., 495–6.

103 "Der Geburtstag" and "Querschnitt" in Benn, *Sämtliche Werke: Band III: Prosa 1*, 50–61 and 82–92. Cf *Primal Vision*, 3–12 (*The Birthday*).

104 In Benn, *Sämtliche Werke: Band III: Prosa 1* (the Schuster/Stuttgart edition), 108–9. There are, among minor others, two noteworthy discrepancies between the Schuster/Stuttgart edition and the version of this text in Benn, *Szenen und Schriften* (the Hillebrand/Frankfurt edition), 153–4. These are the absence of the title in the Hillebrand/Frankfurt edition, as well the variant "Rauch und Qualen" (fume and agonies), rather than the tautological "Rauch und Qualm" (fume and smoke) of the Schuster/Stuttgart edition (and of Benn's actual novella *Querschnitt*, also in the Hillebrand/Frankfurt version). I have chosen to insert the title, but have reverted to the *Erstdruck* rather than the tautology, hence "agonies." N.B. While the Frankfurt edition indicates *Erstdrucke* in its title, the Stuttgart edition is based on *Fassungen letzter Hand*, as its editorial report explains; hence, textual discrepancies between the two editions are self-explanatory. German original and English translation are reprinted with the kind permission of J.G. Cotta'sche Buchhandlung Nachfolger GmbH Stuttgart, which owns the rights to Benn's work.

105 For Benn's own commentaries on these travels, cf "Einiges Private" in *Prosa und Autobiographie in der Fassung der Erstdrucke*, 475–7; "Frankreich und Wir" in *Essays und Reden in der Fassung der Erstdrucke*, 77; and "Produktive Eindrücke auf Reisen" in *Szenen und Schriften in der Fassung der Erstdrucke*, 173, where Benn writes informatively about mental touring and protopoetic evocation: "Die speziellen Eindrücke meiner Reisen in Frankreich habe ich beschrieben. Aber es gibt noch andere Reiseeindrücke, Ein-

drücke allgemeinerer und dunklerer Art: Schauer der Fremde, land-
schaftliche oder ozeanische Berauschungen, Einbrüche aus Stätten die
waren und vorüberziehen, wiederholt habe ich aus solchen Zuständen
Material für meine Verse und Sätze gewonnen" (I have described my
specific impressions on my journeys in France. But there are other travel
impressions as well, impressions of a more general and of a darker kind:
shudder vis-à-vis the unknown, landscape-related, or oceanic ecstasies,
the invasion by places that have been and have gone by; I have repeatedly
found material for my verses and sentences in such states of being.)

106 Ziebarth, "Es ist schön, an Orpheus zu denken," in *Hexenspeise*, 111. Cf
also "Kann keine Trauer sein," which is Benn's very last poem (1956) and
explicitly remembers, in an act of mourning against mourning, as it were,
not only Nietzsche's dark dead eyes on his Weimar pillow, but Droste's
small death bed in Meersburg as well (*Gedichte in der Fassung der Erstdrucke*,
476).

107 Friedrich, "Plädoyer für die schwarzen Kutten"; and Ziebarth, *Reisen mit
Benn*.

108 "Probleme der Lyrik," in *Essays und Reden in der Fassung der Erstdrucke*, 523.

109 *Prosa und Autobiographie in der Fassung der Erstdrucke*, 459.

110 J.P. Jacobsen, *Niels Lyhne*, 149. Incidentally, Sigmund Freud read *Niels Lyhne*
in 1895 and was considerably moved by its final chapters in particular.

111 Ziebarth, *Hernach*, 36.

112 *Gedichte in der Fassung der Erstdrucke*, 195.

113 *Essays und Reden in der Fassung der Erstdrucke*, 306. It is essential to distinguish between Benn's Ligurian-Provençal poetological placements
and his early poems, in which places range from "Wüste" (desert) and
"Schädelstätte" (Golgotha) to "Arkadien" (Arcadia) and "Urwald" (rain
forest); from "Ithaka" (Ithaca) and "Hölle" (hell) to "Rom" (Rome),
"Sansibar," (Zanzibar),and "Dschungel" (jungle); from "Palmen"(palm
trees) to "Muschelmeer" (sea of shells). Cf "Schöne Jugend," "Der Arzt,"
"Nachtcafé," "Prolog 1920," "Alaska," "Fleisch," "Innerlich," "Banane,"
"Fürst Kraft," "Annonce," "Zwischenreich," "Widmung," "Hyperämische
Reiche," "Qui sait," "Alaska," "Ostafrika," "Jena," "Osterinsel," "Sils-Maria"
(Nietzsche), "Turin" (Nietzsche), and "März: Brief nach Meran," all in
Gedichte in der Fassung der Erstdrucke.

114 Meli, "Il giardino di Arles," 189–221. And Secci, "Il complesso ligure di
Gottfried Benn" (unpaginated).

115 *Prosa und Autobiographie in der Fassung der Erstdrucke*, 96.

116 Ibid., 91–100.

117 *Szenen und Schriften in der Fassung der Erstdrucke*, 193. While commenting
on the pastor's home, he mentions himself and various other cases such

as Nietzsche and van Gogh as examples of a thoroughly educational but
psychologically questionable kind of upbringing. This religious-cultural
lens offers another interesting perspective from which to look at Nietzsche,
van Gogh, and Benn's clichéd dichotomies as south-Catholic-Romance versus north-Protestant-Germanic. It does not, however, fully explain Benn's
specific attraction to things Ligurian.

118 Hillebrand, *Gottfried Benn*, 165.

119 *Gedichte in der Fassung der Erstdrucke*, 82, 11, and 384.

120 The biblical patriarch Methuselah is the oldest person in the Old Testa-
ment (Genesis 7:4), upon whose passing God delayed the flood in order to
grant seven days of mourning for him. Benn was attracted to the power of
this name (which is Hebrew for either "man of the dart" or "his death shall
bring"), to yet another Ur, which accords with Benn's interest in age and
aging as well as in origins and genealogies. It is interesting in the context
of the present study's elaboration on ligurianity to mention Aubrey de
Gray's notion of *methuselarity*, a vision of future life that eliminates death
and thus addresses the state of being alive, regardless of age, with no death
approaching, and as such diametrically opposed to *arcadianity*.

121 Gauguin, *Avant et après*, 12, 113, and 122.

122 In *Szenen und Schriften in der Fassung der Erstdrucke*, 223. Cf Gauguin, *Avant
et après*, 15. Gauguin and van Gogh lived together for about two months
in the yellow house at the Arlesian Place Lamartine, before the legendary
quarrel between the two painters erupted, at the end of which van Gogh
began his acts of self-mutilation, while Gauguin escaped to more exotic
pastures (such as the Marquesas).

123 *Essays und Reden in der Fassung der Erstdrucke*, 223 and 89.

124 See Benn's "Antwort an die literarischen Emigranten" (*Prosa und Autobiographie*, 295–302), in which he defends the position that German history
could be judged only by those who stayed in Germany, not by the emigrés
on Mediterranean lidos. Cf Reinhard Alter, *Gottfried Benn*. Instead of emi-
grating in the 1930s with his fellow Expressionists, who relocated primarily
to the French Riviera, Benn briefly became a fellow-traveller of the nascent
regime in that he judged the rise of National Socialism in Germany far too
idealistically, criticizing the emigrant writers in their "französische Bade-
orte" (French Riviera beach towns, or "Latin shores," as Ashton translates
it in Benn, *Primal Vision*, 48) and eventually, in 1944–5, living a life in
inner emigration as a military doctor in the Landsberg barracks. Cf *Prosa
und Autobiographie in der Fassung der Erstdrucke*, 298 and 415. That Benn's
post-Nietzschean Ligurian territory, which increasingly became his poetic
alibi, should geographically coincide with the exact Mediterranean shore

to which Klaus Mann and many others emigrated in 1933 makes Benn's retreat all the more complex and controversial. Cf Grandjonc, *Emigrés français en Allemagne*, and Herzer, *The Italian Refuge* (who confirms Genoa's liberalism).

125 Brode, ed., *Benn Chronik*, 34.

126 *Essays und Reden in der Fassung der Erstdrucke*, 495 and 501. Benn borrows the phrase "Welle und Spiel" from Nietzsche's *Dionysos-Dithyramben*.

127 Nietzsche wrote this in a letter from Rapallo to Heinrich Köselitz in 1882. Cf *Briefwechsel*, 288.

128 Both "which distance provides" and "which provides distance" are possible renderings of this syntactically ambiguous German passage. *Essays und Reden in der Fassung der Erstdrucke*, 93.

129 Luce, *Celebrating Homer's Landscapes*, 5.

130 Benn's early Rönne prose is clearly autobiographical. Dr Rönne is Dr Benn's *alter ego*, which Benn later on confirms in his autobiography, *Doppelleben*. In similar fashion, Nietzsche's Zarathustra is an *alter ego*, as Nietzsche explains in his autobiographical retrospection *Ecce Homo*.

131 *Essays und Reden in der Fassung der Erstdrucke*, 510.

132 *Prosa und Autobiographie in der Fassung der Erstdrucke*, 273–4. *Theogony* means "birth of the gods" and is likely an allusion to the poem by Hesiod.

133 Pound, *Literary Essays*, 4. While defining the image, Pound mentions a connection between his understanding of "complex" and that of psychologists such as Bernard Hart.

134 *Gedichte in der Fassung der Erstdrucke*, 304; Ritchie, *Gottfried Benn*, 114; and Benn, *Primal Vision*, 251.

135 *Prosa und Autobiographie in der Fassung der Erstdrucke*, 173 and 418.

136 Ibid., 487.

137 Fisher, *Making and Effacing Art*, 196.

138 Benn, *Prosa und Autobiographie*, 60.

139 Benn's note in the manuscript. Deutsches Literaturarchiv Marbach/Neckar, Benn Estate. D86.258.Handschriftenabteilung. Benn wrote an alternative word above "Farben" (colours), which is difficult to decipher but may be "Schleier" (veil, veils).

140 *Gedichte in der Fassung der Erstdrucke*, 55.

Postface

1 *La strada di San Giovanni*, 97; *The Road to San Giovanni*, 129.

2 Kermode, *The Sense of an Ending*, 3 and 156.

3 Quoted in Müller-Buck, "Nihilismus und Melancholie: Nietzsches Denken

im Spiegel Sigmund Freuds" 266. The German "fertig werden" can either mean "to finish" / "be done with," or else "to cope with" / "to overcome" – "coming to terms" captures both semantic dimensions, that of dealing as well as that of ending. In his revisiting of *Dawn* in *Ecce Homo*, Nietzsche writes in a similar vein: "Dies Buch [*Die Morgenröthe*] schliesst mit einem 'Oder?' – es ist das einzige Buch, das mit einem 'Oder'? schliesst ..." (This book ends in an "or"? – it is the only book that ends in an "or"? ...). *Ecce Homo*, 330.

4 *Die fröhliche Wissenschaft*, 521 and *The Gay Science*, 221.

5 *Morgenröthe*, 9. T.S. Eliot also quotes from the Vedas in *The Waste Land*.

6 *Inferno*, 12–13.

7 *Italienische Reise*, 9; and *Italian Journey*, 23.

8 *Also sprach Zarathustra*, 11.

9 Among these are Pourtalès, *Nietzsche en Italie*; Harrison, *Nietzsche in Italy*; Buddensieg, *Nietzsches Italien*; and Simmons, *Freud's Italian Journey*.

10 Woolf, *A Room of One's Own*, 3.

11 I have begun this sort of investigation in Kolb, "Gottfried Benn's Return to the Future."

12 Woolf, *A Room of One's Own*, 98–9.

13 Nietzsche, *Menschliches, Allzu Menschliches* I (*Human, All Too Human* I), and *Zarathustra*, 92 and 122. Cf. Don McKay, "Between Rock and Stone: A Geopoetic Alphabet."

14 Mitchell, trans. and ed., *Gilgamesh*, 70.

15 Cf the aforementioned "methuselarity," and the recent popularity of "italicity" to combine metalingualism with a plurality of ethnicities.

16 White, *On the Atlantic Edge*, 52.

17 *Die fröhliche Wissenschaft*, 574, and *The Gay Science*, 280.

18 White, *On the Atlantic Edge*, 76.

Bibliography

Abrams, Meyer H. *The Mirror and the Lamp: Romantic Theory and the Critical Tradition*. Oxford: Oxford University Press, 1971.

Alter, Reinhard. *Gottfried Benn: The Artist and Politics (1910–1934)*. Bern, Frankfurt, Munich: Herbert Lang, 1976.

Andriuoli, Elio. *Venticinque poeti:Ricerche sulla poesia del novecento in Liguria*. Liguria: Sabatelli, 1987.

Andronik, Catherine M. *Wildly Romantic – The English Romantic Poets: The Mad, the Bad, and the Dangerous*. New York: Henry Holt, 2007.

Anselmi, Gian Maria G. *Mappe della letteratura europea e mediterranea*. Milan: Mondadori, 2000.

Apollinaire, Guillaume. *Fenêtres*. Paris: Éditions des Cendres, 1983.

Apollinaire, Guillaume. *Selected Writings of Guillaume Apollinaire*. Ed. and trans. Roger Shattuck. New York: New Directions, 1971.

Armstrong, Richard H. *A Compulsion for Antiquity: Freud and the Ancient World*. Ithaca, NY: Cornell University Press, 2006.

Assereto, Giovanni. *Storia d'Italia: Le regioni dall'unità ad oggi: La Liguria*. Turin: Einaudi, 1994.

Assmann, Jan. *Das kulturelle Gedächtnis*. Munich: Beck, 2007.

Assoun, Paul-L. *Freud et Nietzsche*. Paris: Presses Universitaires de France, 1980.

Auden, W.H. *Selected Poems*. Ed. Edward Mendelson. New York: Vintage, 1989.

Auerbach, Erich. *Gesammelte Aufsätze zur romanischen Philologie*. Bern: Francke, 1967.

Augé, Marc. *Non-Lieux: Introduction à une anthropologie de la surmodernité*. Paris: Éditions du Seuil, 1992.

Bachelard, Gaston. *La poétique de l'espace*. Paris: Presses Universitaires de France, 1998.

Bacigalupo, Massimo, ed. *Ezra Pound: Un poeta a Rapallo*. Genoa: Edizioni San Marco di Giustiniani, 1985.

Baedeker's Italien: Von den Alpen bis Neapel. Leipzig: Karl Baedeker, 1903.

Baedeker's Ober-Italien: Handbuch für Reisende. Leipzig: Karl Baedeker, 1886.

Bainton, Roland H. *A Life of Martin Luther: Here I Stand.* New York: Meridian, 1995.

Banville, John. *Shroud: A Novel.* New York: Alfred A. Knopf, 2003.

Barchiesi, Alessandro. *The Geopoetics of Virgil's Aeneid.* Cambridge: Cambridge University Press, 2004.

Barni, Gianluigi. *Storia di Rapallo e della gente del Tigullio.* Genoa: Sabatelli, 1983.

Battafarano, Italo M. *Die im Chaos blühenden Zitronen: Identität und Alterität in Goethes Italienischer Reise.* Bern: Peter Lang, 1999.

Battafarano, Italo M., ed. *Italienische Reise, Reisen nach Italien.* Gardolo di Trento: Luigi Reverdito, 1988.

Bauerkämpfer, Arnd, Hans E. Bödeker, and Berhard Struck, eds. *Die Welt erfahren: Reisen als kulturelle Begegnung von 1780 bis heute.* Frankfurt, New York: Campus, 2004.

The Beach Boys. "Kokomo." In *Still Cruisin'* (1989).

Bec, Pierre. *La langue occitane.* Paris: Presses Universitaires de France, 1963.

Bec, Pierre, ed. *Nouvelle anthologie de la lyrique occitane du Moyen Âge: Initiation a la langue et la poésie des troubadours.* Avignon: Éditions Aubanel, 1970.

Benatti, Luigi, M. Angela Bacigalupo, and Emilio Carta. *Rapallo ha visto … hanno visto Rapallo.* Rapallo: Edito dal Comune di Rapallo, 1997.

Benn, Gottfried. *Briefe an F. W. Oelze.* Wiesbaden, Munich: Limes, 1977.

Benn, Gottfried. *Essays und Reden in der Fassung der Erstdrucke.* Ed. Bruno Hillebrand. Frankfurt: Fischer, 1989.

Benn, Gottfried. *Frühe Lyrik und Dramen.* Wiesbaden: Limes, 1952.

Benn, Gottfried. *Gedichte in der Fassung der Erstdrucke.* Ed. Bruno Hillebrand. Frankfurt: Fischer, 1982.

Benn, Gottfried. *Primal Vision: Selected Writings of Gottfried Benn.* Ed. E.B. Ashton. New York: New Directions, 1971.

Benn, Gottfried. *Prosa und Autobiographie in der Fassung der Erstdrucke.* Ed. Bruno Hillebrand. Frankfurt: Fischer, 1984.

Benn, Gottfried. *Prose, Essays, Poems.* Ed. Volkmar Sander. New York: Continuum, 1987.

Benn, Gottfried. *Sämtliche Werke I: Gedichte 1.* Ed. Gerhard Schuster. Stuttgart: Klett-Cotta, 1986.

Benn, Gottfried. *Sämtliche Werke III: Prosa 1.* Ed. Gerhard Schuster. Stuttgart: Klett-Cotta, 1987.

Benn, Gottfried. *Sämtliche Werke IV: Prosa 2.* Ed. Gerhard Schuster. Stuttgart: Klett-Cotta, 1989.

Benn, Gottfried. *Sämtliche Werke VI: Prosa 4.* Ed. Holger Hof. Stuttgart: Klett-Cotta, 2001.

Benn, Gottfried. *Szenen und Schriften in der Fassung der Erstdrucke.* Ed. Bruno Hillebrand. Frankfurt: Fischer, 1990.

Bernardini, Enzo. *Liguria.* Rome: Newton Compton, 1981.

Bernstein, Charles. *A Poetics.* Cambridge, MA: Harvard University Press, 1992.

Berri, Pietro. *Rapallo nei secoli: Rievocazioni e scorribande.* Rapallo: Ipotesi, 1979.

Berthold, Helmut. *Die Lilien und den Wein: Gottfried Benns Frankreich.* Würzburg: Königshausen und Neumann, 1999.

Bertolotti, Davide. *Viaggio nella Liguria marittima.* Turin: Eredi Botta, 1834.

Bertone, Giorgio. *Letteratura e paesaggio: Liguri e no.* Lecce: Manni, 2001.

Bertram, Ernst. *Nietzsche: Attempt at a Mythology.* Trans. Robert E. Norton. Urbana, Chicago: University of Illinois Press, 2009.

Bertram, Ernst. *Nietzsche: Versuch einer Mythologie.* Bonn: Bouvier, 1965.

Bettelheim, Bruno. *Freud and Man's Soul.* New York: Alfred A. Knopf, 1983.

Billig, Michael. *Freudian Repression: Conversation Creating the Unconscious.* Cambridge: Cambridge University Press, 1999.

Blanton, Casey. *Travel Writing: The Self and the World.* New York, London: Routledge, 2002.

Block, Richard A. *The Spell of Italy: Vacation, Magic, and the Attraction of Goethe.* Detroit: Wayne State University Press, 2006.

Bloom, Harold. *The Anxiety of Influence: A Theory of Poetry.* New York, Oxford: Oxford University Press, 1997.

Bloom, Harold. *Poetics of Influence.* New Haven: Henry R. Schwab, 1988.

Blume, Mary. *Côte d'Azur: Inventing the French Riviera.* New York: Thames and Hudson, 1992.

Boccaccio, Giovanni. *Decamerone.* Ed. Carlo Salinari. Bari: Laterza, 1986.

Bohusch, Otmar, ed. *Interpretationen moderner Lyrik.* Frankfurt, Berlin, and Munich: Diesterweg, 1978.

Borges, Jorge L. *Selected Non Fictions.* London, New York: Penguin, 1999.

Bonta, Mark, and John Protevi. *Deleuze and Geophilosophy: A Guide and Glossary.* Edinburgh: Edinburgh University Press, 2004.

Bowd, Gavin, Charles Forsdick, and Norman Bissell, eds. *Grounding a World.* Glasgow: Alba Editions, 2005.

Boyer, Marc. *L'invention de la Côte d'Azur: L'hiver dans le Midi.* Paris: Édition de l'Aube, 2002.

Bradford, Ernle. *Mediterranean: Portrait of a Sea.* New York: Harcourt Brace Jovanovich, 1971.

Brandt, Joan. *Geopoetics: The Politics of Mimesis in Poststructuralist French Poetry and Theory.* Stanford: Stanford University Press, 1997.

Brandt, Reinhard. *Arkadien in Kunst, Philosophie und Dichtung.* Freiburg, Berlin: Rombach, 2005.

Braudel, Fernand. *Les mémoires de la Méditerranée: Préhistoire et antiquité.* Paris: Éditions de Fallois, 1998.

Braudel, Fernand. *Memory and the Mediterranean.* Trans. Siân Reynolds. New York: Alfred A. Knopf, 2001.

Brilli, Attilio. *Quando viaggiare era un'arte*. Bologna: Il Mulino, 1995.

Brilli, Attilio. *Il viaggio in Italia*. Milan: Banca Popolare di Milano, 1987.

Brinkmann, Richard. *Expressionismus: Internationale Forschung zu einem internationalen Phänomen*. Stuttgart: Metzler, 1980.

Brode, Hanspeter, ed. *Benn Chronik*. Munich and Vienna: Carl Hansser, 1978.

Brooks, Peter, and Alex Woloch, eds. *Whose Freud? The Place of Psychoanalysis in Contemporary Culture*. New Haven, London: Yale University Press, 2000.

Browning, Robert, and Michael Hamburger, eds. *German Poetry from 1750 to 1900*. New York: Continuum, 1984.

Buddensieg, Tilmann. *Nietzsches Italien: Städte, Gärten und Paläste*. Berlin: Wagenbach, 2002.

Burckhardt, Jacob. *Der Cicerone*. Leipzig: Seemann, 1869.

Cahill, Susan, ed. *Desiring Italy*. New York: Fawcett, 1997.

Calvino, Italo. *The Road to San Giovanni*. Trans. Tim Parks. New York: Pantheon, 1993.

Calvino, Italo. *La strada di San Giovanni*. Milan: Mondadori, 1990.

Calvino, Italo, and Folco Quilici. *Liguria*. Silvana: Cinisello Balsamo, 1973.

Cameron, Kenneth N., ed. *Romantic Rebels: Essays on Shelley and His Circle*. Cambridge, MA: Harvard University Press, 1973.

Campioni, Giuliano, Paolo D'Iorio, Maria Cristina Fornari, Francesco Fronterotta, and Andrea Orsucci, eds. *Nietzsche's persönliche Bibliothek (Supplementa Nietzscheana)*. Berlin, New York: Walter de Gruyter, 2003.

Carson, Anne. *Eros, The Bittersweet: An Essay*. Princeton: Princeton University Press, 1986.

Casa di Goethe. *Finalmente in questa capitale del mondo! Goethe a Roma*. Rome: Artemide Edizioni, 1997.

Casey, Edward S. *The Fate of Place: A Philosophical History*. Berkeley: University of California Press, 1997.

Casey, Paul F., and Timothy J. Casey, eds. *Gottfried Benn: The Galway Symposium*. Galway: Galway University Press, 1990.

Cattanei, Giovanni. *La Liguria e la poesia italiana del '900*. Milan: Silva, 1966.

Chamberlain, Lesley. *Nietzsche in Turin: An Intimate Biography*. New York: Picador, 1998.

Chamberlain, Lesley. *The Secret Artist: A Close Reading of Sigmund Freud*. New York: Seven Stories Press, 2000.

Chapelle, Daniel. *Nietzsche and Psychoanalysis*. Albany: State University of New York Press, 1993.

Chard, Chloe. *Pleasure and Guilt on the Grand Tour: Travel Writing and Imaginative Geography, 1600–1830*. Manchester, New York: Manchester University Press, 1999.

Cicero, Marcus Tullius. *The Orations of Marcus Tullius Cicero*. Vol. 2. Trans. C.D. Younge. London: George Bell and Sons, 1902.

Clarke, Hyde. *Notes on the Ligurians, Aquitanians, and Belgians.* London: Trübner and Co, 1883.

Columbus, Christopher. *The Four Voyages.* Ed. and trans. J.M. Cohen. London and New York: Penguin, 1969.

Cooke, Miriam, Erdağ Göknar, and Grant Parker, eds. *Mediterranean Passages: Readings from Dido to Derrida.* Chapel Hill: University of North Carolina Press, 2008.

Cordes, Léon. *Troubadours aujourd'hui.* Éditions C.M.P, 1975.

Coverley, Merlin. *Psychogeography.* Harpenden, Herts: Pocket Essentials, 2010.

Crane, Hart. *The Complete Poems of Hart Crane.* Ed. Marc Simon. New York, London: Liveright, 1993.

Curtius, Ernst Robert. *Europäische Literatur und Lateinisches Mittelalter.* Bern: Francke, 1954.

Daboul, Alexander D. *Die artistische Ausnutzung des Nihilismus: Zum Kunstdenken von Benn und Nietzsche.* Frankfurt: Haag und Herchen, 1995.

Dabrowski, Magdalena. *French Landscape: The Modern Vision, 1880–1920.* New York: Museum of Modern Art, 1999.

Dacqué, Edgar. *Das Verlorene Paradies: Zur Seelengeschichte des Menschen.* Munich: R. Oldenbourg, 1953.

Dante Alighieri. *De vulgari eloquentia.* Trans. Sally Purcell. Manchester/England: Carcanet New Press, 1981.

Dante Alighieri. *The Divine Comedy of Dante Alighieri: Inferno.* Trans. Allen Mandelbaum. Toronto: Bantam Books, 1980.

Dante Alighieri. *The Divine Comedy of Dante Alighieri: Purgatorio.* Trans. Allen Mandelbaum. Toronto: Bantam Books, 1982.

Dante Alighieri. *The Divine Comedy of Dante Alighieri: Paradiso.* Trans. Allen Mandelbaum. Toronto: Bantam Books, 1984.

Dante Alighieri. "Egloghe" and "Epistole." In *Tutte le Opere.* Ed. Luigi Blasucci. Florence: Sansoni, 1989.

Dante Alighieri. *Epistola a Cangrande.* Ed. Enyo Cecchini. Florence: Giunti, 1995.

Daudet, Alphonse. *Port-Tarascon: Dernières aventures de l'illustre Tartarin.* Paris: Flammarion, 1890.

de Guglielmi, Ada, ed. *Liguria.* Brescia: La Scuola, 1987.

Deleuze, Gilles, and Félix Guattari. *Mille plateaux.* Paris: Éditions de Minuit, 1980.

de Man, Paul. *The Resistance to Theory.* Minneapolis: University of Minnesota Press, 1986.

de Marinis, Raffaele C., and Giuseppina Spadea, eds. *I liguri: Un antico popolo europeo tra Alpi e Mediterraneo.* Genoa and Milan: Palazzo Ducale and Skira, 2004.

Demetz, Peter. *Worte in Freiheit: Der italienische Futurismus und die deutsche literarische Avantgarde, 1912–1934.* Munich, Zurich: Piper, 1990.

de Nicola, Francesco. *La Liguria dei poeti.* Genoa: Ferrari, 1998.

de Pourtalès, Guy. *Nietzsche en Italie.* Paris : Bernard Grasset, 1929.

Derrida, Jacques. *Archive Fever: A Freudian Impression.* Trans. Eric Prenowitz. Chicago, London: University of Chicago Press, 1996.

Derrida, Jacques. *La carte postale: De Socrate à Freud et au-delà.* Paris: Flammarion, 1980.

Deutsch, Babette, and Avrahm Yarmolinsky, eds and trans. *Contemporary German Poetry: An Anthology.* New York: Harcourt, Brace and Company, 1923.

Dickens, Charles. *Pictures from Italy.* New York: Coward, McGann and Geoghegan, 1974.

Donahue, Neil H., and Doris Kirchner, eds. *Flight of Fantasy: New Perspectives on Inner Emigration in German Literature, 1933–1945.* New York, Oxford: Berghahn, 2003.

Downie, David, and Alison Harris. *Enchanted Liguria: A Celebration of the Culture, Lifestyle and Food of the Italian Riviera.* New York: Rizzoli, 1997.

Downing, Eric. *After Images: Photography, Archaeology, Psychoanalysis and the Tradition of Bildung.* Detroit: Wayne State University Press, 2006.

Dreßler, Roland, Herman Josef Schmidt, and Rainer Wagner. *Spurensuche: Die Lebensstationen Friedrich Nietzsches, 1844–1869.* Erfurt: Verlagshaus Thüringen, 1994.

Duclos, Michèle. *Kenneth White: Nomade intellectuel, poète du monde.* Grenoble: Ellug, 2006.

Duranti, Massimo, ed. *Gerardo Dottori: Catalogo generale ragionato.* Perugia: Fabrizio Fabbri, 2006.

Ďurišin, Dionyz. *Il Mediterraneo: Una rete interletteraria.* Rome: Bulzoni, 2000.

Dwyer Hickey, Christine. *Last Train from Liguria.* London: Atlantic Books, 2009.

Dyck, Joachim, Holger Hof, and Peter D. Krause, eds. *Benn-Jahrbuch, Vol. I.* Stuttgart: Klett-Cotta, 2003.

Eliot, T.S. *Four Quartets.* San Diego, New York, and London: Harcourt Brace Jovanovich, 1988.

Eliot, T.S. "Introduction." In *Ezra Pound, Selected Poems.* London: Faber and Faber, 1977.

Eliot, T.S. *The Sacred Wood: Essays on Poetry and Criticism.* New York: Barnes and Noble, 1976.

Epicurus. *Letter on Happiness.* San Francisco: Chronicle Books, 1994.

Fehr, Michael, Clemens Krümmel, and Markus Müller, eds. *Platons Höhle: Das Museum und die elektronischen Medien.* Cologne: Wienand, 1995.

Figl, Johann, ed. *Von Nietzsche zu Freud: Übereinstimmungen und Differenzen von Denkmotiven.* Vienna: Wiener Universitätsverlag, 1996.

Fisher, Philip. *Making and Effacing Art: Modern American Art in a Culture of Museums.* Cambridge, MA, and London: Harvard University Press, 1991.

Formaggio, Dino, ed. *Il Dante di Guttuso: Cinquantasei tavole dantesche disegnate da Renato Guttuso.* Milan: Mondadori, 1970.

Frankland, Graham. *Freud's Literary Culture.* Cambridge: Cambridge University Press, 2000.

Fraser, Veronica M. *The Songs of Peire Vidal: Translation and Commentary.* New York: Peter Lang, 2006.

Freud, Sigmund. *Bildende Kunst und Literatur: Studienausgabe X.* Ed. Alexander Mitscherlich, Angela Richards, James Strachey and Ilse Grubrich-Simitis. Frankfurt: Fischer, 1997.

Freud, Sigmund. *Briefe an Wilhelm Fließ, 1887–1904.* Ed. Jeffrey M. Masson. Frankfurt: Fischer, 1986.

Freud, Sigmund. *Briefe, 1873–1939.* Frankfurt: Fischer, 1960.

Freud, Sigmund. *Five Lectures on Psycho-Analysis.* Ed. and trans. James Strachey. New York, London: Norton, 1989.

Freud, Sigmund. *Letters of Sigmund Freud.* Ed. Ernst L. Freud; trans. Tania Stern and James Stern. New York: Basic Books, 1960.

Freud, Sigmund. *On Dreams.* Ed. and trans. James Strachey. New York, London: Norton, 1980.

Freud, Sigmund. *Psychologie des Unbewußten: Studienausgabe III.* Ed. Alexander Mitscherlich, Angela Richards, James Strachey, and Ilse Grubrich-Simitis. Frankfurt: Fischer, 1997.

Freud, Sigmund. *Psychologische Schriften: Studienausgabe IV.* Ed. Alexander Mitscherlich, Angela Richards, James Strachey and Ilse Grubrich-Simitis. Frankfurt: Fischer, 1997.

Freud, Sigmund. *Schriften zur Behandlungstechnik: Studienausgabe Ergänzungsband.* Ed. Alexander Mitscherlich, Angela Richards, James Strachey, and Ilse Grubrich-Simitis. Frankfurt: Fischer, 1997.

Freud, Sigmund. *Die Traumdeutung: Studienausgabe II.* Ed. Alexander Mitscherlich, Angela Richards, James Strachey, and Ilse Grubrich-Simitis. Frankfurt: Fischer, 1996.

Freud, Sigmund. *Vorlesungen zur Einführung in die Psychoanalyse: Studienausgabe I.* Ed. Alexander Mitscherlich, Angela Richards, James Strachey, and Ilse Grubrich-Simitis. Frankfurt: Fischer, 1997.

Freud, Sigmund. *Der Wahn und die Träume in Jensens Gradiva: Mit der Erzählung von Wilhelm Jensen.* Frankfurt: Fischer, 2003.

Frey, Hans-Jost, and Otto Lorenz. *Kritik des freien Verses.* Heidelberg: Lambert Schneider, 1980.

Friedrich, Heinz. "Plädoyer für die schwarzen Kutten zu Gottfried Benns 20. Todestag." *Merkur* 39 (1976): 628–37.

Frye, Northrop. *The Anatomy of Criticism*. Princeton: Princeton University Press, 1990.

Gabrielli, Bruno. *Storia d'Italia*. Turin: Einaudi, 1994.

Galley, Micheline, and Leïla Ladjimi Sebai, eds. *L'homme méditerranéen et la mer: Actes du Troisième Congrès International d'Études des Cultures de la Méditerranée Occidentale*. Tunis: Éditions Salammbô, 1985.

Garton, Janet, ed. *Facets of European Modernism*. Norwich: University of East Anglia, 1985.

Gasser, Reinhard. *Nietzsche und Freud*. Berlin, New York: Walter de Gruyter, 1997.

Gauguin, Paul. *Avant et après: Avec les vingt-sept dessins du manuscrit original*. Paris: Les Éditions G. Crès, 1923.

Gay, Peter. *Freud: A Life for Our Time*. New York: Anchor Books Doubleday, 1989.

Gehrke, Hans-Joachim. *Auf der Suche nach dem Land der Griechen*. Heidelberg: Universitätsverlag Winter, 2003.

Gibbons, Herbert Adams. *Riviera Towns*. New York: Robert M. McBride and Company, 1920.

Gibbons, John. *To Italy at Last*. London: Methuen, 1933.

Gibelli, Antonio, and Paride Rugafiori, eds. *La Liguria*. Turin: Einaudi, 1994.

Gildenhard, Ingo, and Martina Ruehl. *Out of Arcadia: Classics and Politics in the Age of Burckhardt, Nietzsche and Wilamowitz*. London: Institute of Classical Studies, 2003.

Gilman, Sander. *Reading Freud's Reading*. New York: New York University Press, 1995.

Gilmour, David. *The Pursuit of Italy: A History of a Land, Its Regions, and Their Peoples*. New York: Farrar, Straus and Giroux, 2011.

Girani, Alberto, and Cristina Galletti. *Una terra fatta a scalini*. Genoa: Sagep, 1991.

Girard, François. *Gênes, ses environs et les deux Rivières (Ponente et Levante)*. Munich: Bruckmann, 1893.

Goethe, Johann Caspar. *Viaggio per l'Italia*. Rome: Farinelli, 1932–3.

Goethe, Johann W. von. *Dichtung und Wahrheit*. Frankfurt: Insel, 1975.

Goethe, Johann W. von. *Gedichte*. Berlin and Weimar: Aufbau-Verlag, 1988.

Goethe, Johann W. von. *Italian Journey*. Trans. W.H. Auden and Elizabeth Mayer. London: Penguin, 1970.

Goethe, Johann W. von. *Italienische Reise*. Ed. Herbert von Einem. Munich: Beck, 1981.

Goethe, Johann W. von. "Noten und Abhandlungen zu besserem Verständnis des West-östlichen Divans." In *Werke in vier Bänden III*. Ed. Gerhard Stenzel. Salzburg: Caesar, 1983.

Goethe, Johann W. von. *Die Wahlverwandtschaften*. Munich: DTV, 1997.

Goethe, Johann W. von. *Wilhelm Meister's Apprenticeship.* Ed. and trans. Eric Blacka-ll. New York: Suhrkamp, 1989.

Grandjonc, Jacques, ed. *Emigrés français en Allemagne, Emigrés allemands en France: 1685–1945.* Paris: Institut Goethe, 1983.

Grimm, Reinhold. *Gottfried Benn: Die farbliche Chiffre in der Dichtung.* Nuremberg: Hans Carl, 1962.

Grundlehner, Philip. *The Lyrical Bridge: Essays from Hölderlin to Benn.* Rutherford: Fairleigh Dickinson University Press, 1979.

Gsell-Fels, Theodor. *Italien in sechzig Tagen.* Leipzig: Bibiographisches Institut Leipzig, 1878.

Gugelberger, G.M. *Ezra Pound's Medievalism.* Frankfurt: Lang, 1978.

Guiccioli, Teresa. *Lord Byron's Life in Italy.* Trans. Michael Rees. Newark: University of Delaware Press, 2005.

Günzel, Stephan. *Geophilosophie: Nietzsches philosophische Geographie.* Berlin: Akademie Verlag, 2001.

· Haarhaus, Julius R. *Auf den Spuren Goethes in Oberitalien.* Leipzig: C.G. Naumann, 1896.

Hale, Julian. *The French Riviera: A Cultural History.* Oxford: Oxford University Press, 2009.

Hallet, Wolfgang, and Birgit Neumann, eds. *Raum und Bewegung in der Literatur: Die Literaturwissenschaften und der Spatial Turn.* Bielefeld: Transcript, 2009.

Hamburger, Michael. *Modern German Poetry.* New York, Philadelphia: Chelsea House, 1989.

Hamburger, Michael, ed. *German Poetry, 1910–1975.* New York: Urizon Books, 1976.

Harries, Karsten. "The Philosopher at Sea." In *Nietzsche's New Seas: Explorations in Philosophy, Aesthetics, and Politics.* Ed. Michael A. Gillespie and Tracy B. Strong, 21–44. Chicago, London: University of Chicago Press, 1988.

Harrison, Thomas. *Nietzsche in Italy.* Saratoga, CA: Anma Libri, 1988.

Hartman, Geoffrey H. *Beyond Formalism.* New Haven, London: Yale University Press, 1970.

Hawthorne, Nathaniel. *The French and Italian Note-Books.* Boston: Houghton, Osgood and Company, 1878.

Hay, Daisy. *Young Romantics: The Tangled Lives of English Poetry's Greatest Generation.* New York: Farrar, Straus and Giroux, 2010.

Heinrichs, Hans-J. *Fenster zur Welt: Positionen der Moderne.* Frankfurt: Athenäum, 1989.

Heintel, Helmut. *Block II, Zimmer 66: Gottfried Benn in Landsberg, 1943–1945.* Stuttgart: Urachhaus, 1988.

Hellingrath, Norbert von. *Hölderlin-Vermächtnis.* Munich: Bruckmann, 1936.

Hennig, Christoph. *Italienische Riviera: Ligurien.* Cologne: DuMont, 1999.

Herzer, Ivo, ed. *The Italian Refuge: Rescue of Jews during the Holocaust.* Washington, DC: The Catholic University of America Press, 1989.

Hewitt, Andrew. *Fascist Modernism: Aesthetics, Politics and the Avant-Garde.* Stanford: Stanford University Press, 1993.

Hibbert, Christopher. *The Grand Tour.* London: Thames Methuen, 1987.

Highet, Gilbert. *Poets in a Landscape.* London: Prion Books, 1999.

Hillebrand, Bruno. *Gottfried Benn.* Darmstadt: Wissenschaftliche Buchgesellschaft, 1979.

Hillebrand, Bruno, ed. *Über Gottfried Benn: Kritische Stimmen, 1912–1956.* Frankfurt: Fischer, 1987.

Hillebrand, Bruno, ed. *Über Gottfried Benn: Kritische Stimmen, 1957–1986.* Frankfurt: Fischer, 1987.

Hof, Holger. *Benn: Sein Leben in Bildern und Texten.* Stuttgart: Klett-Cotta, 2007.

Hoffmeister, Gerhart, ed. *Goethe in Italy, 1786–1986.* Amsterdam: Rodopi, 1988.

Hohmann, Werner L. *Vier Grundthemen in der Lyrik Gottfried Benns: Gesehen unter der Wirkung der Philosophie Nietzsches.* Essen: Die Blaue Eule, 1986.

Hormes, Stephan, and Silke Peust. *Atlas der wahren Namen: Deutschland, Europa und die Welt in etymologischen Karten.* Hamburg: Carlsen, 2009.

Howarth, David A. *The Greek Adventure: Lord Byron and Other Eccentrics in the War of Independence.* New York: Atheneum, 1976.

Hunt, Leigh. *Lord Byron and Some of His Contemporaries: With Recollections of the Author's Life and of his Visit to Italy.* New York: AMS Press, 1966.

Huyssen, Andreas, and David Bathrick, eds. *Modernity and the Text: Revisions of German Modernism.* New York: Columbia University Press, 1989.

Ibbeken, Hillert. *The Other Italy/Das andere Italien: Stories from Liguria and Calabria.* Fellbach: Edition Axel Menges, 2010.

Ipser, Karl. *Mit Goethe in Italien: 1786–1986.* Berg: Türmer Verlag, 1986.

Irion, Ulrich. *Eros und Thanatos in der Moderne: Nietzsche und Freud als Vollender eines anti-christlichen Grundzugs im europäischen Denken.* Würzburg: Königshausen und Neumann, 1992.

Istituto Geografico De Agostini. *Liguria.* Novara: De Agostini, 2000.

Italia Benedettina II: Liguria Monastica. Ed. Centro Storico Benedettino Italiano. Badia del Monte: Cesena, 1979.

Italia Benedettina V: Storia monastica Ligure e Pavese: Studi e documenti. Ed. Centro Storico Benedettino Italiano. Badia del Monte: Cesena, 1982.

Ivancich, Gianfranco, ed. *Spots and Dots: Ezra Pound in Italy. Photographs by Vittorugo Contino.* New York: Rizzoli, 1970.

Jacobsen, Jens P. *Niels Lyhne.* Trans. Tiina Nunnally. Seattle: Fjord Press, 1990.

Jakobson, Roman. "Linguistics and Poetics." In *Language in Literature*, ed. Krystyna Pomorska and Stephen Rudy, 62–94. Cambridge, MA, and London: Belknap Press of Harvard University Press, 1987.

Jakobson, Roman. "Poetry of Grammar and Grammar of Poetry." In *Selected Writings III*. The Hague: Mouton, 1981.

Jakobson, Roman. "Two Aspects of Language and Two Types of Aphasic Disturbances." In *Language in Literature*, ed. Krystyna Pomorska and Stephen Rudy, 95–113. Cambridge, MA, and London: Belknap Press of Harvard University Press, 1987.

James, Henry. *Collected Travel Writings: The Continent: A Little Tour in France, Italian Hours, Other Travels.* New York: Library of America, 1993.

James, Henry. *The Complete Tales of Henry James.* Philadelphia, New York: J.B. Lippincott Company, 1964.

Janz, Curt P. *Friedrich Nietzsche Biographie in drei Bänden.* Munich, Vienna: Carl Hanser, 1993.

Jensen, Wilhelm. *Gradiva: Ein pompeijanisches Phantasiestück.* Dresden, Leipzig: Carl Reissner, 1903.

Jirat-Wasiutyński, Vojtěch, and Anne Dymond, eds. *Modern Art and the Idea of the Mediterranean.* Toronto: University of Toronto Press, 2007.

Jodice, Mimmo, ed. *Mediterranean: Essays by George Hersey and Predrag Matvejević.* Verona: Aperture, 1995.

Johnson, Ruth Laurie. *Aesthetic Anxiety: Uncanny Symptoms in German Literature and Culture.* Amsterdam, New York: Rodopi, 2010.

Jones, Ted. *The French Riviera: A Literary Guide for Travellers.* London: Tauris Parke, 2007.

Kanceff, Emanuele, ed. *Viaggiatori stranieri in Liguria.* Geneva: Slatkine, 1992.

Kaufmann, Walter. *Discovering the Mind.* New Brunswick, NJ: Transaction Publishers, 1992.

Kaufmann, Walter, ed. *Twenty German Poets: A Bilingual Collection.* New York: The Modern Library, 1962.

Kaufmann, Walter, and R.J. Hollingdale. *Nietzsche: Philosopher, Psychologist, Antichrist.* Princeton: Princeton University Press, 1974.

Kaufmann, Walter, and R.J. Hollingdale, ed. and trans. *The Portable Nietzsche.* London: Penguin, 1982.

Keith, Thomas. *Nietzsche-Rezeption bei Gottfried Benn.* Cologne: Teiresias, 2001.

Keller, Harald. *Die Kunstlandschaften Italiens.* Munich: Prestel, 1965.

Kenner, Hugh. *The Pound Era.* Berkeley, Los Angeles: University of California Press, 1971.

Kermode, Frank. *The Sense of an Ending.* Oxford, London: Oxford University Press, 1967.

Kienitz, Friedrich-K. *Das Mittelmeer: Schauplatz der Weltgeschichte von den frühen Hochkulturen bis ins 20. Jahrhundert.* Munich: Beck, 1976.

Kivland, Sharon. *Freud on Holiday, Volume 1: Freud Dreams of Rome.* York: Information as Material, 2006.

Kivland, Sharon. *Freud on Holiday, Volume II: A Disturbance of Memory.* York: Information as Material and CubeArtEditions, 2007.

Klenze, Camillo. *The Interpretation of Italy during the Last Two Centuries: A Contribution to the Study of Goethe's Italienische Reise.* Chicago: University of Chicago Press, 1907.

Knowlson, James, ed. *The Theatrical Notebooks of Samuel Beckett: Waiting for Godot.* New York: Grove Press, 1993.

Kolb, Martina. "Erwanderte Lyrik: Ezra Pound's Walk of Life." *Parapluie* 16 (Summer 2003) <http://parapluie.de>.

Kolb, Martina. "Gottfried Benn's Return to the Future: Four Translations and Commentaries." *Italian Poetry Review* 5 (2010): 125–44.

Kolb, Martina. "Guilt Trips on Royal Roads: Freud's Mediterranean Affinities." *Quaderni di Studi Indo-Mediterranei* II (2009): 329–46.

Kolb, Martina. "In His Image: Pound at Pisa." *Yale Italian Poetry* V–VI (2001–2): 315–28.

Kolb, Martina. "Poetry Must Be as Well Written as Prose." *Yale Italian Poetry* VIII (2006): 259–60.

Koschorke, Albrecht. *Die Geschichte des Horizonts: Grenze und Grenzüberschreitung in literarischen Landschaftsbildern.* Frankfurt: Suhrkamp, 1990.

Krell, David F., and Donald L. Bates. *The Good European: Nietzsche's Work Sites in Word and Image.* Chicago: The University of Chicago Press, 1999.

Krohn, Claus-Dieter, Erwin Rotermund, Lutz Winckler, and Wulf Koepke, eds. *Exilforschung 12: Ein internationales Jahrbuch: Aspekte der künstlerischen inneren Emigration 1933–1945.* Munich: Edition Text und Kritik, 1994.

Kuhn, Dorothea. *Auch ich in Arcadien: Kunstreisen nach Italien 1600–1900. Eine Ausstellung im Schiller-Nationalmuseum Marbach/Neckar 1966.* Stuttgart: Turmhaus, 1966.

Küster, Bernd, and Eberhard Grames. *Van Goghs Provence.* Hamburg: Ellert and Richter, 1985.

Lagorio, Gina. *Cultura e letteratura ligure del '900.* Genoa: Sabatelli, 1972.

Lammert, Eberhard, and Giorgio Cusatelli, eds. *Avantgarde, Modernität, Katastrophe: letteratura, arte e scienza fra Germania e Italia nel primo 900.* Florence: Olschki, 1995.

Laplanche, Jean, and J.-B. Pontalis. *Vocabulaire de la psychanalyse.* Paris: Presses Universitaires de France, 1967.

Le Corbusier. "Other Icons: The Museums." In *The Decorative Art of Today*, trans. James I. Dunnett, 15–23. Cambridge: MIT Press, 1987.

Lees, Frederic, and Edith S. Lees. *Wanderings on the Italian Riviera: The Record of a Leisurely Tour in Liguria.* Boston: Little, Brown, and Company, 1913.

Lehmann, Herbert. *Essays zur Physiognomie der Landschaft.* Ed. Anneliese Krenzlin and Renate Müller. Stuttgart: Franz Steiner Wiesbaden, 1986.

Lehrer, Ronald. *Nietzsche's Presence in Freud's Life and Thought.* Albany: State University of New York Press, 1995.

Lennig, Walter. *Gottfried Benn in Selbstzeugnissen und Bilddokumenten.* Hamburg: Rowohlt, 1964.

Levy, Emil. *Petit dictionnaire provençal-français.* Raphèles-les-Arles: Marcel Petit, 1991.

Liégeard, Stéphen. *La Côte d'Azur.* Paris: Maison Quantain, 1887.

Lindberg, Kathryne V. *Reading Pound Reading: Modernism after Nietzsche.* New York, Oxford: Oxford University Press, 1987.

Lohner, Edgar, ed. *Gottfried Benn: Dichter über ihre Dichtungen.* Munich: Heimeran, 1969.

Lohner, Marlene. "Das Blau erlogener Meere: Wirkungen des *West-östlichen Divans* auf Gottfried Benn." *Goethe Jahrbuch* 109 (1992): 145–57.

Luce, John V. *Celebrating Homer's Landscapes: Troy and Ithaca Revisited.* New Haven: Yale University Press, 1998.

Luchsinger, Martin. *Mythos Italien: Denkbilder des Fremden in der deutschen Gegenwartsliteratur.* Cologne: Böhlau, 1996.

MacKay, Agnes E. *An Anatomy of Solitude: Towards a New Interpretation of the Sources of Creative Inspiration.* Glasgow: MacLellan, 1978.

McDougal, Stuart Y. *Ezra Pound and the Troubadour Tradition.* Princeton: Princeton University Press, 1972.

McKay, Don. "Between Rock and Stone: A Geopoetic Alphabet." *Antigonish Review* 140 (Winter, 2005): 101–28.

McManus, Tony. *The Radical Field: Kenneth White and Geopoetics.* Dingwall: Sandstone Press, 2007.

Makin, Peter. *Provence and Pound.* Berkeley: University of California Press, 1978.

Mann, Erika, and Klaus Mann. *Das Buch von der Riviera.* Reinbek: Rowohlt, 2002.

Margatin, Laurent. *Kenneth White et la géopoétique.* Paris: L'Harmattan, 2006.

Marinetti, Filippo T. *Teoria e invenzione futurista.* Ed. Luciano De Maria. Milan: Mondadori, 1983.

Marszałek, Magdalena, and Sylvia Sasse. *Geopoetiken: Geographische Entwürfe in den mittel- und osteuropäischen Literaturen.* Berlin: Kadmos, 2010.

Martinet, Marie-Madeleine. *Le voyage d'Italie dans les littératures européennes.* Paris: Presses Universitaires de France, 1996.

Martini, Dario G., and Divo Gori. *La Liguria e la sua anima: Storia di Genova e dei Liguri.* Genoa: ECIG, 1965.

Martini, Fritz. *Das Wagnis der Sprache: Interpretationen deutscher Prosa von Nietzsche bis Benn.* Stuttgart: Ernst Klett Verlag, 1954.

Matvejević, Predrag. *The Mediterranean: A Cultural Landscape.* Trans. Michael H. Heim. Berkeley, Los Angeles, London: University of California Press, 1999.

Maugham, Somerset. *Strictly Personal.* Garden City, NY: Doubleday, Doran and Company, 1941.

Mead, Edward W. *The Grand Tour in the Eighteenth Century.* New York: Benjamin Blom, 1972.

Meli, Marco. "Il giardino di Arles: L'idillio dell'ultimo Io nell'opera giovanile di Gottfried Benn." In *Idillio e anti-idillio nella letteratura tedesca moderna,* ed. Rita Svandrlik, 189–221. Bari: Palomar-Athenaeum, 2002.

Menocal, María R. "The Etymology of Old Provençal *trobar, trobador.* A Return to the Third Solution." *Romance Philology* 36, 2 (November 1982): 137–53.

Menocal, María R. *Shards of Love: Exile and the Origins of the Lyric.* Durham, London: Duke University Press, 1994.

Mertens, Pierre. *Les éblouissements.* Paris: Éditions du Seuil, 1987.

Mertens, Pierre. *Shadowlight.* Trans. Edmund Jephcott. London: Peter Halban, 1997.

Miller, J. Hillis. *Topographies.* Stanford: Stanford University Press, 1995.

Miltoun, Francis, and Blanche McManus. *Rambles on the Riviera: Being Some Account of Journeys Made "en automobile" and Things Seen in the Fair Land of Provence.* Boston: L.C. Page, 1906.

Mitchell, Stephen, trans. and ed. *Gilgamesh: An English Version.* New York, London, Toronto, Sydney: Free Press, 2006.

Moen, Randi L., ed. *Intrecci culturali tra Italia ed Europa del nord.* Rimini: Panozzo, 2003.

Montale, Eugenio. *Ossi di seppia: Cuttlefish Bones, 1920–1927.* Ed. and trans. William Arrowsmith. New York, London: Norton, 1994.

Monteverde, Franco. *I Liguri, un'etnia tra Italia e Mediterraneo.* Florence: Vallecchi, 1995.

Mörike, Eduard. In *Du bist Orplid, mein Land: Ausgewählte Gedichte und Erzählungen.* Ed. Will Vesper. Düsseldorf, Leipzig: Langerwiesche, 1911.

Müller-Buck, Renate. "Nihilismus und Melancholie: Nietzsches Denken im Spiegel Sigmund Freuds." *Jahrbuch für Internationale Germanistik: Reihe A: Kongressberichte* 62 (2003): 261–8.

Müller-Jensen, ed. *Gottfried Benn zum 100. Geburtstag: Vorträge zu Werk und Persönlichkeit von Medizinern und Philologen.* Würzburg: Königshausen und Neumann, 1988.

Nestmeyer, Ralf. *Cinque Terre und Ligurien.* Munich: Gräfe und Unzer, 2000.

Niedermayer, Max, and Marguerite Schlüter, eds. *Das Gottfried Benn Buch: Eine innere Biographie in Selbstzeugnissen.* Frankfurt, Hamburg: Fischer, 1968.

Nietzsche, Friedrich. *Also sprach Zarathustra: Ein Buch für alle und keinen.* Stuttgart: Alfred Kröner, 1988.

Nietzsche, Friedrich. *Briefwechsel.* Ed. Giorgo Colli and Mazzino Montinari. Berlin, NewYork: Walter de Gruyter, 1981.

Nietzsche, Friedrich. *Die fröhliche Wissenschaft.* In *Sämtliche Werke 3,* ed. Giorgio Colli and Mazzino Montinari, 343–651. Munich: DTV, 1980.

Nietzsche, Friedrich. *Die Geburt der Tragödie aus dem Geiste der Musik.* In *Sämtliche Werke 1,* ed. Giorgio Colli and Mazzino Montinari, 11–156. Munich: DTV, 1980.

Nietzsche, Friedrich. *Dionysos-Dithyramben.* In *Sämtliche Werke 6,* ed. Giorgio Colli and Mazzino Montinari, 375–411. Munich: DTV, 1980.

Nietzsche, Friedrich. *Ecce Homo: Wie man wird, was man ist.* In *Sämtliche Werke 6,* ed. Giorgio Colli and Mazzino Montinari, 255–374. Munich: DTV, 1980.

Nietzsche, Friedrich. *Jenseits von Gut und Böse.* In *Sämtliche Werke 5,* ed. Giorgio Colli and Mazzino Montinari, 9–244. Munich: DTV, 1980.

Nietzsche, Friedrich. *Morgenröthe.* In *Sämtliche Werke 3,* ed. Giorgio Colli and Mazzino Montinari, 9–331. Munich: DTV, 1980.

Nietzsche, Friedrich. *On the Genealogy of Morals, Ecce Homo.* Trans. Walter Kaufmann and R.J. Hollingdale; ed. Walter Kaufmann. NewYork: Vintage, 1989.

Nietzsche, Friedrich. *Thus Spoke Zarathustra: A Book for All and None.* Trans. Walter Kaufmann. NewYork: The Modern Library, 1995.

Nietzsche, Friedrich. *Über das Pathos der Wahrheit.* In *Gesammelte Werke 4,* 139–47. Munich: Musarion, 1921.

Nietzsche, Friedrich. *Über Wahrheit und Lüge im außermoralischen Sinne.* In *Werke in Sechs Bänden 5,* ed. Karl Schlechta, 309–22. Munich: Karl Hanser, 1980.

Nietzsche, Friedrich. *Werke in drei Bänden.* Ed. Karl Schlechta. Munich: Carl Hanser, 1966.

Nietzsche, Friedrich. *Zur Genealogie der Moral.* In *Sämtliche Werke 5,* ed. Giorgio Colli and Mazzino Montinari, 245–412. Munich: DTV, 1980.

Nitsche, Roland. "Zur Typologie der Einsamkeit: Nietzsche – Rilke – Benn – Schönwiese." *Forum* 8 (1961): 328–31.

Nitzschke, Bernd. *Aufbruch nach Inner-Afrika: Essays über Sigmund Freud und die Wurzeln der Psychoanalyse.* Göttingen: Vandenhoeck and Ruprecht, 1998.

Novelletto, Arnaldo, Gianni Eugenio Viola, and Franca Rovigatti. *L'Italia nella psicoanalisi / Italy in Psychoanalysis.* Rome: Istituto della Enciclopedia Italiana, 1990.

Oliensis, Ellen. *Freud's Rome: Psychoanalysis and Latin Poetry.* Cambridge: Cambridge University Press, 2009.

Omar, Bsaithi. *Land and Mind: Kenneth White's Geopoetics in the Arabian Context.* Cambridge: Cambridge Scholars Publishing, 2008.

Onfray, Michel. *Le crépuscule d'une idole: L'affabulation freudienne.* Paris: Éditions Grasset et Fasquelle, 2010.

Ornston, Darius G., ed. *Translating Freud*. New Haven, London: Yale University Press, 1992.

Ortheil, Hanns-J. "Schön in der Schwebe." In *Merian: Ligurien*, 27–91. Hamburg: Hoffmann und Campe, 2002.

Ovid. *Metamorphoses*. Trans. Charles Martin. New York and London: Norton, 2004.

Paganelli, Giovanni, ed. *Liguria e arte: Pittori dal 1900 al 1940: Catalogo della mostra*. Genoa: Sagep, 1994.

Pamuk, Orhan. *Kara Kitap*. Istanbul: Can Yayınları Ltd. Şti, 1990.

Pamuk, Orhan. *The Black Book*. Trans. Maureen Freely. London: Faber and Faber, 2006.

Pamuk, Orhan. *The Black Book*. Trans. Güneli Gün. London: Faber and Faber, 1995.

Paolucci, Anne. "Benn, Pound, and Eliot: The Monologue Art of German Expressionism and Anglo-American Modernism." *Review of National Literatures* 9 (1978): 10–24.

Parente, James A., and Richard Erich Schade, eds. *Studies in German and Scandinavian Literature after 1500*. Columbia, SC: Camden House, 1993.

Parks, George P. *The English Traveler to Italy*. Rome: Edizioni di Storia e Letteratura, 1954.

Pelizza, Tito, and Giovanni Paganelli, eds. *Realtà e magia del novecento italiano in Liguria*. Genoa: Sagep, 1995.

Pellegrino, Charles. *Ghosts of Vesuvius: A New Look at the Last Days of Pompeii, How Towers Fall, and Other Strange Connections*. New York: William Morrow, 2004.

Pemble, John. *The Mediterranean Passion: Victorians and Edwardians in the South*. Oxford: Clarendon Press, 1987.

Perkins, David. *A History of Modern Poetry: From the 1890s to the High Modernist Mode*. Cambridge, MA, and London: The Belknap Press of Harvard University Press, 1976.

Perloff, Marjorie. *The Futurist Moment: Avant-Garde, Avant-Guerre, and the Language of Rupture*. Chicago, London: University of Chicago Press, 1986.

Petrarca, Francesco. *Africa*. Ed. and trans. Thomas G. Bergin. New Haven: Yale University Press, 1972.

Phillipotts, J. Surtees. *Stories from Herodotus in Attic Greek: Story of Rhampsinitus, The Battle of Marathon*. Whitefish: Kessinger, 2009.

Pinthus, Kurt, ed. *Menschheitsdämmerung: Ein Dokument des Expressionismus*. Hamburg: Rowohlt, 1959.

Plato. *Complete Works*. Ed. John M. Cooper. Indianapolis, Cambridge: Hackett, 1997.

Pottle, Frederick A., ed. *Boswell on the Grand Tour: Italy, Corsica and France, 1765–1766*. London: Heinemann, 1955.

Pound, Ezra. *The Cantos of Ezra Pound*. New York: New Directions, 1998.

Pound, Ezra. *Literary Essays.* Ed. T.S. Eliot. New York: New Directions, 1968.

Pound, Ezra. *Personae: The Shorter Poems of Ezra Pound.* Ed. Lea Baechler and A. Walton Litz. New York: New Directions, 1990.

Pound, Ezra. *The Spirit of Romance.* New York: New Directions, 1968.

Powers, Alice L., ed. *Italy in Mind.* New York: Vintage, 1997.

Preiß, Martin. *Daß es die Wirklichkeit nicht gäbe: Gottfried Benns Rönne-Novellen als Autonomieprogramm.* St Ingbert: Röhrig Universitätsverlag, 1999.

Preminger, Alex, and T.V.F. Brogan. *The New Princeton Encyclopedia of Poetry and Poetics.* Princeton: Princeton University Press, 1993.

Raabe, Paul, and Max Niedermayer, eds. *Gottfried Benn: Den Traum alleine tragen: Neue Texte, Briefe, Dokumente.* Wiesbaden: Limes, 1966.

Raddatz, Fritz J. *Gottfried Benn: Leben – niederer Wahn: Eine Biographie.* Munich: Propyläen, 2001.

Ragazzi, Franco. *Liguria futurista.* Milan: Mazzotta, 1997.

Ragazzi, Franco. *Marinetti: Futurismo in Liguria.* Genoa: DeFerrari, 2006.

Ragazzi, Franco, ed. *Gaetano Previati: Vent'anni in Liguria (1901–2000).* Genoa: DeFerrari, 2005.

Ragazzi, Franco, ed. *Kandinsky, Vrubel', Jawlensky e gli artisti russi a Genova e nelle Riviere: Passaggio in Liguria.* Milan: Mazzotta, 2002.

Ranicki, Marcel, R., ed. *1000 Deutsche Gedichte und ihre Interpretationen: Von Trakl bis Gottfried Benn.* Frankfurt: Insel, 1944.

Requadt, Paul. "Gottfried Benn und das südliche Wort." *Neophilologicus* 46 (1962) 50–66.

Reynolds, Susan, and Daniel Minter. *The First Marathon: The Legend of Pheidippides.* Park Ridge, IL: Albert Whitman and Company, 2006.

Richardson, Leslie. *Things Seen on the Riviera: A Description of Its Interesting Peoples and Their Ways and the Charming Scenes of the French and Italian Rivieras Lying between Marseilles and Genoa.* New York: Dutton, 1923.

Ricœur, Paul. *De l'interprétation: Essai sur Freud.* Paris: Éditions du Seuil, 1965.

Ridley, Hugh. *Gottfried Benn.* Opladen: Westdeutscher Verlag, 1990.

Ring, Jim. *Riviera: The Rise and Fall of the Côte d'Azur.* London: John Murray, 1988.

Ritchie, J.M. *Gottfried Benn: The Unreconstructed Expressionist.* London: Oswald Wolff, 1972.

Robinson, Jeffrey C. *The Walk: Notes on a Romantic Image.* Norman, London: University of Oklahoma Press, 1989.

Rolleston, Maud. *Talks with Lady Shelley.* London: George G. Harrap, 1925.

Room, Adrian. *Placenames of the World: Origins and Meanings of the Names of 6,600 Countries, Cities, Territories, Natural Features and Historic Sites.* Jefferson, NC: McFarland, 2006.

Ross, Michael. *From Liguria with Love: Capture, Imprisonment and Escape in Wartime Italy.* London: Minerva Press, 1997.

Rossi, Luisa, ed. *Dora d'Istria: Autunno a Rapallo: I bagni marini di una principessa in Liguria.* Genoa: Sagep, 2000.

Rothenberg, Jerome, and Jeffrey C. Robinson, eds. *Poems for the Millennium.* Vol. III. Berkeley, Los Angeles, London: University of California Press, 2009.

Rübe, Werner. *Provoziertes Leben: Gottfried Benn.* Stuttgart: Klett-Cotta, 1993.

Russo, Lucio. *Nietzsche, Freud e il paradosso della rappresentazione.* Rome: Istituto della Enciclopedia Italiana, 1986.

Saine, Thomas P., and Jeffrey L. Sammons, eds. *Goethe: Italian Journey.* Trans. Robert R. Heitner. New York: Suhrkamp Publishers, 1989.

Salin, Sophie. *Kryptologie des Unbewußten: Nietzsche, Freud und Deleuze im Wunderland.* Würzburg: Könighausen & Neumann, 2008.

Santos, Luis Martín. *Encuentro en Sils-Maria.* Madrid: Akal, 1986.

Sbarbaro, Camillo. In *L'opera in versi e in prosa.* Ed. Gina Lagorio and Vanni Scheiwiller. Milan: Garzanti, 1985.

Scartazzini, Giovanni Andrea. *Enciclopedia dantesca: Dizionario critico e ragionato di quanto concerna la vita e le opere di Dante Alighieri.* Milan: U. Hoepli, 1895–1905.

Schellenberger-Diederich, Erika. *Geopoetik: Studien zur Metaphorik des Gesteins in der Lyrik von Hölderlin bis Celan.* Bielefeld: Aisthesis, 2006.

Schinaia, Cosimo. "Freud e Genova." *Rivista di Psicoanalisi* 51 (2005): 475–87.

Schlechta, Karl. *Nietzsches Grosser Mittag.* Frankfurt: Vittorio Klostermann, 1954.

Schlögel, Karl. *Im Raume lesen wir die Zeit.* Munich: Carl Hanser, 2003.

Schneede, Uwe M. *Vincent Van Gogh: Leben und Werk.* Munich: Beck, 2003.

Schröder, Jürgen. "Es knistert im Gebälk: Gottfried Benn – Ein Emigrant nach innen." *Exilforschung* 12 (1994): 31–52.

Schuster, Gerhard, ed. *Gottfried Benn, Max Rychner: Briefwechsel 1930–1956.* Stuttgart: Klett-Cotta, 1986.

Schwebell, Gertrude C., ed. *Contemporary German Poetry: An Anthology.* New York: New Directions, 1964.

Secci, Lia. "Il complesso ligure di Gottfried Benn." *Genova*, 11 (November 1966): n.p.

Self, Will, and Ralph Steadman. *Psychogeography: Disentangling the Modern Conundrum of Psyche and Place.* New York: Bloomsbury, 2007.

Shapiro, Gary. *Archaeologies of Vision: Foucoult and Nietzsche on Seeing and Saying.* Chicago, London: The University of Chicago Press, 2003.

Sherry, Vincent. *The Great War and the Language of Modernism.* Oxford, New York: Oxford University Press, 2003.

Siculus, Diodorus. *Biblioteca storica.* Milan: Rusconi, 1985–1998.

Sieburth, Richard, ed. *A Walking Tour in Southern France: Ezra Pound among the Troubadours.* New York: New Directions, 1992.

Silver, Kenneth. *Making Paradise: Art, Modernity, and the Myth of the French Riviera.*
Cambridge, MA, and London: The MIT Press, 2001.

Simmons, Laurence. *Freud's Italian Journey.* Amsterdam, New York: Rodopi, 2006.

Staten, Henry. *Nietzsche's Voice.* Ithaca, London: Cornell University Press, 1990.

Stein, Gertrude. *Gertrude Stein's America.* Ed. Gilbert A. Harrison. Washington,
D.C.: Robert B. Luce, 1965.

Stein, Gertrude. *Wars I Have Seen.* London: Batsford, 1945.

Stein, Howard F., and William G. Niederland, eds. *Maps from the Mind: Readings in
Psychogeography.* Norman and London: University of Oklahoma Press, 1989.

Steinhagen, Harald. *Die Statischen Gedichte von Gottfried Benn: Die Vollendung seiner
expressionistischen Lyrik.* Stuttgart: Klett, 1969.

Stierle, Karlheinz. "Im Zwischenreich der Dichtung: Zum poetischen Werk
Eugenio Montales." *Italienisch: Zeitschrift für italienische Sprache und Literatur* 37
(May 1997): 2–22.

Stoppard, Tom. *Arcadia: A Play.* London: Faber and Faber, 1993.

Stork, Charles Wharton, trans. *The German Classics: Masterpieces of German Literature Translated into English.* Vol. 7. New York: AMS Press, 1969.

Sugarman, Susan. *Freud on the Acropolis: Reflections on a Paradoxical Response to the
Real.* Boulder, CO: Westview Press, 1998.

Tappert, Birgit, and Willi Jung, eds. *Heitere Mimesis: Festschrift für Willi Hirdt zum
65. Geburtstag.* Tübingen, Basel: Francke, 2003.

Tauxe, Henri Ch. *Le tunnel du fou: Pièce en un acte.* Lausanne: L'Âge d'Homme,
2000.

Taylor, Charles, and Patricia Finley. *Images of the Journey in Dante's Divine Comedy.*
New Haven, London: Yale University Press, 1997.

Theweleit, Klaus. *Buch der Könige: Orpheus und Eurydike.* Basel, Frankfurt: Stroem-
feld/Roter Stern, 1988.

Tögel, Christfried. *Berggasse – Pompeji und zurück: Sigmund Freuds Reisen in die
Vergangenheit.* Tübingen: Edition Diskord, 1989.

Tögel, Christfried, ed. *Sigmund Freud: Unser Herz zeigt nach dem Süden: Reisebriefe
1895–1923.* Berlin: Aufbau-Verlag, 2002.

Touring Club Italiano. *Liguria: Genova, le valli, i borghi interni, l'alta via dei monti
liguri, le riviere di levante e ponente.* Milan: Touring Editore, 2001.

Touring Club Italiano, ed. *Attraverso l'Italia del 900: Immagini e pagine d'autore.*
Milan: Touring Editore, 1999.

Toynbee, Paget. *A Dictionary of Proper Names and Notable Matters in the Works of
Dante.* Oxford: Clarendon Press, 1968.

Traverso, Paola. *Psyche è una parola greca: Forme e funzioni della cultura classica
nell'opera di Freud.* Genoa: Compagnia dei Librai, 2000.

Urmes, Dietmar. *Handbuch der geographischen Namen.* Wiesbaden: Marix, 2004.

Uzuner, Buket. *Istanbul Blues*. Trans. Pelin Arıner. Istanbul: Epsilon, 2004.

Vaihinger, Hans. *Die Philosophie des Als-Ob: System der theoretischen, praktischen und religiösen Fiktionen der Menschheit aufgrund eines idealistischen Positivismus*. Berlin: Reuther and Reichard, 1911.

Vartzbed, Eric. *Troisième oreille de Nietzsche: Essai sur un précurseur de Freud*. Paris: Harmattan, 2003.

Vietta, Silvio, and Hans-Georg Kemper. *Expressionismus*. Munich: Wilhelm Fink, 1994.

Villa, Edoardo. *I mercanti e le parole: Letteratura in Liguria*. Genoa: La Querica, 1983.

Virgil. *The Aeneid*. Trans. Allen Mandelbaum. Toronto: Bantam Books, 1981.

Virgil. *Georgics*. Trans. Janet Lembke. New Haven, London: Yale University Press, 2005.

Völker, Ludwig. *Gottfried Benn: Sprache – Form – Wiklichkeit: Zwei Vorträge*. Münster: Kleinheinrich, 1990.

Waters, Helena. *The French and Italian Rivieras*. Boston, New York: Houghton Mifflin, 1924.

West, Rebecca. *Eugenio Montale: Poet on the Edge*. Cambridge, MA: Harvard University Press, 1981.

Westphal, Bertrand. *La géocritique: Réel, fiction, espace*. Paris: Les Éditions de Minuit, 2007.

White, Kenneth. *Geopoetics: Place, Culture, World*. Glasgow: Alba Editions, 2003.

White, Kenneth. *On the Atlantic Edge: A Geopoetics Project*. Dingwall: Sandstone Press, 2006.

White, Kenneth. *Open World: Collected Poems, 1960–2000*. Edinburgh: Polygon, 2003.

White, Kenneth. *Travels in the Drifting Dawn*. Edinburgh, London: Mainstream Publishing, 1989.

White, Kenneth. *Van Gogh and Kenneth White: An Encounter*. Paris: Flohic Éditions, 1994.

White, Kenneth. *The Wanderer and His Charts*. Edinburgh: Polygon, 2004.

Wilkins, Ernest H., and Thomas G. Bergin, eds. *A Concordance to the Divine Comedy of Dante Alighieri*. Cambridge, MA: The Belknap Press of Harvard University Press, 1965.

Williams-Ellis, Amabel. *An Anatomy of Poetry*. Oxford: Basil Blackwell, 1922.

Wirtz, Ursula. *Die Sprachstruktur Gottfried Benns: Ein Vergleich mit Nietzsche*. Göppingen: Alfred Kümmerle, 1971.

Witte, Bernd, and Mauro Ponzi, eds. *Goethes Rückblick auf die Antike: Beiträge des deutsch-italienischen Kolloquiums Rom 1998*. Berlin: Erich Schmidt Verlag, 1999.

Wodtke, Friedrich W. *Die Antike im Werk Gottfried Benns*. Wiesbaden: Limes, 1963.

Woolf, Virginia. *A Room of One's Own*. San Diego, New York, London: Harcourt, 1981.

Wunberg, Gotthart, ed. *Nietzsche und die deutsche Literatur: Texte zur Nietzsche-Rezeption 1873–1963*. Tübingen: Max Niemeyer, 1978.

Yalom, Irvin D. *When Nietzsche Wept: A Novel of Obsession*. New York: Harper Perennial Modern Classics, 2003.

Yeats, William B. *Collected Poems*. London: Macmillan, 1963.

Young, Julian. *Friedrich Nietzsche: A Philosophical Biography*. Cambridge: Cambridge University Press, 2010.

Ziebarth, Ursula. *Hernach: Gottfried Benns Briefe an Ursula Ziebarth*. Munich: DTV, 2003.

Ziebarth, Ursula. *Hexenspeise*. Pfullingen: Neske, 1978.

Ziebarth, Ursula. *Reisen mit Benn: Erinnerungen an einen Dichter*. Dir. Andreas Chr. Schmidt, 1998.

Zilcosky, John, ed. *Writing Travel: The Poetics and Politics of the Modern Journey*. Toronto: University of Toronto Press, 2008.

Zintzen, Christiane. *Von Pompeji nach Troja: Archäologie, Literatur und Öffentlichkeit im 19. Jahrhundert*. Vienna: Universitätsverlag, 1998.

Index

GERMAN AND EUROPEAN STUDIES
General Editor: Rebecca Wittmann